Brave NUI World

Brave NUI World

Designing Natural User Interfaces for
Touch and Gesture

Daniel Wigdor
User Experience Architect, Microsoft Surface

Dennis Wixon
Research Manager, Microsoft Surface

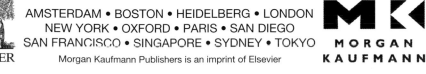

AMSTERDAM • BOSTON • HEIDELBERG • LONDON
NEW YORK • OXFORD • PARIS • SAN DIEGO
SAN FRANCISCO • SINGAPORE • SYDNEY • TOKYO

Morgan Kaufmann Publishers is an imprint of Elsevier

Acquiring Editor: Rachel Roumeliotis
Development Editor: David Bevans
Project Manager: Andre Cuello
Designer: Joanne Blank

Morgan Kaufmann Publishers is an imprint of Elsevier
30 Corporate Drive, Suite 400, Burlington, MA 01803, USA

Notices
Knowledge and best practice in this field are constantly changing. As new research and experience
broaden our understanding, changes in research methods or professional practices, may become
necessary. Practitioners and researchers must always rely on their own experience and knowledge
in evaluating and using any information or methods described herein. In using such information or
methods they should be Mindful of their own safety and the safety of others, including parties for
whom they have a professional responsibility.

To the fullest extent of the law, neither the Publisher nor the authors, contributors, or editors,
assume any liability for any injury and/or damage to persons or property as a matter of products
liability, negligence or otherwise, or from any use or operation of any methods, products,
instructions, or ideas contained in the material herein.

Library of Congress Cataloging-in-Publication Data
Wigdor, Daniel.
   Brave NUI world : designing natural user interfaces for touch and gesture / Daniel Wigdor,
   Dennis Wixon.
     p. cm.
   ISBN 978-0-12-382231-4
1. User interfaces (Computer science) 2. Haptic devices. 3. Human-computer interaction.
   I. Wixon, Dennis. II. Title.
   QA76.9.U83W537 2010
   004.01'9—dc22
                                           2010047830

British Library Cataloguing-in-Publication Data
A catalogue record for this book is available from the British Library.

Printed in the United States of America

11 12 13 14   10 9 8 7 6 5 4 3 2 1

Working together to grow
libraries in developing countries

www.elsevier.com | www.bookaid.org | www.sabre.org

ELSEVIER   BOOK AID International   Sabre Foundation

For information on all MK publications visit our website at www.mkp.com

Dedication

This book is dedicated to Jo Anne Bennett and Amy Wigdor, without whose support and encouragement it would not have been a reality, and to Chia Shen, who taught Daniel that nothing is truly understood until "you can feel it in your bones." This book is a marrow sample drawn from very deep indeed. It is further dedicated to the new generation of researchers and practitioners who will be the inhabitants of the Brave NUI World of human-computer interaction, and to the professors of engineering, computer science, art, and design who will be your guides. We hope that this book will serve to help you reach the shores of this promised land—how that world will be formed will be limited only by your imagination, creativity, and perseverance.

Contents

Preface

If you have already purchased this book, thank you. We hope you find it interesting and useful. If you're planning on building an application or platform for next-generation input hardware, we hope that this book convinces you of the necessity, as well as the opportunities and challenges, of creating fundamentally new user interfaces for that hardware. We hope that our vision of the NUI helps shape your thinking, and that you take the ideas and guidance contained within and apply and extend them.

If you haven't purchased this book yet, then what are you waiting for?

However, regardless of whether you are an owner, a possible purchaser, or a user, it will be helpful for you to know something about our view of the NUI and how it evolved.

Decades of cumulative experience in creating interfaces for new technology led us to two important realizations. First, that new input devices do not, in and of themselves, facilitate a better user experience—we argue that the iPhone and Microsoft Surface UIs are highly successful in spite of, rather than because of, the use of a touchscreen. The second realization is that these input devices, while not themselves creating a better user experience, could be enablers for the creation of a UI that is more natural to use, and could fundamentally change the way we interact with technology. We dub this the *natural user interface*.

Ironically a natural user interface does not occur naturally. In our view creating a natural user interface is a design goal. To achieve that goal takes a clear viewpoint, hard work, careful design, rigorous testing, and some luck. The clear viewpoint starts with an understanding and vision of what a natural interface is. Our vision is that a natural user interface is one that provides a clear and enjoyable path to unreflective expertise in its use. It makes skilled behavior seem natural in both learning and expert practice. It makes learning enjoyable and eliminates the drudgery that distracts from skilled practice. It can make you a skilled practitioner who enjoys what you are doing. Natural in this sense does not mean raw, primitive, or dumbed down. The meaning is best captured by the phrase "that person is a natural." When we hear a person referred to in that way, we have the sense that their performance is ideal and that it seems effortless and graceful.

We came to this view over time as a result of painful lessons. This book incorporates our learning from those lessons. They are embodied in both the guidance we provide at the end of each chapter and our discussion of the history and background that opens each chapter. The book represents not only our learning but also the learning of the teams at Microsoft that created Microsoft Surface and a slew of other touch- and gesture-based products. As such, it represents the hard work and lessons of many. Our acknowledgment of them and their work does not do them justice; hopefully this volume does.

Perhaps this preface has convinced you to buy this book. But more importantly it will have succeeded if it convinces you to use the book as a starting point for your thinking about and/or building a NUI, as an ongoing reference for your work, and as a basis for reflection on your particular design and on natural user interfaces in general. We challenge you to take the design, development, research, and philosophy of natural user interfaces to the next stage. After all, you've already gotten this far.

Daniel Widgor

Dennis Wixon

Acknowledgments

The team that came together to create the Microsoft Surface product was composed of hundreds of engineers, researchers, designers, marketers, computer scientists, testers, technicians, planners, artists, and program managers. This team built the first of a generation of NUI devices and experiences and started to infuse Microsoft with the spirit of the NUI, which is now spreading across product teams in every division of the company. Absent the hard work and dedication of any one member of this team, this book would never have been a reality. A full acknowledgment of everyone's contributions to our shared vision for NUI would require a second book. For their support and assistance in ensuring that this title reached the shelves, we thank August de los Reyes, Lisa Anderson, Brad Carpenter, Panos Panay, Stuart Ashmun, Pete Thompson, Robbie Bach, Kay Hofmeester, Paul Hoover, Sarah Williams, Jarrod Lombardo, John Pella, Jennifer McCormick, Steve Seow, Mike Cronin, Robert Levy, Katie White, Maxim Mazeev, Maxim Oustiougov, Nigel Keam, Luis Cabrera-Cordon, Gretchen Richter de Medeiros, Nabeeha Mohamed, and Brett Pearce. We also acknowledge Kristin Alexander, who drove the research that helped convinced Microsoft to build Surface and name it.

A special thanks to Leslie MacNeil, who, in addition to being chief visual designer for Surface, also created the illustrations for this book.

Several people at Microsoft Research and Microsoft Hardware's Adaptive Systems team have also been instrumental; we thank Hrvoje Benko, Merrie Morris, Andy Wilson (co-inventor of the first Surface prototype, along with Steven Bathiche), Ken Hinckley, Paul Dietz, our intern Dustin Freeman (of the University of Toronto), Bill Buxton, and the gracious support of Eric Horvitz. Team NUI in the Entertainment and Devices division was also incredibly supportive—we thank Don Coiner, Steve Kaneko, Steve Herbst, Michael Medlock, Noah Spitzer-Williams, Karon Weber, Nicole Coddington, and Jenny Rodenhouse.

This book is greatly enhanced by the thoughtful sidebars included alongside several chapters. We thank Andy Wilson, Patrick Baudisch, Johnny Lee, Gord Kurtenbach, and Kay Hofmeester for their insights. It is further enhanced by references to significant works by significant researchers around the world, and by other inspiration drawn from the HCI community. In particular, the DiamondSpace and DiamondTouch teams at Mitsubishi Electric Research Labs, made up of Chia Shen, Clifton Forlines, Paul Dietz, Darren Leigh, Sam Shipman, Frederic Vernier, Kathy Ryall, Alan Esenther, and Adam Bogue. Our work has truly been built on the shoulders of giants.

We would also like to thank our editors and the team at Morgan Kaufmann who helped make this book a reality: Mary James, Rachel Roumeliotis, and David Bevans, as well as the dozen or so external reviewers who scrutinized and vastly improved the text. Thank you for your support, and for sharing our vision of this Brave NUI World.

About the Authors

Daniel Wigdor is an Assistant Professor of computer science at the University of Toronto. Before joining U of T, he worked at Microsoft in nearly a dozen different roles, among them serving as the User Experience Architect of the Microsoft Surface product and as a cross-company expert in the creation of natural user interfaces. Before joining Microsoft, he conducted research in advanced user interfaces and devices at Mitsubishi Electric Research Labs and at the Initiative in Innovative Computing at Harvard University. He is also co-founder of Iota Wireless, a company dedicated to the commercialization of NUI technologies for mobile phones. Daniel's work has been described in dozens of publications in leading international conferences, journals, and books. His is the recipient of a Wolfond Fellowship and multiple ACM Best Paper awards.

Dennis Wixon is currently Discipline Lead for Microsoft US BPD. Prior to this role he was the head of research for Microsoft Surface, and he has also managed research teams at Microsoft Game Studies and MSN/Home Products. Before joining Microsoft, Dennis managed the usability team at Digital Equipment Corporation, where a number of important usability methods such as usability engineering and contextual inquiry were developed. Dennis has been an active member of the user research community for over 25 years. He co-chaired CHI 2002 and served as Vice President for Conferences for ACM SIGCHI. Dennis has co-authored over 60 articles, book chapters, and presentations on research methods and theory. He is an adjunct Full Professor in the Human Centered Design and Engineering Department at University of Washington and co-edited with Dr. Judy Ramey the book *Field Methods Case Book for Software Design*. Dennis holds a Ph.D. in Social Psychology from Clark University.

Introducing the NUI

Introduction

All things will be produced in superior quantity and quality, and with greater ease, when each man works at a single occupation, in accordance with his natural gifts, and at the right moment, without meddling with anything else.

—Plato

In the decades since the first digital computers were programmed using mechanical switches and plug boards, computing and the ways in which people interface with computers have evolved significantly. Some aspects of this evolution have both been anticipated and withstood the test of time. Moore's law is an example. The law states that *the number of transistors that can be placed inexpensively on an integrated circuit will double approximately every two years.* The trend that this law describes has created opportunities for the growth of computing and its adoption into many aspects of our lives. As computers have increased in power and decreased in size and cost, new form factors have been created (e.g., smart phones, PDAs, and digital cameras), new platforms have evolved (e.g., the Internet), new infrastructures have become widely available (e.g., GPS), new industries have arisen (e.g., computer games), and new application families (e.g., spreadsheets, document processing, image creation, modification and sharing) have flourished. All of these trends have resulted in the democratization of computing as the number of people directly interacting with computers has steadily increased. This proliferation of computing has transcended national boundaries and permeated nearly all economic classes. It has changed the way people work, play, and interact with one another.

While the increase in computing power has been more or less continuous, the interfaces between human and computers have evolved more discontinuously. A widely held perspective is that interfaces have passed through phases. These phases are loosely defined but can be thought of as the phase of typing commands (the command line), followed by the graphical user interface (GUI). More specifically, most computers with which people interact regularly are based on the desktop metaphor (so called because windows are allowed to overlap, like paper atop a desk) and rely on a known set of user interface elements, commonly referred to as WIMP: windows, icons, menus, and pointers.

During that evolution some other contenders for the predominant interface, such as menu-only systems, did not attain dominance or widespread use. Instead, they were limited to niche applications, such as ATMs and televisions. A deeper analysis would show that many popular applications contain elements of each style. In effect, they are hybrids. For example, typical GUIs make use of menus (pull-down menus) and forms (dialog boxes and property sheets). In some cases, such as spreadsheets, the interaction style includes command-like elements, that is, complex formulas and sophisticated functions. Similarly, another class of successful applications, document processing, also introduces new concepts such as "what you see is what you get," (WYSIWYG) that is, what is on the screen is a reasonably faithful rendition of what will be printed. In both cases, the elements of the GUI are accompanied by particularly useful and appealing aspects that propelled these applications to wide adoption. It is important to be cognizant of the fact that these approaches are neither preordained nor task neutral. WYSIWYG, for example, fundamentally shapes the way people spend their time composing text—simultaneously focusing on both form and content.

While a thoughtful interpretation of the history of human-computer interaction is complex and nuanced, certain generalizations are evident. The way in which humans interact with computers has evolved. That evolution has enabled more people to do more things with computers. It has led to a vast and rapid increase of the volume, scope, and diversity of the computer business.

There are many perspectives from which we could view this evolution. Some are merely tautological. For example, a common view is that more people use more computation because the barriers have been reduced and the functionality of the machines has increased. While true, that characterization provides precious little insight. To provide it some intellectual weight, we need to be clearer with respect to what barriers have been reduced and which functions have been provided. It is also useful to examine closely the development of certain computing "niches," which thrive in limited but well-defined contexts.

Some of the early analysis of the GUI provided just this kind of deeper insight. Analysts pointed out that recognizing and choosing were easier than remembering then typing. In other words, with its menus, dialog boxes, icons, and familiar work spaces, the WIMP GUI represented a lower barrier for users than a command line interface. This difference becomes clearer if we consider specific applications. By and large, it is easier to learn and use a word processor to create simple documents than to edit in a markup language. In addition, the often-overlooked advantage of the computer, that is, that it produces revisable work products, was fully realized with a word processing system.

Functionality gains are also apparent for most users. Before the computer, a skilled typesetter could produce formatted documents, but the average citizen was confined to typing final work products in a mono-spaced font, with cumbersome correction tools. The combination of reduced thresholds for learning, easier recall, increased functionality for the average user, the reduced cost promised by Moore's law, and the widespread capability to revise one's work without redoing it signaled the explosive growth of a number of well-featured and -designed applications that adopted the desktop computer and the subsequent consignment of more traditional approaches to specialized niches.

When the desktop GUI was first created and made widely available, its ultimate fate was unclear. It was derided by many experts who coined its current name: the WIMP interface. Although WIMP stood for windows, icons, menus, and a pointer, it implied that the users of the GUI were not the manly men who had mastered the previous, more arcane ways of interacting with computers. Ultimately, those supposedly more manly folks were consigned to the social position of specialists or hobbyists. We can see this pattern in many other domains: personal transport, cooking, penmanship, and CB radio operators.

Now we stand at the brink of another potential evolution in computing. Natural user interfaces (NUIs) seem to be in a position similar to that occupied by the GUI in the early 1980s. Like the desktop GUIs, NUIs promise to reduce the barriers to computing still further, while simultaneously increasing the power of the user, and enabling computing to access still further niches of use. But just as GUIs did not simply make command systems easier, NUIs are not simply a natural veneer over a GUI. Instead, like GUIs, NUIs have a set of strengths based on *what* they make easier, *how* they make those things easier, *how* they shape the user's interaction with technology, *which* niches they fit in, and whether or not these niches expand to dwarf the space occupied by traditional GUIs.

When examining this history and anticipating the future, we should not be distracted by single instances. Many of these will be failures and will not represent any overall trend. The failure of makes and models of some cars did not end the phase of personal transport. The failure of many GUI products and the inevitable consolidation of the marketplace did not impede the overall growth of personal computing or prevent GUIs from pre-eminence. It is as dangerous to generalize to the future based on a few examples as it is hard to anticipate the future when looking from our current perspective.

In this book we do not aim to provide an exhaustive overview of the NUI. We do not predict the future of human-computer interaction. We do not assume the predominance of NUI-based designs. We do not provide a complete set of rules for creating a successful NUI, because NUI is not yet at a state of evolution or standardization to allow for such a definition.

We can make some relatively safe predictions. NUIs are here to stay. They either will find a successful niche, like menu system ATMs, or will come to dominate the computer landscape. If the latter comes to pass, we can still expect GUIs to persist in specialized environments. The ultimate evolution of the NUI will be determined not by the analysts and the critics, but by those who step forward and take the risk to build true NUI applications. Here we offer a way to think about NUIs that is counter to the predominant metaphor. This perspective on the NUI suggests that NUIs provide an enjoyable way for novices to move quickly and seemingly effortlessly to skilled practitioners. This approach involves more than being "natural" or intuitive. It means that the domain of use and the requirements of context are carefully assessed. It also means that the conventions of the GUI should be studiously ignored. It requires careful design and rigorous research. We give some guidance on how to do those things and how to re-conceptualize the NUI.

We offer a number of essays on the NUI and on methods that can be utilized to achieve it, written from the perspective of two journeyman user experience experts who have had the opportunity to immerse themselves in the nitty-gritty of designing, engineering, building, testing, researching, and shipping multiple products that have come to define the category. Overall, the essays are intended to provide a nuanced set of perspectives on NUI systems. These perspectives range from specific descriptions of the syntax and semantics of the NUI to broad analyses of the NUI in terms of the history of computing. Each essay is composed of the same essential elements. Each concludes with specific, concrete design guidelines meant to help take words into action. Those guidelines are divided into three types: *must*, those that we believe are necessary conditions to achieving a natural-feeling experience; *should*, those elements that, while nonessential, have been found to add greatly to achieving such an experience; and *could*, those guidelines that may apply only to certain contexts or situations.

To frame our collection, we offer a framework that we have evolved for the general process of the creation of a gesture-based natural user interface. The sections of this book reflect the phases of this process, and individual chapters provide thoughts, tools, and methods for implementing it. This framework is an evolution of classic methods for designing interactive systems, with the addition of elements unique to the creation of a fundamentally new way of interacting (Figure 1.1).

Different elements of this book will appeal to different pieces of team building a touch- and gesture-based product. Chapters 2 and 3 will best be consumed by planners and business managers. Chapters 4–11 will feel most familiar to designers, who think broad thoughts early and whittle toward the final product. Chapters 12–15 might seem most approachable by program managers, who seek quickly to understand where they are, where they need to be, and the pitfalls along the way. Chapters 16–21 may seem best suited to software developers and testers, who seek to carefully define goals and test cases. Chapters 22–26 might, at first glance, be targeted to hardware engineers, who are seeking to find the uses for different sensing capabilities in the hardware. And Chapters 27–29 might be seen as targeting user researchers, who seek methods for guiding the design process and goals.

Approaching this text with such a discipline-centric viewpoint, however, would be a missed opportunity. This book has been lovingly composed by a philosopher-researcher and a computer scientist-designer who had the opportunity to work together closely in multidisciplinary teams to create something special. We highly encourage all members of a team creating a NUI application to deeply engage with this material, to understand fully our vision for natural user interfaces and our guidance for how to achieve them.

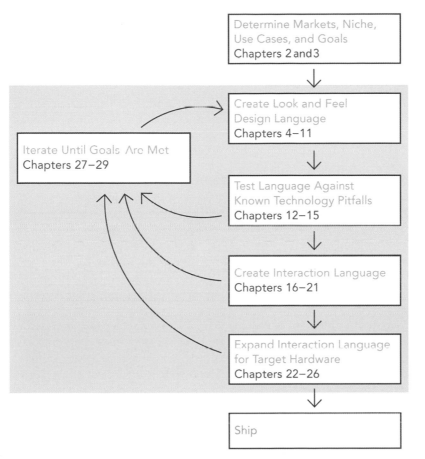

FIGURE 1.1

Our framework for the creation of natural user interfaces (NUIs).

Our broader goal is to move both the consideration of the NUI and the implementation of NUI systems forward. We hope that other thinkers and practitioners will take the material here as a starting point for reflection, elaboration, construction, and, yes, even contradiction. We want to move the conversation of what is a NUI and how do we create one forward to more sophisticated discussion. We want to make reflection on the NUI more insightful and sophisticated. We are optimistic that exciting and popular NUI applications will flourish. More than anything else, we wish our fellow NUI explorers, researchers, designers, developers, and business leaders well. Together, you will determine the future history of the NUI approach to human-computer interaction.

The Natural User Interface

Free like freedom, not like beer.

—Richard Stallman

DESCRIPTION

The term *natural* is often understood to mean mimicry of the "real world." In our view, it is a design philosophy and a source for metrics enabling an iterative process to create a product. In this book, we discuss touch and gestural interaction as one modality enabling the construction of a natural user interface. However, we believe that a NUI can be created with other input modalities as well. Indeed, one could imagine following the design guidelines we lay out to create a new kind of interface for the mouse and keyboard, voice commands, in-air gesturing, mobile phones, and so on. Input and output technologies offer us the opportunity to create a more natural user interface; they do not, in and of themselves, define or guarantee it. The natural user interface lies in the UI and experiences we create for use with those technologies and how we leverage the potential of new technologies to better mirror human capabilities, optimize the path to expert, apply to given contexts and tasks, and fulfill our needs.

The term *natural* is a powerful one, in that it quickly evokes a range of imagery in those who hear it. The first, and most important, thing to understand is that we use it to describe a property that is actually external to the product itself. The natural element of a natural user interface is not about the interface at all. Quite the opposite. We see *natural* as referring to the way users interact with and feel about the product, or more precisely, what they do and how they feel while they are using it.

Most of us can only imagine how a major-league pitcher feels while standing atop the mound. He works the dirt with his foot so that it does exactly what he expects it to when he moves. He grips the ball in a way so familiar, it feels like part of his body. He stares down at the catcher's mitt. He feels at home.

This is exactly the feeling we want to evoke in our users. Your product must mirror their capabilities, meet their needs, take full advantage of their capacities and fit their task and context demands. The trick, of course, is in helping them to feel that way the moment they pick it up, instead of after decades of practice (the UI minor leagues?).

The introductory quote by Richard Stallman of the free software movement illustrates a similar point in the ambiguity in the word *free*. In the natural user interface, *natural* refers to the user's behavior and feeling during the experience rather than the interface being the product of some organic process. The production of this conclusion is the end result of rigorous design, leveraging the potential of modern technologies to better mirror human capabilities.

Direct, multi-touch devices hold the promise as a natural input modality. Potentially dozens of degrees of freedom allow a level of expressiveness not possible with a mouse alone. Work in the field has demonstrated that direct-touch systems better leverage spatial memory, and multi-touch shows the promise of easily wielded high-bandwidth input from the user. The goal of those creating a NUI, therefore, is properly leveraging this potential. It is far too easy to fall into the trap of simply copying the WIMP GUI, which is designed for mouse-based interaction. Instead, an all-new interface must be designed with new input actions, new affordances—in short, a new paradigm.

A device that feels truly natural to the user means taking full advantage of the user's bandwidth, a device that behaves as a sort of appendage. By designing and building natural user interfaces, taking advantage of modern input technology, we stand at the brink of a new era, one in which technology can truly integrate into our lives, liberating us from the past of frustration and mediocrity.

APPLICATION TO NUI

It is with this understanding that we begin our exploration of natural user interfaces. While natural is an emergent property, it can be reliably achieved by following the various principles, processes, and examples we will describe in this book. Achieving the goal of creating a user interface that, to its user, *feels* natural is NOT best achieved by mimicry of some other experience, by relying on familiar metaphors, or even by directly asking users what kind of experience they would like to have.

We must *design, research,* and *engineer* these user interfaces. This will be a challenge. Most designers have never had to truly design a user interface. Instead, they have relied on the designs of others, provided within the connective tissue of decades of iterative design. Buttons. Scrollbars. Check boxes. Radio buttons. Each of these comes from this iterative design process, started by Engelbart and English, and continued by the designers at PARC, Apple, Microsoft, and elsewhere. Creating natural user interfaces, which leverage new technologies and human capabilities, will require no less. Similarly, many researchers are familiar with techniques that refine or evaluate designs within an existing paradigms. While the techniques of research may not change in a fundamental way, their goal and their specific application may change dramatically.

The main point of this chapter is to help designers, researchers, and managers avoid a dead-end street: the belief that a NUI can be created by simply mimicking existing experiences. This dead end avoided, we will then examine the many lessons that we and others have learned in the process of creating some of the very early work in natural user interfaces.

LESSONS FROM THE PAST: THE FIRST APPLE PAD

In 1989, Apple Computer began work on a new kind of platform—one that would provide a device that would fit easily into the user's lifestyle by, among other things, recognizing the *natural* means of output for a human: handwriting. Well, we all know what happened: the Newton Message Pad was fraught with problems, among them that the handwriting recognition was insufficiently robust—so bad, in fact, that it earned a place of honor as the butt of a Doonesbury cartoon (Figure 2.1). The Newton has been long forgotten, except by those of us who follow the industry. Its successor, however, found far more success.

In 1997, Jeff Hawkins and his team at US Robotics, gave us the Palm Pilot, and history seemed ready to repeat itself. Once again, a product promised to fit itself neatly into our mobile lifestyles and featured handwriting recognition as the method of entry. Unlike the Newton, however, the Palm Pilot was a critical and popular bonanza. Millions were sold worldwide, and several versions were produced over many years.

A key difference was that Hawkins and his team recognized the limitations of their technology. Instead of trying to build a robust recognizer for regular handwriting, they developed a special input language, known as Graffiti—a variation of

FIGURE 2.1

When Doonesbury dedicates a strip to your UI, you really want it to be for a good reason.

(From http://images.ucomics.comics/db/1993/db930827.gif.)

the Unistroke technique invented by David Goldberg of Xerox's Palo Alto Research Center (Figure 2.2). Graffiti simplified the input language in a number of ways, but was similar enough to standard Roman characters that it was easy to learn. By shifting the burden of learning from the device to the user, the Palm was no less *natural* than the Newton. Indeed, because the recognizer worked so well, it enabled an experience that could be felt to be natural, if only by experts who had mastered the language. This is one of the goals in creating a NUI—that your system continues to feel natural to its most expert users, rather than have them feel perpetually stuck in *beginner mode*. A NUI requires learning.

It must be understood that this does not give free reign to the engineer to ignore user needs and prior knowledge. What it does, however, is free us from the potential pitfall of believing that mimicry of an existing experience or phenomenon will necessarily yield a natural user interface.

This lesson embodies the key thesis underlying our definition of the natural user interface: that our goal is a product that creates an experience and context of use that ultimately leads to the user feeling like the pitcher atop the mound: completely comfortable, expert, and masterful—a virtuoso of the user experience. The goal is to achieve this from the very beginning, for complete novices, and to carry this feeling through as the users become experts. And a product that creates the potential for this experience at minimal cost in learning time and effort.

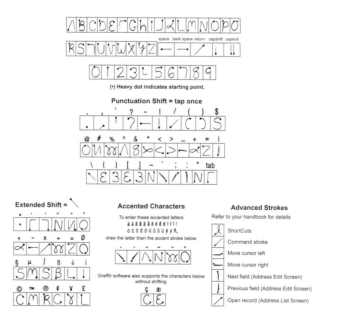

FIGURE 2.2

The Palm Pilot's Graffiti text input language.

How this is achieved is the subject of this book. With a deep understanding of human capabilities, technologies, and unique design processes, you will be armed to create them.

DESIGN GUIDELINES

The complete design guidelines for NUI are embodied in the various chapters of this book. For now, it will suffice to understand that the goal is to build a user experience that is natural to your user, rather than somehow intrinsically natural.

Must

- Create an experience that, for expert users, can feel like an extension of their body.
- Create an experience that feels just as natural to a novice as it does to an expert user.
- Create an experience that is authentic to the medium—do not start by trying to mimic the real world or anything else.
- Build a user interface that considers context, including the right metaphors, visual indications, feedback, and input/output methods for the context.
- Avoid falling into the trap of copying existing user interface paradigms.

Should

- Forget your understanding of what *natural* means.

Could

- Leverage innate talents and previously learned skills. Making an interface that mimics some other experience at which your user is already an expert is one technique for making them feel like a natural—but it's not the only one.

Not
NATURAL USER INTERFACE,

but
NATURAL USER INTERFACE

FIGURE 2.3

Creating this type of experience is the topic of the chapters that follow.

SUMMARY

A NUI is not a natural *user interface*, but rather an interface that makes your user act and feel like a natural. An easy way of remembering this is to change the way you say "natural user interface"—it's not a *natural* user interface, but rather a *natural user* interface (Figure 2.3).

Ecological Niche: Computing, the Social Environment, and Ways of Working

Adapt or die.

—Anonyomus

DESCRIPTION

There is an interdependency between any system and the environment in which that system operates. While many would regard this conclusion as obvious, it is all too often obscured when we look at the history of computing.

Even considering biological evolution, there is no uniform march forward with new species reliably replacing older species. Some species die. New species emerge. Some species survive countless years. Cockroaches, horseshoe crabs, and tube worms live for millions of years as other species die. In addition, some species change so much that their ancestors would be almost unrecognizable today, eohippus, for example.

It might be more productive to think of species as fitting into a niche and surviving if their niche endures and if they face "manageable" competition or predation in that niche. This is very different from a "conventional" view of evolution, which sees life as becoming ever more "advanced" and "adapted." We could call this view the *niche view* and contrast it with the *unidirectional view*, that is, more advanced species uniformly replace less advanced ones.

We can look at the history of computing in a similar way. Conventional wisdom sees computing as "unidirectional," that is, with each new "generation" the previous generation of computing is swept away, like an extinct species. Applying this viewpoint to hardware platforms, we could conclude that the mainframe was supplanted by the minicomputer; the minicomputer was supplanted by the personal computer in its various forms; and the personal computer will be supplanted by the smaller connected computers or mobile phones. This is a unidirectional view of evolution of hardware.

Some data would seem to support this view, for example, a view of the growth of PC sales in unit numbers and dollar volume in the United States (USA) and the **15** world (WW) as shown in Figure 3.1—depicts increases of between 4200 and 15,000%!

But did mainframes actually go away? In human-computer interaction (HCI), was the command language replaced by the graphical user interface (GUI)? Will the GUI be replaced by the natural user interface (NUI)?

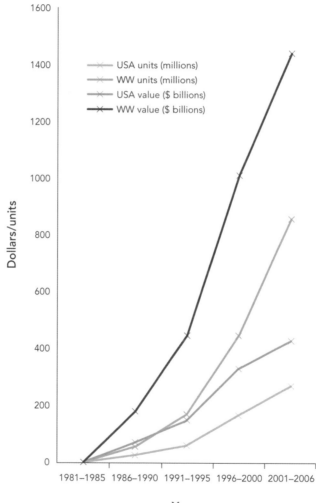

FIGURE 3.1

Sales of PCs.

(From http://www.thefreelibrary.com/Computer+Industry+Almanac%3A+25-Years+PC+Anniversary +Statistics%3B...-a0149450229.)

A more careful examination of this history leads to a more nuanced and complex view. In fact, the various forms of computing morph, adapt, and coexist with new forms of computing. For example, the mainframe did not go away as the smaller and more personal computers became popular. Instead, the mainframe continued to exist in its domain, processing large-scale routine jobs (e.g., payroll). The size of the mainframe market (measured in revenue) has been surprisingly stable over the years. The mainframe market and range of its use just seem tiny because they have been dwarfed by an incredible explosion of smaller and more flexible computers. Factors such as low cost, wide range of applications, and an ever-increasing ease of use worked in true synergy to make these personal computers ubiquitous. Ironically, medium-size computers morphed into server arrays where they connect smaller and cheaper computers into useful networks. So we see great growth in the number of and value of new hardware platforms that support a wider range of activities.

The same kind of evolution exists in the human-computer interface space. Command languages continue to exist in the form of programming languages and command procedures and as a way to execute more specialized and technical operations. Considered broadly, there are more commands running computers than there ever were. Every equation in every spreadsheet is a command, and the universality and power of command systems are surprisingly large. Within spreadsheets, this "command ecology" coexists with a GUI ecology of pull-down windows, icons, and menus.

The apparent ubiquity of the graphic user interface stems from several sources. First, the GUI is well suited to office work, where it is ubiquitous and obvious. Many people labor in cubicles and offices using GUIs and are painfully aware of the interface they are using to access functionality they need. Interestingly, there is as much or more computing power and as many hours of use in the population of gaming consoles as there are in personal computers. Gaming is very widespread. The consoles are very powerful. Game players spend a lot of time playing games. We might group the various gaming system interfaces as the fun user interface, or the FUI. Unlike the GUI, the FUI is mostly invisible to players. They are immersed in the game. Similarly, almost everyone who uses a computer today interacts with the World Wide Web in one form or another. The web presents its own unique interface of links that change the content of the display and the available choices (links). The interactive element links are spread throughout the page and not confined to a menu bar or button ribbon. We could call this interface the web user interface, or the WUI. The WUI and the FUI peacefully coexist and in some cases (e.g., World of Warcraft) work together to the users' delight.

APPLICATION TO NUI

The historical context outlined above gives us a vantage point from which to consider any natural user interface.

First, despite the enthusiasm of its proponents, the natural user interface will not supplant the GUI. The GUI is too well adapted to its ecological (i.e., business and social) niche of office work. Keyboards and pointing devices serve the office worker very effectively. A NUI would be out of place. Imagine typing a long report on a virtual keyboard. That said, the NUI will create a new "niche" of computing. How large that niche will be is impossible to say at this time. The NUI is like the GUI in that both are examples of an underlying driver that is expanding the overall computing universe in terms of both size and range/diversity. This underlying driver is the reduction in time and effort that users incur in adopting new ways of interacting with machines. In other words, as the barriers to functionality contained within, or the fun enabled by computing, are reduced, the scope of computing is expanded. Second, the NUI and the GUI will likely coexist, leading both to prosper. For example, the NUI is well adapted to the niche of leisure and entertainment. There the NUI contributes to the fun of viewing content, for example, pictures, or playing games. At the same time, the content comes from the GUI world of transferring photos from cameras to computers. The games are developed using GUI and command systems. Considering NUI in the home, we are likely to see an even tighter integration, for example, someone browsing the web for pictures, downloading them, then manipulating them using the NUI.

The NUI itself may well exist in different "flavors," much as the GUI systems do. For example, the GUI controls of buttons are readily transferred to control systems on touchscreens in cars. In contrast, the hierarchy of GUI menus and a separate pointing control (usually a joystick-like control that employs pushing and twisting) is not well adapted to a driving environment. Similarly, a NUI interface that works well for horizontal interfaces will be used differently when placed vertically. Horizontally, it is a table well adapted to games like hockey or bowling. Vertically, a NUI would be used more like a white board on steroids, for example, moving and merging content from other sources, or even writing. But we would not expect the sustained and intense use in the vertical form as we see in the horizontal form. Here we see a fundamental principle in action—the new interface accommodates to the traditional use that existed in the "old" environment.

LESSONS FROM THE PAST

As we have seen, the past is often misread by the causal observer and the superficial historian. A deeper examination leads to the following generalizations:

- Hardware platforms and forms of interaction do not replace each other as the universe of computing grows. They continue to exist in the "niche" in which they always prospered. Their absolute size (revenue) and range (uses) may be undiminished in an absolute sense but may seem reduced dramatically as new ways of computing and interaction emerge and dwarf them.

- Types of computing often combine into useful hybrids that borrow interface elements from each other to form systems that are well adapted to a particular niche. The spreadsheet, for example, contains command and NUI elements.

- New types of computing often evolve into subspecies that are well adapted to one particular environment or another. Horizontal NUIs will be used differently than vertical ones. This adaptation reflects the constraints of the context and the possibilities that the new interface and technology bring.

DESIGN GUIDELINES

In the context of an ecological niche, the design guidelines for the NUI are not different than the design guidelines for any genre of computing. That is, the same general principles apply.

Must

- Consider the context of use and the new possibilities that the interface brings to interaction in that context.
- Do not simply translate from one genre of computing to another. For example, copying a web application to a NUI will result in an interface that does not exploit the possibilities of the NUI.

Should

- Be aware that in different environments the patterns of use of an interface may be dramatically different.

Could

- If the context demands it, consider a judicious mixing of interface elements from various styles. This is risky and needs to be done with care.

SUMMARY

The NUI may represent a revolution in computing, not because it replaces existing ways of interacting with computers, but because it enables computing to expand into new niches that could be of tremendous size and importance. Like previous interfaces, the NUI draws its power from reducing interface learning cost. Finally, the NUI will evolve into subspecies that will be well adapted to given social and business niches.

Design Ethos of NUI

II

Less Is More

4

DESCRIPTION

Start simple and look for every opportunity to build on simple interactions to support more complex tasks.

APPLICATION TO NUI

With each new generation of interfaces, developers and designers are faced with a challenge—building applications that exploit the advantages that the new interface offers. A risk in building these new applications is that the designers and developers rely on concepts and approaches that worked in the past. In the most extreme case, the unintended result is that the new application is merely a transcription of an old application interface to the new genre. Often clients who have an existing application will directly ask for a translation. In that case the NUI becomes a GUI with touch. Replacing the mouse with fingers does not make an interface a NUI and is not likely to work very well for users. Even when there is no pre-existing interface to copy, the team is likely to simply not consider the more novel aspects of the new medium and thus is likely to produce a pedestrian interface embedded in an undistinguished application.

LESSONS FROM THE PAST

While it may seem unbelievable, I have seen GUIs that drew from the programmers' experience with command interfaces. In one particular example the user **23** was expected to select an operation first, which would render objects as selectable. This proved very confusing to users since it introduced a kind of mini-mode, that is, when I choose the print function only printable objects are selectable. In fact, this interface abandoned a fundamental tenet of the GUI: select first then choose an operation. Needless to say, users found it very confusing.

Given the challenge of building an application in a new genre, teams should start with the fundamental interactions of a system, perfect them, and then extrapolate them to more advanced functionality. When considering a family of applications, a team would be wise to start with small and simple applications, and when those are perfected, take on more complex applications. Together, these two approaches will help the team develop insight about designing for a NUI and increase the likelihood that each application is successful.

Admittedly, we are advocating a very "conservative" approach to developing a GUI application or a family of such applications. One motive for this approach is that when other approaches such as copying an existing interface have been tried, the projects have either failed completely or had to restart with a focus on fundamentals. However, examining the "definition" we have offered for a NUI application also suggests such a conservative approach. The NUI promises a relatively rapid and enjoyable progress from novice to skilled practitioner. In addition the NUI "promises" that the process of developing skills and the interaction itself will be fun. It also promises that this transition will begin with interaction primitive, a simple action accompanied by system feedback that is fundamental to interacting with the system, that are derived from interactions in the real world. Those requirements make the development of a NUI a daunting task. In contrast, the essential promise of a GUI is that it will use some fundamental interaction conventions (e.g., menus, dialog boxes, "what you see is what you get") to build a system that supports a given set of tasks. From its inception, the inventor of the GUI did not think of it as a way to create easy-to-use systems or systems that were "fun" to interact with. Rather, it was a way to "augment" human capabilities. Analogously, developing a NUI system is more like creating a game. That is, the interaction should be fun, and should introduce new challenges in a gradual way. However, game interfaces differ from NUIs in that most games offer a challenge as part of the game. In contrast, NUI only offers a path to skilled practice. The development of skilled practice may be challenging in and of itself. But the NUI promises to make that transition as progressive and seamless as possible.

The recommendation of starting with the fundamental interactions begs the question of how does one distinguish fundamental interactions from other required interactions. There is no simple rule, but there are three good "clues" for identifying such interactions. The first is what interactions are the most frequent, the second is what interactions are most likely to be done first, and the third is what interactions can serve as building blocks for more advanced actions. For example, a hypothetical NUI program for landscape design would begin by presenting the user with a number of possible designs for different contexts. Landscape elements could be moved only to appropriate places. Goals for the design would such as cost would be tracked as the design was created. The growth of all the plants used could be simulated over time so that the designer could see how her design would look 10 or 20 years into the future. Only plants appropriate for a given environment would be offered on "plant pallets" (e.g., no tropical plants for northern climates).

We have focused on how a team "should" approach the development of NUI application or a family of NUI applications. We are not saying that the NUI can only be applied to relatively simple tasks such as viewing pictures or playing simple games. Instead, because it removes the additional complexity of describing actions in terms of a complex language (command systems), or expressing interaction through a relatively artificial but conventional interaction paradigm (GUI), it promises to make complex tasks and rules easier to learn and perform. For example, the design of complex architectural drawings could be made more accessible by allowing users to manipulate the architectural objects directly. Their constraints are expressed in how they behave, for example, an object that cannot be resized in the real world cannot be resized in the application. Objects can only be moved to where they logically fit. Objects will by default do the "right" thing when placed in the proper context.

DESIGN GUIDELINES

The design guidelines for NUIs are similar to those for any new genre or medium.

Must

- Forget past interaction styles. Don't simply transcribe an application rendered in a traditional medium (web or GUI) as a NUI.

- Choose a promising niche for developing a family of NUI apps. Thus far, the NUI has shown the most success in social and entertainment contexts. Its application to other domains requires an analysis of the way in which the interaction would support and teach the rules of the interaction domain.

- When developing a single NUI application, start with the most fundamental interactions. Perfect them through careful design and testing. Then extrapolate those designs to more complex regions in an interaction domain.

Should

- Test the fundamental mechanics of the primary interactions before building out the entire interaction. When these are working well (i.e., users enjoy doing them), build on them.

- In building a family of NUI applications, start with simple ones (i.e., those with few possibilities and a clear and familiar model of interactions) and perfect them. Apply those learnings to more advanced applications.

Could

- Study existing NUI applications. Are they fun to use? Do the interactions seem seamless and intuitive? Did users hate to stop using them? If the answer to all these questions is yes, then apply what you have learned to your application.

SUMMARY

Creating successful NUI applications requires attention to the mechanics of interaction and the constraints of the domain. Imagining a skilled practitioner in the domain and designing the system to work the way she does is a good approach.

Contextual Environments

> *All science is experiential; but all experience must be related back to and derives its validity from the conditions and context of consciousness in which it arises, i.e., the totality of our nature.*
>
> **—Wilhelm Dilthey**

DESCRIPTION

In Chapter 2 we provided a definition of the NUI. NUIs are not thoughtless applications of new modalities of input that either mimic actions in the real world or mimic existing interface paradigms. Instead, NUIs reframe design and research in terms of the following questions:

1. How can I create an interface in which users quickly become expert while using actions that feel natural to them and build on and extrapolate from natural actions? (the design question)

2. How can I be sure that I succeeded in creating an interface that feels natural to the user? (the research question)

In that chapter we used the example of the major league pitcher. To him, standing on the mound, choosing the pitch, and throwing it are "natural," that is, they feel natural and his behavior is natural. The challenge of the NUI is to move users from clumsy and self-conscious novice performance to accomplished, fluid, and comfortable performance as quickly as possible. NUIs do this by beginning with "self-evident" evident actions, for example, defining the ways of propelling a sphere (underhand or overhand) using only one's body and shaping these actions quickly and continuously in the context of skilled performance by the professional.

In Chapter 3, we examined the contextual environment. Drawing on the example in Chapter 2, pitching is "natural" in baseball. It fits in the context of baseball. The same action would be unnatural in cricket or American football and illegal in soccer. **27**

Each of these environments is highly artificial and stylized with arcane rules and traditions. How could the behavior in any of these environments be construed as "natural"? What natural means to us is *not* primitive or unrefined. A natural user interface is not one that magically responds to any action, somehow correctly guessing the user's intent. Instead, a NUI fosters the development of skilled behavior and engenders a feeling of mastery by eliciting appropriate actions from users and shaping them into skilled behavior smoothly, efficiently, and enjoyably.

But what role do context and environment play in creating a NUI? Practically, the team creating a NUI is faced with three questions.

1. What are the characteristics of contexts in which a touch-based NUI is likely to be ultimately successful?

2. What about the environment is likely to elicit actions that will be initially successful and that can be shaped and extended to meet the ultimate task requirements in a way that is quick and fosters a sense of mastery and enjoyment in the user?

3. What does skilled and fluid action look like in a given context?

It follows that careful reflection on the context and environment in terms of how they elicit action that is congruent with the actions of the skilled practitioner and enjoyable is the key to the success of that particular NUI in terms of gaining initial acceptance, promoting rapid learning, and achieving skilled performance.

APPLICATION TO NUI

When we look at specific contexts in which touch-based NUIs have shown promise, they tend to embody some common characteristics. First, they are social contexts—leisure environments, where people gather to interact, retail environments, where people meet to transact business, demonstration environments, where the user employs technology to perform before an audience, and public environments, where people are enticed to walk up and explore the technology. These latter environments are a kind of interactive public art. The NUI enhances those interactions. So the NUI works well for tightly "coupled" tasks, where multiple people are working closely together toward a common goal. Playing games, sharing experiences, and completing a complex transaction are good examples. These environments are also characterized by intermittent use of indeterminate duration. Again, playing a game, sharing experiences, and completing complex social/commercial transactions are good candidates. Some of these are social contexts where groups gather and dissipate spontaneously and at will. Others are contexts in which people gather to complete a shared task that involves complex information and multiple possible outcomes (e.g., buying a product that has multiple alternatives.) They often take place in public places. The intermittent and indeterminate use of these systems necessitates easy introduction and a quick ascension to "expert" use. The fact that they are mostly voluntary means that the interaction must be fun and rewarding for all. In many cases the technology will offer enhanced capabilities that make the interaction more enjoyable. Another characteristic of these environments is that users are focused on content—the representation of the game pieces, the sharing of photos or other content, or the examination or configuration of products.

In addition to these obvious characteristics of the areas where the touch-based NUIs seems to work well, there is a more subtle aspect of the contexts in which NUIs are effective. That is, the deep context of interaction is a relationship between the two or more parties in which the interface is acting as facilitator not only for the outcome of the transaction but also for the relationship between the actors.

These contexts contrast sharply with the domain in which the traditional graphical user interface (the GUI) has been most successful. The typical GUI environment is one where users are working in isolation, with their interactions occurring not here and not now. For example, they are sending email to each other or they are interacting through instant messaging, which has been characterized as "CB radio for typists."

At this point we should review the definition of the NUI in relation to our discussion of context. The "leading skilled effortless practice" aspect of the definition of NUI is in some tension with the "most appropriate for context," and both of those are in tension with "social". Interestingly, "content first" is just another way of saying controls disappear, which is congruent with all the aspects of the NUI definition.

For example, wouldn't a voice interface for giving commands be more "natural" in the context of driving a car? The argument would be that typing while driving is not natural. Few would disagree. Would that make speaking while driving "natural"? It's certainly more appropriate to context. You can keep your eyes on the road and your hands on the wheel. We'll leave aside the subtlety of where your attention is focused. (The researchers argue that talking on the phone [or dictating] is almost as bad as typing, but for some reason listening to the radio or talking with passengers is not as cognitively demanding as those activities.)

However, the NUI is defined by three elements:

- Enjoyable

- Leading to skilled practice

- Appropriate to context

These elements are joined by "and." A NUI must have all of these elements in varying degrees. Games are enjoyable, but many have nothing to do with NUI. Many training systems (e.g., Mavis Beacon teaches typing) lead to skilled practice, but are not NUIs. An ATM is appropriate to context but is not a NUI.

This could be seen as an elaborate evasion, but it's true of most sophisticated definitions. Chess is not defined by any single attribute but by all its elements in combination. This is a type of definition that prevents one from falling into intellectual cul-de-sacs. These cul-de-sacs are common with definitions that rely on a single attribute. For example, "humans are defined by tool making." Okay, then monkeys,

Japanese otters, and many birds are also humans since they make and use tools. This explains why all these species also build cathedrals, create theories of the universe, and have wars. In fact, if we consider what makes a human a human to be a combination of many characteristics, we can escape such absurdities. The same logic applies to the definition of the NUI.

LESSONS FROM THE PAST

Thinking from a NUI perspective, how do we elicit behaviors that are likely to be successful and can form a trajectory of learning that leads to mastery? In creating a truly natural user interface it's helpful to consider the original definition of "affordance." While some recent authors have narrowed that definition, originally it was conceived quite broadly and was rooted in a spontaneous and holistic relationship between the actor and the environment, that is, "an affordance is a property of whatever the person interacts with, but to be in the category of affordances it has to be a property that interacts with a property of an agent in such a way that an activity can be supported." The statement is complex and requires some unpacking. First, it says that an affordance is a property of the environment or context. Second, the affordance elicits an action. Third, the action elicited by the environment is supported by the environment. Stated simply, the user is likely to "do the right thing" without training. The "right thing" is an action that is successful in the near term and increases the likelihood that the next action will be successful.

The naturalness of the NUI begins with a symbiotic relationship between the actor and the acting system (the environment). This symbiosis is the starting point for design, the touchstone for evaluation, and the determinant of initial success. The NUI system reacts in such a way as to show the user the next step or foreshadow the final outcome. For example, cupping one's hands allows one to "pick up" liquids to drink. The success of retrieving liquids with one hand leads one to try two hands. The way in which the hands are held is gradually shaped by the way the water reacts.

This symbiosis between the environment and the user leads to several implications for design and evaluation.

DESIGN GUIDELINES

As we noted, the first step is forget what you know about designing for GUIs or the web. The GUI is interaction mediated by a mouse (or some other pointing device). The web interaction is very simple: just point and click. The challenge of web design is knowing where to click to get the desired result. The NUI designer should forget all she knows about the these highly successful designs and should instead begin with a clean sheet. But how do you "fill that paper"?

Must

- Begin with what actions are elicited in this environment. For example, a game can begin with the environment and actions typical of that game. Where to begin in designing a NUI game of checkers is relatively clear.

- Next, consider content. Users focus on content and so should the interface. Provide the absolute minimal number of interface elements that are required for the interaction. For some interactions that is no interface beyond the content.

- Third, consider how these interactions might be logically extended so that the new actions are easily learned and present the expected result.

For example, one of the popular application on Microsoft Surface is a bowling game. The only interface is the pins, the bowling ball, and the lane. The action is obvious: roll the ball to knock down the pins. The game is enhanced by the fact that you can stretch the bowling ball to cover the entire lane. It is also enhanced by the fact you can knock over pins by hand. (Note: An astute reader will object that this simple bowling game does not prepare one to be a skilled bowler. That is true. In this case the game is an end in itself, just as "pong" or Tetris are games that are ends in themselves: the goal of the NUI in this case is to facilitate playing of this game, and not of the physical game which it represents).

Should

- Interface control elements should not be presented if they are not needed. For example, if the user is resizing an object, he simply stretches it with by touching it in two places and moving his fingers apart.

- Most interface elements should emerge in response to user action only to communicate the state of the system and suggest the next action or the consequence of the current action.

- The number of system states should be few, and the gestures required to invoke them should be obvious.

- The system should be judicious about changing state mid-gesture.

Could

- Start with the beginning and end state of an application, remove all the interface controls, and imagine how the user would interact with the objects of the application to move from the start state to the end state.

SUMMARY

We considered the relationship of environmental context to a gestural NUI. In doing so we described the characteristics of environments where a gestural NUI would be successful. We also considered the environment inside the application itself. What elements would elicit responses from the user? How could we shape those responses to teach the user the entire system?

FURTHER READING

Gibson's theory of affordances offers an important and useful alternative to the cognitive perspective often assumed by researchers and practitioners in HCI. Its importance and usefulness derives (in part) from its emphasis on the environment as eliciting behavior. This focus on the environment steers researchers and designers to look to the visual and interactive design of a system for incremental improvements and breakthroughs. At the same time, the theory uses a specialized and somewhat arcane language to describe affordances. The third chapter, "The Theory of Affordances," in *Perceiving Acting and Knowing* (Lawrence Earlbaum, 1977) provides a good overview of the theory and a perspective on its origins in Gestalt psychology.

For an early and prescient overview of the future of computing, Mark Weiser's article "The Computer of the 21st Century," which appeared in a special issue of *Scientific American* in 1991 (Sept. 1991, pp. 94–104), shows considerable insight into the future of touch computing. It can be read to predict the iPhone (active badge), the iPad (pad), and Microsoft Surface (live board).

The Spatial NUI

> *Space is big. You just won't believe how vastly, hugely, mind-bogglingly big it is.*
> *I mean, you may think it's a long way down the road to the drug store, but that's just*
> *peanuts to space.*
>
> —Douglas Adams

DESCRIPTION

Traditional GUI interaction models are flat, planar, and two-dimensional (2-D). You can use some *two-and-a-half dimensional* (2.5-D) techniques (such as skewing planes, adding shadows, and overlapping elements) to make some objects look as if they have depth. In contrast, in a touch NUI interaction, models go beyond a simple plane to provide depth, encourage immersion, and make objects appear to have volume or take on real-world three-dimensional (3-D) behaviors so people can navigate spatially in all dimensions.

APPLICATION TO NUI

You should not always use 3-D environments. Sometimes, 3-D environments are disorienting and overly complex, but your application's behaviors, transitions, and navigation should always consider the *z*-axis. For example, photos and videos in the Photos application on Microsoft's Surface are inherently resting on a flat canvas, but they rise to the surface when users touch them to give the feeling of depth and realism.

Experiences can represent objects volumetrically and leverage a user's depth perception and spatial memory. Environments can extend well off screen, and users can drag the environment around to relocate content. Objects can be stacked in 3-D space, **33** using depth to sort, distribute, or focus on content. As long as users can use gestures to navigate the environment and orient themselves, they can create a mental model of the space, its content, and the gestures that they need to access that content without needing to see it all on-screen. Users naturally develop associations between what they want to do (for example, play a game) and where they do it (for example, in a game application) from memory-triggered context.

LESSONS FROM THE PAST

For many users the GUI was their first experience of "space" on a computer. The desktop and the icon view of folders allowed them to use two-dimensional space to organize objects. In addition, the WYSIWYG elements of a new generation of applications (word processors, drawing programs) allowed them to use space in input. Previous editors used markup languages to format text; as a result, the text was just a series of commands and text objects. The commands controlled layout and appearance and thus manipulated the output space. GUIs and the generation of applications associated with them changed that. Users could now interact with documents in the same two dimensions (horizontal and vertical) that the document would be rendered in. The same was true (more or less) of drawing programs.

Systems that used 3-D representations of objects have been tested in experiments. The results have been encouraging, even though these interfaces used a traditional mouse and keyboard.

DESIGN GUIDELINES

Support Using 2-D Planar Space

Depending on your application's scenarios and context, the viewable space might be constrained. In some cases, the canvas is fixed, with a limited content presentation. In other cases, the canvas is flexible, enabling users to zoom in and out. Use spatial memory in situations where the canvas is larger than what appears in the screen. In either case, backgrounds, objects, and controls must consider the z-axis for their behaviors and movements.

Must

- Create an environment that is optimized for touch in its layout, feedback, metaphors, and behaviors. Any item that responds to users' touch must be at least 15 mm in size in all directions, and there must be at least 5 mm between minimally sized touch targets.

Should

- Leverage spatial memory by enabling users to change the screen layout themselves, and consistently position content and controls within your application.

In situations with large canvases, make sure that the spatial relationship of objects is clear and consistent.

- Consider the meaning of spatial relationships. Geographical and other naturally spatial content lends itself well to spatial relationship. For nonphysical information, consider carefully how the spatial relationship between elements is considered and remembered. (For example, an organizational hierarchy's levels are strictly hierarchical, because the physical distance between elements has no meaning. However, viewers tend to associate vertical position with power, so the relative position of two equally "ranked" individuals should be the same, and not necessarily moved up because one person reports to a more senior leader.)

- In a multi-user system do not allow one user to shift the views of all users, unless the task is highly coupled. In loosely coupled or uncoupled tasks, users are disrupted if the entire canvas moves because of one user's actions.

Could

- Use spatial navigation (flat and wide) in place of hierarchical navigation (that is, menus).

- Make sure that the application does not become too cluttered or too sparse. Enable users to quickly and dynamically repopulate the screen with an optimal information density for the task that they are performing (for example, if users are viewing hierarchical data visualizations, provide preferred views of the data and note important information such as organizational or educational boundaries).

Adhere to Principles of 3-D Space Utilization (the z-Axis)

Users can clearly see and recognize objects, content, and other elements from a distance. When users view them at a closer distance, they see more detail, such as additional information, subtle textures, or hints of reflected light. When users interact with interface elements, they reveal an even finer level of detail through sound, visual feedback, and movement. For example, icons in Launcher transform into application previews when they are touched, and then they change into the live application when they are touched again. These actions all provide progressively more detail with deeper interactions. As users zoom in closer to objects, the objects should reveal unexpected visual or audible details.

Must

- For all movable and free-form elements, use visual feedback (depth) to acknowledge objects or controls that users successfully touch by moving the item toward the user along the z-axis. (The exception to this guideline is when the z-axis is already being used for another purpose, or where precise placement is required.)

- Adhere to the standard gesture for moving forward and back in the z-axis.

Should

- Use an appropriate 3-D projection. A standard perspective projection does not work because users can approach a display from any side.

- Use 3-D space in a semantic way, so that the relative z-axis position of each element has meaning to the user.

- Make the structure of every element feel like it has volume. The experience must feel exploratory and invite users to navigate through the volume as if it is their own world.

Could

- Use the zoom gesture to move the view in and out, rather than to change the size of content. The functional difference is that all elements move toward the viewer, rather than a single element growing larger relative to the others.

- Give 3-D behaviors to 2-D elements, so that, for example, users can turn over flat elements and interact with the other side.

- Remember that the potential volume of interactive space can be larger than what users can view on the screen at any given moment. Allow users to understand that volume can be a vast 2-D canvas and also a fully 3-D volume in which content is located and activities occur.

SUMMARY

The use of effective 3-D space can significantly enhance the experience with a NUI. Some of these benefits could also be present in GUI interfaces also if it was decided to use them. However, in addition to the fact that the use of 3-D space aids in finding documents for the NUI, they are even more significant. NUI systems make users comfortable by providing environments similar to the real world. This ability moves the NUI beyond the traditional desktop.

FURTHER READING

Three-dimensional interfaces can provide a wide variety of benefits regardless of where they are realized on a NUI or a GUI. These benefits are well documented in two papers by George Robertson et al. See Data Mountain: Using Spatial Memory for Document Management, G. Robertson and M. Czerwinski, UIST, San Francisco, 1998; http://delivery. acm.org/10.1145/290000/288596/p153-robertson.pdf?key1=288596&key2= 3134091821&coll=ACM&dl=ACM&CFID=98229772&CFTOKEN=82307336; and The Task Gallery: A 3D Window Manager, G. Robertson, M. van Dantzich, et al., CHI 2000, The Hague, Amsterdam; http://delivery.acm.org/10.1145/340000/332482/p494-robertson.pdf?key1=332482 &key2=4114091821&coll=ACM&dl=ACM&CFID=98229772&CFTOKEN=82307336.

A *projection* is the mathematical mechanism by which 3-D images are mapped onto a 2-D plane, usually in such a way that the images appear to be in 3-D.

The Social NUI

A dream you dream alone is only a dream. A dream you dream together is reality.
—**John Lennon**

DESCRIPTION

In standard GUIs, social barriers occur because of the input and output system. For example, experiences are inherently single-person when users have only one mouse, one keyboard, and no touchscreen. The standard GUI supports a classic view of the information worker; she is alone in her office working on various documents (e.g., spreadsheets, reports) or analyzing data. In contrast, many modern NUIs are designed for multi-person input, so multiple users can gather around the display and interact with it. For example, they can play the same instance of a game at the same time. In this way they elevate the activity from a solitary experience to a social experience.

The social experience is not limited to the interactions between people and the user interface. For a "social interface," the less communication that happens between an individual and the UI, the better. The more communication that happens between the people around it, the better. People focus more on each other than the computer, so the computer becomes secondary to the group using it.

In the video game industry, competitive and cooperative games rival traditional single-player games as the exciting games in the market. Console games have increasingly become the mediator for social interaction that occurs between people who are engaged in a game. These cooperative and competitive games occur in two forms: "shoulder to shoulder," where people play side by side, or mediated, where people are distant from each other in space or time or both.

You can reuse cooperative techniques from video game design to make other NUI applications more engaging, fun, and social.

APPLICATION TO NUI

Not all NUI interfaces are designed for shoulder-to-shoulder social interaction. Some use NUI principles and approaches to facilitate solitary consumption of content such as electronic books or movies online. Other NUI devices are designed to simplify tasks in specific environments, such as using a touchscreen or issuing voice commands while driving. Conversely, much of social computing does not involve the use of a NUI. Often social computing systems use a classic GUI to provide sharing of information and enable collaborative working with other members of a work team who are displaced in space or time or both. In this chapter we focus on NUIs that are intended to support shoulder-to-shoulder social interaction.

In order to succeed, the designer of this type of NUI, the social NUI, needs to supplement her NUI design principles with some "social design" principles. Similarly, the researcher needs to evaluate the system using pairs or groups of people. Below, we list some of these principles for testing and designing social NUI.

LESSONS FROM THE PAST

Considering the history of HCI since the early 1980s, some consistent themes are breaking down the barriers between humans and technology and breaking down the barriers between people. An overall trend in interface design has been to move away from interfaces that require people to express their requests in a specific, detailed, precise syntax and an arcane semantics that closely mirrors the way the system operates. Instead, the trend in interface design has been toward systems that allow for more immediate and natural communication.

For example, early programming consisted of plugging wires in patch panels of circuits. As such, it required the programmers to express themselves in the "language" of current flow. A great step forward occurred with command languages, which allowed people to express their desires in a symbolic way using arbitrary and precise command languages that the user mastered over time. Initially these languages were often awkward to use—they were logical, with regular syntax and systematic semantics—and complete—they covered a domain of work/action. They were often intended for specific domains of human activity as reflected in their names, for example, COBOL (COmmon Business Oriented Language) and FORTRAN (FORmula TRANslation). Command languages for operating systems, for example, UNIX and VMS, had similar properties. Most importantly for our purposes here, it should be noted that they reflected a "relationship" between a single user and a machine (others were involved only peripherally). In addition, interaction was often temporally displaced, for example, the user input a long series of commands (a program or command file) and the system responded with voluminous output.

With the modern GUI the gulf between the user and the computer decreased. With menus and dialog boxes, the GUI eliminated syntax and simplified semantics. The user did not have to memorize and recall commands but could recognize menu items. The syntax of commands was totally eliminated or effectively subsumed in a dialog box. Combined with the personal computer and its WYSIWYG (what you see is what you get) environment, the user could see the immediate effects of her interaction. With the introduction of "undo," the cost of experimentation was greatly reduced. However, the GUI was no more "social" than the command systems that preceded it.

Computing became more social with the broad adoption of the Internet and Ethernet technology. Providing a relatively fault tolerant and standard way for computers to share information naturally resulted in people being able to share information. The architecture and its protocols were particularly suited to sharing by people who were separated by space and time (not here, not now). Applications such as mail (anywhere, anytime) and IM messaging (anywhere, now) exploited this technology and were widely adopted. While these developments represented a significant advance in bringing people together, they involved a mediated and displaced kind of sharing.

The advent of touch computing and relatively large sharable screens combined to produce systems that are not limited to relatively specific and routinized transactions (like grocery check out). This enables a new kind of computing: the social NUI, where people can share experiences in the here and now and use the computer simply as a supporting mechanism.

The field of supporting multiple users on a single screen is known as *single display groupware*, a term coined by James Stewart and his colleagues. Of particular interest is a piece of work done by Mark Hancock and his colleagues, who where investigating how to give audio feedback to multiple users simultaneously. Their paper provides a variety of recommendations and some surprising findings worth reading more about. Another issue of particular interest is known as "inter-user task coupling," which is of critical importance whenever an application is intended to be used by more than one user simultaneously.

INTER-USER TASK COUPLING

A critical element of social computing is considering the issue of task coupling. At any given time, multiple users who are working around a multi-user device might be engaged in multiple levels of *task coupling*. There are three distinctive levels of task coupling:

- *Highly coupled tasks*: Users help each other accomplish the same task. For example, two users touch two portions of the same object to perform a manipulation, or two users look for the same album in a large collection.

- *Lightly coupled tasks*: Two users try to achieve a result that depends on them both, but they are engaged in different tasks to achieve it (sometimes called *divide and conquer*). For example, one user searches for an album in a large collection while the other user searches for album art to apply to it. Another example is when the Chief of Fire and Chief of Police can manage different elements of a crisis.

- *Uncoupled tasks*: Users share the same space, but they are engaged in separate tasks. For example, two users search through the same collection of photographs, but each user is looking for different pictures, or one user is searching for photographs, while the other user is checking his e-mail.

How well your system supports these different levels of inter-user task coupling will affect how successful it will be as a social NUI.

DESIGN GUIDELINES
Must

- Test designs with multiple users simultaneously interacting.
- Consider how you want to support different levels of coupling in the tasks, and how to support varying levels of coupling within the same application. Consider how multiple users will utilize your application. Will it be on a mobile device that is passed around? Will it be on a single screen that multiple users will view shoulder to shoulder? Will it be on a table where users will sit across from one another?

Should

- Create an experience that comes alive with several users, so that the experience is more fun or efficient when many hands are working simultaneously.
- Enable a single user to enjoy the experience without requiring other users.
- Enable new users to join, so that the approval of additional users allows them to easily engage with your application, without disrupting other users already present.
- Be able to continue with fewer users, allowing one user to leave without disrupting all others' experience.
- Support multiple coupling levels by enabling users to perform tasks together to varying degrees. Do not segment the space into areas for particular functions (for example, this side is for performing task A, and the other side is for task B). Allow any function to be performed in any space.
- Enable many users to simultaneously use content and controls. Do not block progress by requiring all users to use a common set of controls. Instead, allow users to break up portions of the task by dividing up the controls.
- Do not break from the paradigm of direct-touch input when users are performing highly coupled or lightly coupled tasks because direct manipulations

beneficially create consequential communication. For example, if users are searching through objects by physically moving them, their progress is clear by the speed of their movement and its location on the screen, and can be seen effortlessly by other users through peripheral vision. Changing this to a virtual device removes this communication.

- Support consequential communication by making system changes clear to all users. For example, when a person uses two hands to zoom in on a map, any observer can clearly see how and why the zoom changed.

- Avoid the use of ambiguous audio feedback by making sure that the success or error of a touch is not tied to an audio cue. There is no mechanism to help users distinguish the cause of two simultaneous audio cues.

- Do not provide multiple system modes for input touches. For example, in a GUI application, when a user selects a property to apply to an object, the mouse pointer changes mode (such as turning into a paint brush). This concept does not work with any multi-touch system: which of the 52 contacts should become a paint brush? This is an important, fundamental difference between single-touch and multi-touch systems. This problem is worse in multi-user applications, because one user who puts the system into a particular mode can significantly disrupt all other users.

- Do not attach shared controls to one side of the display, because users will be forced to reach uncomfortably close to another participant to use the control. Instead, enable users to move controls and share them or to dedicate the control to a particular user while he performs some lightly coupled or uncoupled task.

- Communicate ownership through the location of content. If new content is "owned" by a particular user, place it in front of that user. If the group shares ownership, place the content in the center.

Could

- Enable users to divide up their tasks and to decide for themselves whether they will be engaged in a shared-display, single-user session, or in a truly multi-user session.

- Provide methods of dividing up a task with various levels of coupling so that users can work in parallel. For example, enable users to define interaction areas that they can dedicate to a particular function, by specifying what is performed in a particular region of the screen.

- Provide modal spaces that allow input to change modes based on the location of the touch. For example, if you want users to be able to paint and annotate an object, provide regions of the screen where they can drag the object and where touches are then mapped to either paint or annotate. Make sure that users can also move these regions to enable users to divide their task.

FURTHER READING

Stewart, J., Bederson, B., and Druin, A. Single display groupware: A model for co-present collaboration. *Proceedings of Human Factors in Computing Systems (CHI 99)*. ACM Press, 286–293. In this work, Stewart et al. define the term single display groupware, discuss the model, and compare it to traditional computer collaboration with remote participants. They also describe the requirements that SDG places on computer technology, and their understanding of the benefits and costs of such systems. They also present the results of tests run with 60 elementary school children using their technology.

Hancock, M. S., Shen, C., Forlines, C., and Ryall, K. Exploring non-speech auditory feedback at an interactive multi-user tabletop. *Proceedings of Graphics Interface 2005*, 41–50. In this work, Hancock et al. point out the inherent ambiguity of giving audio feedback to multiple users simultaneously. They examine various methods of personalizing the audio feedback to reduce cross-talk.

Consequential communication occurs when the behavior of users who are interacting with the system also provides another user with information about that interaction.

Seamlessness

> There are unknown forces in nature; when we give ourselves wholly to her, without reserve, she lends them to us; she shows us these forms, which our watching eyes do not see, which our intelligence does not understand or suspect.
>
> —Auguste Rodin

DESCRIPTION

Seamless experiences enable users to be immersed so they embrace new experiences. You can create seamless experiences by creating an environment that leads users to suspend their sense of disbelief, no longer comparing their actions to a defined pattern, and experience a direct connection between their actions and the objects and operations of the system.

LESSONS FROM THE PAST

Seamless experiences are those in which users are cognitively and emotionally immersed so that they embrace these new experiences and rapidly progress to skilled practice. You can create seamless experiences by designing a system that leads users to suspend their users' sense of disbelief.

The *suspension of disbelief* refers to a person's willingness to accept something as true or sufficiently real even if it is fantastic or impossible in the real world. The combination of the suspension of disbelief and interactivity makes video games appealing and makes them seem even closer to real life. For many years, the game industry has focused on building immersive worlds that simulate a living, breathing environment in an emotionally engaging and approachable way.

A second element of a seamless experience is that the self-monitoring that is often part of learning new skills has disappeared. The actor no longer monitors her actions, comparing them to an idealized template. New learners often approach new skills with a strategy of "objectifying" themselves and monitoring their actions on a moment-by-moment basis. (They may also develop strategies—verbal formulas that "trick" them into skilled performance.) In contrast, experts act as if there is a direct connection between their actions, any tools that they are using, and the resulting effect. Their actions are fluid and whole rather than halting and particularized.

APPLICATION TO THE NUI

One way to suspend disbelief and encourage fluid action is by mimicking real-world objects and using virtual-world capabilities to extend the objects beyond what is possible in the real world. Imagine an object that initially appears as a globe that you can spin by flicking it with your finger. You touch a location on the globe to zoom in closer. Each touch zooms in further until you see points of interest that you touch to create a personalized itinerary. The object is not a spinning globe that can create itineraries, but disbelief is suspended when the virtual object mimics its real-world counterpart.

To suspend disbelief successfully, erase the line between the physical and virtual worlds in a way that is seamless and in which the performance of the technology is flawless. A NUI experience must respond continuously to fingers and physical objects that are placed on it and must immerse users in a better-than-life experience. For example, exploring a virtual database of treasured objects is both real (these are representations of real objects) and magical (I can control them in exciting ways). These actions themselves enhance any experience.

When users directly manipulate objects on-screen and with their fingers the experience can quickly feel seamless and thrilling. The representation of physical objects makes the experience feel seamless between the physical and virtual worlds and between one's self and one's actions. To perpetuate the suspension of disbelief, the system must respond continuously to fingers and by displaying information on the screen in expected ways.

A final word about seamlessness—it is fragile. Any seemingly small disturbance and the entire illusion is broken and the experience is now disjointed. If the system is slow, or if it responds in an unexpected way, then the experience is no longer seamless. The same principle applies in the real world. To use our baseball metaphor, a bat that is too heavy or too light leads to a feeling of clumsiness and inhibits both performance and the experience of seamlessness. Ironically, highly skilled practitioners may be more sensitive to subtle differences in the tools or instruments they use. In a way their senses are more attuned.

Must

- Respond to *every* contact. Feedback shows that the system is responding, and people will not wonder whether the object is broken or malfunctioning.

- Respond *immediately* to every contact. This immediate response blurs the line between the real and the virtual.

- Make every transition fluid. Every object and visible property change must smoothly animate and transition into and out of existence, or between changes. Nothing should abruptly appear or disappear.

Should

- Make feedback whimsical, magical, and either expected or/and informative. By expected we mean that it should make sense to the user. Moving an object by touching and dragging is a good example. Informative means in a subtle but effective way show the users what they should do next. That kind of feedback/ feedforward makes learning seamless.

- Create transition animations that communicate state and relationship changes and contribute to a consistent interaction paradigm. This ultimately provides the personality of the application.

- Mimic the real world in your transitions by using notions such as mass, acceleration, friction, viscosity, and gravity.

- Make sure the controls for starting and ending and for major state changes are always visible. This visibility is in contrast to systems that embed major functions within menus.

- Break from real-world behavior to match user intent. All interaction metaphors start with physical manipulation, and then extend it. (For more information, see Chapters 9, Super Real, and 10, Scaffolding.)

Could

- Play with physical reactions. Users accept a lot of reinterpretations of reality when they are interacting with virtual objects. You can modify the physical responses to meet the needs of your application.

SUMMARY

Seamlessness is one of the necessary characteristics of the NUI. An interface with obvious discontinuity or one the breaks the user's sense of connection to the objects and her own behavior cannot be a NUI. While any interface can become seamless, with practice NUIs are designed to migrate the user quickly and with pleasure to skilled practice. Making seamlessness a goal of the design is a path to the NUI. We have outlined several techniques to design a seamless interface. However, perception of seamlessness is in the hands of the user, so seamlessness must be tested with users.

FURTHER READING

Seamlessness is easy to grasp but difficult to fully explain. One reason is that once one starts to explain seamlessness, it becomes a construct and loses its essence. One of the early attempts to characterize the broad implications of seamlessness was a narrative written by a philosopher who studied archery in an attempt to better understand Zen philosophy: *Zen in the Art of Archery*, by Eugen Herrigel, Pantheon Books, 1953. The book is short and easy to read, but its meaning can be difficult to grasp.

Super Real

Any sufficiently advanced technology is indistinguishable from magic.

—Arthur C. Clarke

DESCRIPTION

Because touch is inherently physical, it creates a sense of direct interaction with and control of technology. You can create more fluid, natural experiences by mimicking real-world physical interactions and augmenting them beyond what is possible in the real world. *Super realism* pushes beyond what is physically natural so that experiences do more than is possible in the real world. At the same time, super real is an intuitive extension of the real. Super interactions are both grounded and magical.

For example, on the iPhone one can contract or expand an image by touching it with two fingers and then moving one's fingers together (contract) or apart (expand) (Figure 9.1). It is as if the image were made of rubber and can be stretched. This ability to zoom in and out by just touching represents a kind of naive physics and is delightful to users

In other applications such as the URP (Urban and Rural Planning system), one can use actual physical models to simulate an urban environment. One can simply pick up buildings and place them on the screen. The system enhances the experience by allowing the user to simulate and change the angle and intensity of sunlight (for example) as the day progresses. One can also inspect the model from different viewpoints, for example, pedestrian vs. birds-eye view. Similarly, one can change the building material by touching the virtual building with a material wand.

These examples and many others illustrate the power of the super real. The system works as we might expect it to because it mimics the way objects work in the world, that is, it's real. At the same time, we can interact with these objects in extraordinary ways (the super) that do not require an abstract language with arcane syntax or a series of interactions with cumbersome controls.

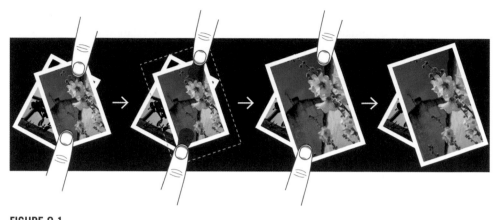

FIGURE 9.1

A user scales a photo by using a two-finger gesture.

To create natural interactions, create the base of the interactions in the real world and then extend them in intuitive ways. To create super real interactions, leverage the possibilities of virtual objects in digital environments to exceed what is possible in the real world.

LESSONS FROM THE PAST

It has been a well-established tradition to design systems that draw from people's knowledge and experience but extrapolate that knowledge and experience in desirable ways. More "traditional" systems like the GUI follow work practice but extend it in ways made possible by technology. These systems and products are also enticing to users because they greatly increase the rate of productivity, create new possibilities for work/creativity, can provide an immediate and positive emotional experience, or some combination of the three.

The GUI and its associated generation of applications were more likely to increase productivity and create new possibilities for work than to excite users. More precisely, experiencing the "thrill" of using a typical GUI application involved learning a new way of working. Admittedly, many GUIs drew on some elements of the user's prior experience and eliminated the need to memorize and correctly type arcane commands with prescriptive syntax. They also capitalized on our knowledge of the electromechanical world. For example, they had buttons that one pressed to activate functions. Even the names of these types of controls drew on analogies from the physical world. For example, "radio buttons" mimicked the action and logic of buttons on electromechanical radios. That is, you push one button and the others are "deactivated" as the station is changed.

However, this approach, while very powerful, creates its own challenges. For example, I no longer have to remember commands; I just have to recognize them.

But I do need to remember where they were in a large maze of menu choices. Even more subtly, the commands often change the user's understanding of their work products. For example, on an electric typewriter the user could hit a return key and simply move the paper up and the point of typing down. In contrast, hitting the return key in a full-screen editor inserts "invisible" characters (carriage return and line feed) that also serve to mark the end of paragraphs. Use of the tab key was even more confusing to the new user.

As the interface and implicit model of a text editor were learned, one could experience the joys of spell-checking, search and replace, and revisable documents. Even more thrilling was the new possibility of creating professional-appearing documents by using fonts, inserting figures, and creating styles.

A NUI promises to shorten the learning curve by replacing a maze of controls and menus with simple actions, gestures, affordances, and feedback. It also promises to keep the interaction fun by making the interaction itself fun. You don't need to wait for a final work product to feel the joy.

But all these goals are easy to discuss and hard to achieve. Below is a set of principles to help the development team create an interface worthy of the NUI title.

APPLICATION TO THE NUI

Must

- Create immediate responses to all user input that will receive a response. Pre-buffer content, provide a transition, or use other mechanisms to make sure that every touch receives an immediate and meaningful response. An application without immediate responses detracts significantly from the user experience.

- Enable single-finger drag and flick movements on movable content. You must always define a single-finger drag and flick to make sure that users can always apply these basic manipulations to all content.

- Enable inertia on objects and content that users can move about the screen. Inertia contributes significantly to the sense of a natural environment.

- Do not use time-based gestures on content. Time-based activations introduce mandatory delays for expert users, and they also detract from the sense of a natural environment.

- Enable users to manipulate content directly, rather than through user interface controls. For example, use a scale manipulation instead of a zoom button.

Should

- Begin the experience with a familiar environment and behaviors, so users quickly feel comfortable in performing explorations. For example, to create this type of experience, mimic the metaphors of Surface Shell or the natural environment around the Microsoft Surface unit.

- Enable quick discovery of delightful interactions, so users can quickly accomplish simple tasks or simply play with the system. Early success creates familiarity, confidence, and a willingness to explore.

- Consistently use transitions and make sure the application does not slow the processor unit. Lagging due to processor saturation makes the screen and input display seem to suffer from random movements.

- Make the experience feel user-driven by ensuring that each state change is clearly in response to user actions. For example, if a user prefers a particular orientation of content, do not "snap" to that orientation. Instead, use a slowing technique that does not employ a step function.

- Do not innovate for the sake of novelty. All interactions in your application should be based on the foundations in the toolkit you are using including both the manipulation and inertia processors or should be natural extensions of the interactions that your users perform.

- Always show signs of life, even when the user is not interacting. For example, the Water attract on Microsoft Surface was designed to be constantly in motion, but it is never distracting.

- In creating this feeling of life, make sure that the behavior is subtle to avoid being annoying or distracting. Do not cause the application's state to actually change; instead, change only background and graphical elements.

Could

- Consider what advanced, expert functionality you want to enable in addition to natural interactions. Provide a mechanism that extends natural behavior to transition the user from a novice to an expert. For more information, see Chapter 10, Scaffolding.

- Provide continued delight and discovery over time, in minutes, hours, days, or months. For example, the Water attract application begins with gentle ripples to entice users, responds to every touch to give them success, and ultimately draws their attention to the access points to enable deeper engagement.

- Provide a path to transition novices to experts. If the same user will use your application for an extended period of time, create distinct usage patterns and methods for novices and experts, so experts can interact more efficiently. Enable novices to become experts without instructions so they use the application for the long term.

SUMMARY

One part of the promise of the NUI is to make interaction with technology seem like magic. Magic is delightful. The magician makes the impossible seem easy and wondrous. Her magic often is an extension of the real that seems impossible but that we might extrapolate. It is a kind of "plausible impossible." When cartoon characters run off a cliff but do not fall because they have not realized they have passed the cliff edge, they are making the impossible seem plausible (you won't fall if you don't realize you are in space). The extension of the joke is that the protagonist can "compensate" by running back to the cliff edge quickly and thereby delay the fall just long enough to grab the edge of the cliff before falling.

The same principles apply to our interaction with NUI technology. It works in delightful ways that we might hope and expect. But then when we try something that is plausible but impossible, we discover to our delight that that works, too.

That's easy to say and hard to achieve. But by applying the principles above, being creative, testing your interface, and being fortunate, it can be done.

FURTHER READING

The paper Reality-Based Interaction: A Framework for Post-WIMP Interfaces, *CHI 2008 Proceedings*, April 5–10, Florence Italy, pp. 201–210, by Jacob et al., provides an excellent discussion of the super real. The authors analyze the ways in which an interaction can be reality based, for example, use naive physics to employ body awareness, and build off skills and the like. It also compares these aspects of reality-based interfaces to the enhanced capabilities that technology typically brings, such as expressive power and efficiency. Often these are thought of as being in opposition. What is natural cannot also be powerful. The concept of the super real invites design teams to try to synthesize both ends of the polarity. It promises that an interface can be both intuitive and powerful.

Scaffolding

10

> *When one puts up a building one makes an elaborate scaffold to get everything into its proper place. But when one takes the scaffold down, the building must stand by itself with no trace of the means by which it was erected. That is how a musician should work.*
>
> **—Andres Segovia**

DESCRIPTION

Scaffolding is the creation of a design that promotes autonomous learning by employing actions that encourage users to develop their own cognitive, affective, and psychomotor skills.

APPLICATION TO NUI

Our vision of NUIs is relatively simple to state in principle, but can be very hard to achieve in practice. That vision is that the user moves from "novice" to "expert" quickly and with pleasure. By novice we simply mean someone who uses the system for the first time. By expert we mean someone who uses the system in the way that the designers intended, feels pleasure in those activities, and has achieved that level of competence without the slow and tortuous learning that is typical of mastering many new interfaces. We also imply that the intended use is not a trivial one, for example, using an ATM, where the functions are very limited and the user is led through the interaction step by step and only needs to push the "correct" button. (Note: We don't mean to minimize the importance and challenge of creating and testing effective designs for these types of interfaces; they are just not NUIs.)

One good way to achieve this vision is to use scaffolding. *Scaffolding* is a teaching method that breaks down bigger challenges (such as "How does this whole system work?" or "What are all the possibilities of this system?") and focuses on smaller problem-solving challenges (such as "How do I initiate this one action?" or "What can I do next?"). These small problems are addressed through specific prompts, hints, and leading questions. Scaffolding provides supportive structures and situations that encourage active exploration. It differs dramatically from approaches that use memorization and repetition (the "drill and kill" approach). Scaffolding also eschews the use of reference information in favor of immediate and simple cues that lead the user to the next action. In other words, when done well, scaffolding integrates learning and doing. The user is rewarded by performing successfully throughout the learning process. Using scaffolding requires deconstructing tasks into small, self-evident steps that minimize trial and error and preclude the cul-de-sacs typical of learning functionally rich computer systems.

As part of scaffolding, present users with only the fewest reasonable choices at a given moment. Those few choices should be supported by affordances to lead the user's next action. The action can then be reinforced by confirmation and/or the next affordance. With a relative few and obvious choices, this approach simplifies decision making, discloses information or required choices over time, and simplifies a user's decision making and action. As a result, the system is easier to use and enjoy.

However, simplicity need never mean simplistic; simple processes and tasks can be incredibly rich and powerful.

LESSONS FROM THE PAST

Many of the effective ways of learning to use interfaces can be characterized as scaffolding. For example, the use of familiar metaphors at either the macro or micro level can be thought of as scaffolding. A macro example is the use of columns and rows in a spreadsheet. This representation builds on the ledger book, which also used columns and rows of figures and which was familiar to the existing population of financial analysts. At the micro level, the typical GUI contains scaffolded elements, such as buttons. The virtual buttons look like physical buttons and elicit the intended behavior (pressing) from the user.

Another scaffolding concept is the idea of presenting limited options to the learner. That approach is also characterized as "training wheels." The system prevents the user from "falling" into the deeper complexities of a system's full capabilities. New concepts are introduced when the user has mastered more basic functions and is ready to learn new things. In other words, the training wheels are slowly removed.

This approach contrasts sharply with some traditional approaches in which the user is exposed to a full system model via "reference documentation." It also differs dramatically from many overly simplistic help systems that simply restate the terms already used in the interface, for example, "Use the file menu to save documents." Finally, this approach diverges from video instruction. Video instruction requires users to stop what they are doing, watch a video, and then transfer that knowledge to their task at hand. While the video may make the transfer more straightforward, it still requires that the user switch out of context.

DESIGN GUIDELINES

Must

- Ensure that all likely actions lead to either prompting for the next step in the action sequence or foreshadowing of the state of the system/object when the action is finished.

- At the appropriate time, show users affordances that guide users to access the unseen content or functionality. For example, animate a list of songs when it appears. Users should see the additional content beyond the last song title, for example, a song title partially displayed. This implies that more songs are listed below; in other words, the shown list is incomplete. If the user touches the content, then it should move slightly to show that it can be scrolled.

- Require explicit and intentional user input to activate destructive functions or to cause larger changes or transitions. This input is especially important for transitions that affect more than one user, and even more so when users are engaged in tasks that are not highly coupled. For example, to launch an application, users must touch the application once to see the application preview, and then touch it again to open the application.

- Foreshadow upcoming results so that users can reverse their actions. For example, during the resize of an image, if the image is about to jump to full screen (obscuring other images), show an outline of the image or a transparent version of the image at full-screen size. Then the user can either reverse and negate that action (the image will not jump to full size) or remove her fingers so that the image becomes full size.

Should

- Reduce the number of features in your applications. Additional features add both power and complexity. Instead, provide a premium experience in the primary task that the application offers. Once the primary experience is working well, that is, you have tested it with the intended audience, then judiciously add new features, testing as you go.

- Make sure that the set of features is focused on the particular task. Many applications provide lots of functionality that enables many separate tasks. Make sure that your application's task is clear and that its features focus on performing that task well.

- Provide a clear path from novice to expert so users can move from the initial view of the application to where you ultimately want them to go. For example, if the novice users are individuals who are working on highly coupled tasks, and you want them to perform different loosely coupled tasks, you should visually divide your application with tools to support each task on separate sides of a rectilinear interface.

- Make sure essential features are immediately discoverable, so that users can begin using the system without rote learning. For example, if your application is about creating a document, provide a blank document for creating content immediately. Do not require the user to access a menu to create the blank document or to access the most common tools for document editing. Do not explain saving files and folders until the user has something to save.

- Encourage discovery through exploration, so that further functionality is revealed as users continue through the experience. For example, in a music-browsing application, make album covers become controls, so users can touch them and flip them over to reveal the contents of the album.

- Use consistent interaction metaphors within your application. For example, if you use the flipping technique that is described in the preceding item, make all objects use the flipping technique, providing additional interaction capabilities on the back of each object.

- Hint at deeper possibilities, without taking the focus away from the content. For example, when users first launch a music application, have the albums appear on the display and a few flip over to demonstrate the functionality.

- Make sure visual indications of touch are accurate so that the users are never misled as to what is touchable. For example, disabled buttons must be visually distinct from enabled buttons.

- Make sure feedback contributes to a better understanding of the system and its state. For example, when users touch a control, it moves to the front, grows, and displays a drop shadow, indicating a change in its position along the z-axis and reinforcing its position and demonstrating that it is on top of the content.

- Put users in control, so that they can always understand the state of the application and how to proceed. Do not provide too many automated actions. Keep controls enabled and logical at all times.

Could

- Reduce the number of available paths and choices, so that the next step and available options are always available to users. Achieve the correct balance between the number of choices and paths to ensure that your application meets the functionality needs of its users. The balance is often apparent only by conducting user testing.

- Consider how multiple users will learn together. Users, especially children, invite others to explain the use of the system.

- Provide instructions within the flow of the application, instead of requiring users to break their concentration and search through a help system.

- Make *all* content touchable, so that some visual response is provided no matter where the user touches on the screen.

- Clarify errors, so that when the users touch the application, they can distinguish between hardware errors (the system did not detect the touch), state errors (the touch was detected, but the touched item is not in a state where it responds the way that they expected, such as being disabled), and semantic errors (the touch was detected, the application is in the state they expected, but the application's response to that touch is not what they expected). You can clarify these errors by providing clear visual feedback with information about *all* of these levels.

SUMMARY

Scaffolding is a powerful approach for creating rich NUI applications that are a pleasure to learn and use. Like many powerful approaches, it requires a deft design touch and a sophisticated understanding. It involves an in-depth understanding of the context of use and of users' expectations. It also necessitates a clear vision of skilled performance. The temptation to put reference information in the help system or use video or extensive tutorials should be resisted. By focusing on learning by doing and using a step-by-step approach, users can attain skilled performance enjoyably and feel a sense of accomplishment throughout the learning process.

FURTHER READING

In the 1950s Jerome Bruner introduced the scaffolding approach to describe language learning. This work was based on the seminal thinking of the famous psychologist Vygotsky. A definition of scaffolding and a review of the history of the concept is provided by Susanne Lajoie in Extending the Scaffolding Metaphor in *Instructional Science* (2005), 33, 541-557.

Richard Catrambone and John Carroll provide the first description of a training wheels approach to learning a system in Learning a Word Processing System with Training Wheels and Guided Exploration in CHI + GI 1987, *Proceeding of the CHI Conference*, 1987, 169-174. Available through the ACM Digital Library, http://delivery.acm.org/10.1145/280000/275625/p169-catrambone.pdf?key 1=275625&key2=4722813821&coll=ACM&dl=ACM&CFID=99878216&CFTOKEN=71839147.

User Differentiation

11

Know thy user, for they are not YOU.

—Ancient usability proverb

DESCRIPTION

The classic dictum in HCI, "know your users," has broader implications than is generally realized. Users don't exist in isolation. They live and work in contexts. They have roles, responsibilities, and tasks. All these elements—users themselves, their contexts, their responsibilities, and their goals—shape both the design possibilities and constraints of not only applications but also the rendering of any new interface paradigm.

APPLICATION TO NUI

Working from our definition of the NUI, we can see that it means different things to different people in different ecological, social, and business contexts. A NUI that responds to in-air gestures would make no sense in a car. For most people, the evolved interface for automobiles requires one or two hands and one or two feet to drive. Thus many NUIs in autos employ voice input or rely on simple touchscreens not far away from the common sight lines. This simple example illustrates the interdependence of context, user capabilities, and task goals. Our discussion here is limited to the touch- and gesture-based NUIs offered on an increasing array of products.

LESSONS FROM THE PAST

NUIs that enable touch, gesture, and object recognition are well suited to contexts where users will walk up and use the system and where an interaction with the system is intended to be enjoyable in and of itself. There are many walk up and **59** use interfaces where the interaction is intended to be simply functional. Examples include parking meters, ATMs, and automated airport check-in systems. All of these are purely functional. The user is therefore a result and woe betide the overzealous designer who attempts to incorporate progressive difficulty or arcane mechanics into such a system.

In contrast, the walk up and use NUI needs to be attractive in approach and engaging in use. That is in part because its use is often discretionary, and in many cases its sole goal is to provide engaging diversion while the user waits for something or someone. This engaged waiting state often serves a larger business strategy. For example, for leisure and entertainment businesses, keeping the user amused is an important business goal.

In other environments such as retail stores, the NUI provides a simple and intuitive interface of mutual interaction by two or more users. Thus a customer and salesperson can interact in a natural way much as they would across a desk. But in this case, the "desk" is enhanced by computer technology that allows both users to interact with the content on a equal basis.

In these environments there are different kinds of differentiation and numerous mechanisms to differentiate users when that is required in the interaction. There may also be contexts where user differentiation is not required or even desirable.

- Differentiation by flexible role assignment. This is most readily demonstrated in game interfaces, which are common in leisure and entertainment environments. Here user roles are flexible at the beginning of the game and are often assigned by agreement or simple physical position. The system does not need to identify a specific person.

- Fixed role definition. Sales environments are typical examples. By definition there is a seller and a buyer. They interact across a table. While their task is tightly coupled, their interaction is fluid. The system may or may not need to identify a specific person or role. The buyer and the seller interact with the system in the same way. For those systems that provide information, individual identification is not needed. The further the system moves into the typical business transaction, the more requirement there is for personal identification. The system may need to identify the seller so that he or she can be credited for engaging the customer and making the sale. If the system is designed to complete the transaction, then in most cases the seller and the buyer (or more precisely the payee and the payment source) need to be individuated.

- Personal identification. In this case, the unique user must be indentified at an early stage in the transaction because the nature of the transaction depends on knowing who the user is. A typical example is a loyalty card. Identification of the person cues the system to provide customized options based on who the user is. In some cases, the user may be identified not as an individual but as a member of a class of people, for example, people who bring in a circular or special offer coupon. They are unique only in being part of a class; high rollers are another example.

- Identifying a user for the duration of the interaction. In this case, the user is uniquely identified in relation to the system, for example, this is the user on the "north" side of the system. This capability allows for role-differentiated interactions. For example, the person on the north side will be the goalie in a tabletop hockey game.

- Differentiated roles. All the role differentiation we have discussed so far applies to end users. Any NUI system will also need to identify users in relation to roles with respect to the unit itself. These include end users, system managers, and support and maintenance staff. The system managers need access to tools and capabilities that are barred to end users.

DESIGN GUIDELINES

The class into which users and their actions fall is determined by the type of identification used and in many cases the method of identification.

Must

- Don't attempt to identify users if you don't need to. Except in widely accepted contexts (for example, ATM systems), users prefer to remain anonymous. They are highly suspicious when asked to identify themselves for a system.

- If users are asked to identify themselves, they must see a clear benefit and be assured that there will be no negative consequences to identifying themselves. For example, users readily accept the need to identify themselves when they make a purchase. However, they are reluctant to identify themselves to an automated system early in the shopping process.

Should

- When users are asked to identify themselves, the process should be easy, private, and secure.

- For users with system management roles, user identification can use more traditional methods.

Could

- In some cases, mixing modalities of interaction may be the best way to approach the problem of identifying a specific person. For example, the interface may read a credit card that was supplied as the payment source and key into a database of customers indexed by that card number.

SUMMARY

The challenge of identifying users in the NUI is made more complex by the following facts:

- The system with the NUI is often in a public place.

- The systems with NUIs are relatively novel and therefore don't benefit from traditional social conventions.

- For NUIs to use their native technology, for example, optical recognition, that technology needs to be sufficiently developed to read objects such as credit, ID cards or biometric elements.

New Technologies: Understanding and Technological Artifacts

III

The State-Transition Model of Input

12

> *So Midas, king of Lydia, swelled at first with pride when he found he could transform everything he touched to gold; but when he beheld his food grow rigid and his drink harden into golden ice then he understood that this gift was a bane and in his loathing for gold, cursed his prayer.*
>
> —Claudian, In Rufinum

DESCRIPTION

Input devices come in a staggering array of shapes, sizes, degrees of freedom, and capabilities. But all can be modeled using a very simple tool: the state model of input devices. By understanding this way of thinking, you will immediately transition from thinking about devices in isolation to thinking about them holistically, and will quickly realize that most input devices, while staggeringly different, can all be thought of as fitting into a rather small number of categories. To understand these categories, you will first need to start building some intuition about the state-transition model. First, consider a typical direct-touch input device, like the iPhone. When the user is not touching it, it is sitting idle—it has no idea where the user's fingers are. Even when the fingers are hovering just a fraction of an inch above the screen, it still has no idea. We think of this state as the idle state. Using a state-transition diagram, we model this state as a simple circle with a label.

FIGURE 12.1

Beginning to model the state/transition diagram of a typical direct-touch input device.

Of course, this isn't the only state. When a user touches the device, suddenly it becomes aware of the position of the fingers. We add this engaged state to the model, along with arrows, denoting the transitions, between each of the two states.

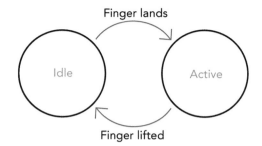

FIGURE 12.2

A more complete model of the state/transition diagram of a typical direct-touch input device.

Now, we're missing just one element: modeling user movement within each state that does not yield a change to another state (e.g., the user moves her hand while touching the screen—this is a change that the system might pick up, but it doesn't actually change the state). We model this movement using transition arrows that reference back to the original state.

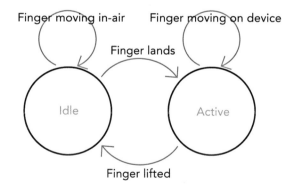

FIGURE 12.3

A complete model of the state/transition diagram of a typical direct-touch input device.

State-transition diagrams are a simple tool that allows us to abstract simple but important elements of the behavior of the input device. If you have done development work, you might begin to note interesting things about the above diagram, such as the fact that each transition arrow (with one exception) corresponds to events in a typical touch input system. We will expand upon this further by using this tool to model the mode and flow of a gesture system in a later chapter. For now, though, you now have a basic understanding of its use for a touch system. Let's start to play with it.

The states of an input device fundamentally affects the design space of gestural systems. Mice and tablets have the luxury of a tracking state, which is used a great deal in the underlying applications. Typical gestural systems do not, as you may have noted in the above figure. Using a model of the states and transitions between states of the input device, and the system's responses, the designer can better understand two things: first, how systems driven by touch input must behave fundamentally differently from those that are driven by other input devices with different state-transition models, and second, how all input devices, from mice to tablets to touch to in-air gesture systems, all share common properties, and how the sophisticated designer can approach them similarly.

APPLICATION TO NUI

The classic WIMP (windows icons menus pointers) GUI is based on not only a set of metaphors (buttons, sliders, check boxes, etc.), but also a particular input device: the mouse. Understanding the states of a mouse will provide an application designer with great insights into how those states map (directly!) onto the states of the graphical user interface. Further, understanding how touch and gestural devices differ in their states will allow a deeper understanding of fundamental issues that require different design.

LESSONS FROM THE PAST

Mouse and Touch: How They're the Same and How They're Different

Much of this book is dedicated to helping the reader break out of the mindset that touch interfaces are the same as mouse interfaces. This chapter is different. Our intention is to help you to place touch input on a spectrum of input devices defined by the number and nature of the states they support. To understand this, let's consider the state-transition model for a one-button mouse. Like the touch device we describe above, it includes both an out of range and an engaged state. But it also includes another state: tracking.

The difference between tracking and engaged is a simple one: the mouse is tracking when it's on the table and in the user's hand. As the mouse is moved around, tracking data are sent to the operating system and to the active application. When the user pushes down on the button, the mouse transitions from tracking to engaged; when the user releases the button, the mouse transitions back to tracking. In old WIMP parlance, tracking is the "pointing," and the transition from tracking to engaged is the "click." The out of range state of the mouse is more important than it appears at first glance: think about how often you lift the mouse in the air to move it somewhere else on the table. You probably do this so often it has become automatic.

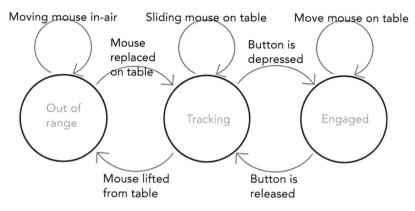

FIGURE 12.4

The state-transition model for a one-button mouse.

As you begin to place input devices on the spectrum, you can begin to think of touch input as equivalent to a mouse that lacks a tracking state. Put in this context, you can begin to see how input devices are really quite similar to one another in terms of their fundamental affordances. This is how touch and mouse input are the same.

How touch and mouse input are different from one another is also obviated by the above figures: most touch devices lack the tracking state present in a mouse. A question worth asking is "Does this matter?" At first glance, it looks like it might not: after all, the purpose of the tracking state is to show you where your disembodied virtual finger (that is, the mouse pointer) is in the system. Direct touch, in contrast, has the user's own actual, embodied (hopefully) finger to serve as a visual representation of itself. But deeper examination reveals that the WIMP GUI has actually been designed with an engrained assumption of the presence of a tracking state. In the Mac OS X, icons grow and shrink as the mouse passes over them. In Windows, buttons are highlighted when the pointer is over them. Hover long enough, and a tooltip pops up to tell the user just what will happen when she transitions to the engaged state. Further, hovering over menu headings, once any one menu is open, causes them to expand to show more options. In all flavors of Linux, the mouse pointer itself serves as a preview of not just the target object, but also the actual pixel that will be selected when the user depresses the button. All of these examples (and many others) point to a generalized definition of the use of the tracking state: it serves as a preview to help guide the user toward successful activation.

So here we are, trying to build a natural user interface, which means we want to make our users feel like naturals, which means we need to guide them toward success—and we're giving away one of the most important guides that our users rely on today to be successful. We can think of this as the "Midas touch" problem.

King Midas discovered that his blessing was really a curse when he tried to lift his food to his mouth and got only gold. What he needed was a way to have two types of touches—those that transmorphed objects and those that simply manipulated them and those that didn't. Touch input suffers from precisely the same problem. Every touch counts, and this leads to a whole host of complexity not present in mouse-based WIMPs, which can (and, it turns out, do) rely rather heavily on the tracking state of the mouse. Our design guidelines, therefore, address the lack of this state and point out the importance of designing software well despite its absence. This is also taken up in Chapter 17, when we describe the need for new primitives, and again in Chapter 21, when we will model the mode and flow of the gesture language, again using state-transition diagrams as a tool.

DESIGN GUIDELINES

Our design guidelines generally fall into two categories: how to recreate a *de facto* (or logical) tracking state despite the input device's inability to differentiate one, and that it's actually a better idea to design fundamentally new UI that does not rely on a state not actually provided by the input device.

Emulating a Tracking State

As we have seen, touch lacks a tracking state. A lingering question in your mind may be, *if touch lacks a tracking state, why is it that the trackpad on my laptop seems to have one?* The answer, of course, is that it doesn't actually have one. But someone has done a pretty good job (in hardware, software, or both) of making you think it does. A trackpad emulates a three-state input device (such as a mouse) in software; the transitions between the tracking and engaged states are managed entirely by the OS. This can be done with a physical button beside the trackpad (common), or operated by a gesture performed on the pad (tapping the pad is the most common). It can also be done by putting the whole pad atop a pressure switch, as has been done on recent Apple laptops, but this obviously works only for single and not for multi-touch.

So, can we do the same thing for direct touch? Clearly, it's trickier, since adding a button to the side of a direct-touch input device makes it, well, less direct. One previously explored trick lies in being creative in how states of the various touchpoints are mapped onto mouse states in software. The naive approach is to simply overlay the touch model atop the mouse one. This model is the most direct, because system events will continue to happen immediately beneath the finger. It is not the best, however, because it omits the tracking state and is imprecise.

The DT Mouse project from Mitsubishi Electric Research Labs is the best example of a good mapping between physical contact and virtual mouse states. Built for the popular DiamondTouch multi-user tables, DT Mouse was developed over the course of several years and was entirely user-centrically designed, with tweaks done in real time. It is highly tuned, and includes many features. The most basic is that it has the ability to emulate a tracking state—this is done by putting two fingers down on the screen. When this is done, the pointer is put into a tracking state, and

FIGURE 12.5

Left: The pointer is displayed between the middle finger and thumb. Right: the transition from tracking to engaged is simulated when the index finger is touched to the display.

positioned between the fingers. The engaged state is entered by tapping a third finger on the screen. An advanced user does this by putting down her thumb and middle finger, and then tapping with the index finger (Figure 12.5).

A project from AutoDesk research explored a plethora of methods for emulating mouse input using multi-touch. Suffice it to say, there are a lot of them, and each has advantages and disadvantages, but most add a logical tracking state. So there are sophisticated ways of doing mouse emulation with touch. But this has to lead you to ask the following question: *if all I'm using touch for is mouse emulation, why not just use the mouse?*

Designing for an Impoverished Input Device

So, touch input is impoverished in terms of the number of states supported by the input device. Of course, this is just one point of view. Many designers of touch software make this mistake. They begin by designing for the mouse, find their new device to be impoverished, and then tweak their software to compensate. In order to be successful, designers of systems for multi-touch applications should start by applying rules about touch and assigning state changes to those events that are easily generated using a touch system, designing fundamentally new interaction methods in the process.

States and transitions in a touch system include the contact state information we have shown above. In a multi-touch system, we can start to think about combining the state and location of *multiple* contacts, and mapping events onto those. This requires a fundamental rethinking of the graphical user interface.

By now you should have picked up a main message of the book, which is that to achieve a natural user interface we are going to require a new kind of graphical user interface. There is no contradiction here: Users feel the most like a natural with your software when they have affordances to lead them and feedback to guide them. The trick is to build a graphical user interface that properly takes advantage of and is designed for your hardware. In the case of touch input, that means designing for a two-state input device. The balance of this book will serve as a series of lessons in how to do this. Take this chapter as a cautionary note about the importance of fundamentally new UI design.

Must

- Understand the limitations of your input device and realize that touch input deprives you of a tool that the WIMP GUI relies on heavily. Design your software so that it does not assume the presence of a tracking state in order for the user to be successful. Use the balance of this book as a guide to do this well.

Should

- Go a step further, and design your UI from the ground up for touch, rather than thinking of it simply as an impoverished mouse.

Could

- Emulate a three-state (or more!) input device in software using multi-touch input. But do this with great care. Simply emulating one input device using another is a recipe for disaster.

SUMMARY

The state-transition model of input devices provides an extremely useful tool to help you to understand the true utility of your input device, how it is the same as a mouse, and how it's different from a mouse. Embracing these similarities and differences not only makes you a better designer of touch and gestural software, but also will equip you to become a designer of software for all manner of hardware.

FURTHER READING

Matejka, J., Grossman, T., Lo, J., and Fitzmaurice, G., The design and evaluation of multi-finger mouse emulation techniques. *CHI 2009 Conference Proceedings*, pp. 1073–1082. In this paper, Matejka et al. examine several mappings of multi-touch input to emulating a mouse. This is worth reading, as it thoroughly explores the space. Do so with the important caveat that the goal of this book is to break you from the habit of thinking of mouse input (and its associated GUI) as the starting point for all software design.

Buxton, W., A Three-State Model of Graphical Input. In D. Diaper et al. (Eds.), Human-Computer Interaction—INTERACT '90. Amsterdam: Elsevier Science Publishers B.V. (North-Holland), pp. 449–456. This chapter draws heavily from Buxton's definitions of the state model of graphical input. Our recasting it as the state-transition model is meant to highlight the importance of transitions.

Fat Fingers

13

The fingers you have used to dial are too fat. To obtain a special dialing wand, please mash the keypad with your palm now.

—**The Simpsons ("King Size Homer")**

DESCRIPTION

The mouse is a tool that easily supports movements that are both precise and rapid. A single pixel among millions can easily be selected with a mouse, meaning that graphical user interface elements can be as small as a single pixel in size. Indeed, some such elements in modern GUIs are almost that small—for example, the handles that allow resizing of windows in both of the most popular operating systems are no larger than 4 pixels in size. This is a small target to select with a mouse—and a nearly impossible one for a touch UI.

The "fat finger" problem is actually a mix of two issues. First, when the user touches her finger to the device, a relatively large area of the finger comes into contact with it. All currently existing touch platforms, however, including the iPhone and Microsoft Surface, use only a single point within this area to do their hit testing. The consequence is that a user can be in physical contact with the item she wishes to target, but the system believes she is not (Figure 13.1).

In and of itself, this wouldn't be such a big deal—after all, the mouse is an object even larger than the finger and is represented as a particular pixel (the tip of the mouse pointer). This brings us to the second portion of the fat finger problem: that because the user's finger is in the way, she can't see the pixel that is being targeted—and because most devices can't sense the finger until it's touching, the pixel can't be shown to the user before it's being occluded.

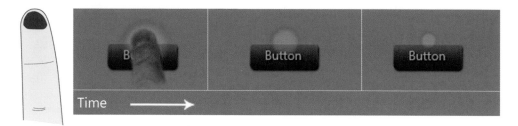

FIGURE 13.1

Left: The area of the user's finger which is in contact with the display is rather large. Right: The Contact Visualizer, described in detail in Chapter 14, shows the user this contact area when they lift their finger.

APPLICATION TO NUI

Designing around this problem, at first, seems relatively straightforward: Make everything in the UI large enough that the user can select it with confidence. Indeed, design guidelines for touch platforms typically include a minimum size that an element can occupy. We see quickly, however, that this does not scale—if everything needs to be a of a minimum physical size, this means we must either severely limit on-screen elements or have very large screens. Further, it ignores the very real possibility that every single pixel, such as on a map, is equally targetable. So, we need to enable precise interaction—and we need to solve the fat finger problem.

LESSONS FROM THE PAST

A problem similar to the fat finger problem has actually reared its head before, but in a totally different context. This came when the producers of the game Halo tried to move the incredibly popular first-person shooter (FPS) genre from the PC to the console. In so doing, they faced a significant challenge: In an FPS, the user must quickly select objects and click on them (that is, shoot them). Rapidly selecting objects is exactly what the mouse was designed for, so this is a genre that lived quite well on the PC. In contrast, when the Halo team attempted to move to the console, they were attempting to move a UI idea from one input device (the mouse) to another (the joystick). And the joystick is a *terrible* pointing device. Where the mouse is meant to control position (*x/y*), a joystick is a *rate control* device: It controls orientation and speed. Anyone who has a laptop with a little eraser head controller on it understands the pain that these designers were about to inflict on their users. The common wisdom was that first-person shooters could never make it onto the console, because a joystick could never be used to control the position of the crosshairs.

Undeterred, the designers set about their task. They quickly realized that they had an advantage over the eraser-head-to-control-the-mouse-pointer problem. Unlike the designers of that device, they knew exactly where on the screen the user was likely to want to point the crosshairs: at the enemy!

With this in mind, they did two things. First, they expanded the area where the user could point their gun and still hit the enemy (in the game, this shows up as the shrapnel flying at the enemy in an arced path, with a "heat seeker"-like quality). Second, they modified the movement of the crosshair as it slides across the screen: When the gun is pointing in the direction of an enemy, the speed of movement slows down, so that the player has a little bit of time to let go of the stick and leave it still pointing at the baddie.

The exact amount that these two tweaks were applied was adjusted through dozens of rounds of play testing. The goal, of course, was to make sure that the users felt like they were the ones pointing their weapons at the bad guys—to make the users feel like a natural.

Of course, we all know how this turned out: Halo turned out to be a flagship game for the Xbox platform, helping to sell millions of consoles.

How this lesson applies to the fat finger problem is clear: Precise selection with a joystick is hard, so the developers of the experience adjusted the physics of their world to make it easier. Touch UI requires no less refinement.

DESIGN GUIDELINES

A lot of work that has attempted to address this problem, and it generally falls into one of two categories. The first is to design the UI in such a way that the fat finger problem is irrelevant. The second is to provide a mechanism to allow users to vary their precision: quick movements for large targets, but add a tool to allow them to select things more precisely.

Make Stuff Bigger

The first, and easiest, guideline is to always make stuff in your UI big enough to touch. As we saw above, you can't base the size of your controls on pixels, since displays vary widely in terms of the density of pixels. Instead, you must determine the *physical* size of your screen, and design controls and objects to a minimum size. In our testing, we have found that for large touchscreens, where users will be moving their entire arms, a target size of 1.6 cm is the minimum that they can hit reliably. On smaller touchscreens that users hold in their hand, and thus move only their fingers or thumb to make a selection, a smaller target size of 0.9 cm is sufficient.

Consider User Perception to Adjust the Touch Point

Smaller on-screen objects can be selected if you take into consideration the user's perception of the precise touch point under the user's finger. In one extreme, a pair of researchers at the Hasso Plattner Institute in Berlin used fingerprint scanners to carefully model that perception, taking into account the roll, pitch, and yaw of the finger to decide on the touch point. A more simplistic version can be seen as part of the Microsoft Surface platform. When the user touches the device, the entire contact area is sensed. Rather than taking the simple center of the contact area to be the point, the point is pushed out toward the tip of the user's finger.

You can do something similar by asking users to come and perform basic tasks on your device. Provide objects on the screen that you ask your user to select, and record the point that your system reports for the touch. After several users, you will have a reliable data set to give you a good understanding of where the users believe they are touching versus where your system believes they are touching. Using this data, you can easily compute a calibration that you can apply to your device to make its reported touch point more closely mimic users' expectations. Holtz and Baudisch's data collection technique can be applied generically to your device.

Iceberg Targets

Also worth considering is the use of the iceberg targets technique: making the on-screen object that the user is asked to touch smaller than the actual area that will result in it being selected. The extreme version of this would be to compute the object closest to every pixel on the screen, so that when the user selects that pixel, the closest object is selected. The selection area for each object would then look like the one shown in Figure 13.2.

This approach is a bit extreme, since on a screen with a single button the user might select it accidentally by tapping a full foot away from it. But you get the idea. It also assumes that your system knows where all the touch targets are—believe it or not, this is not always the case.

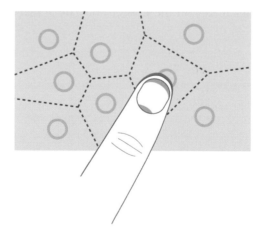

FIGURE 13.2

Iceberg targets can theoretically be so large that touching anywhere on the screen will activate the nearest touch visible target.

Reduce the Role of Land On

Improving the accuracy of the reduction from *touch area* to *touch point* and expanding target sizes will get you a long way. But even with this accuracy, targets will still be missed. To do even better, you should consider changing more elements of the user experience.

Two general approaches have been explored before and are worth considering; both involve changing the selection event. Consider four possible ways by which a finger can come into or leave contact with an object. It can slide onto the object (A in Figure 13.3), it can land on the object (B), it can be lifted away from the object (C), or it can slide off of an object (D).

Engaging a key on a keyboard requires only (B): Landing on a key causes text to be entered. Engaging a button in a GUI usually requires both (B) and (C), so that the user has an opportunity to slide off the button. One approach for solving the fat finger problem is to require only (C): lifting off of the screen while touching the object. Consider the keyboards on the Android, Windows Phone, and iPhone platforms: When a finger lands on the keyboard, no text is entered. The button the user is touching grows to show an approximation of where the finger is, so that the user can slide around on the keyboard to find the right key. Where the user lifts (C) is what counts.

This approach gives users the opportunity to correct their selection before they confirm it, but it does have the disadvantage that small targets require a good amount of time to be made. An alternative method was described by researchers at the University of Toronto. Their technique, dubbed "Escape," was a variation of selection using the (D) event: The selection is made by examining the *direction* of the user's finger as it slides off of an object.

Figure 13.4 makes the technique clear. The user wishes to select the green object (1). She puts her finger on the cluster (2). The actual land-on point is used only to make everything nearby a candidate—it doesn't matter if he actually lands

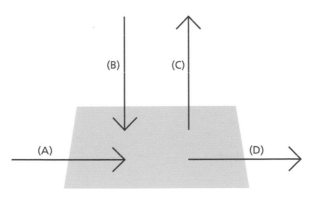

FIGURE 13.3

Four different finger/object interactions: slide on (A), land on (B), lift off (C), slide off (D).

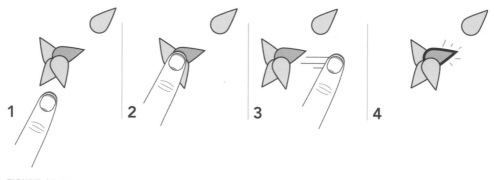

FIGURE 13.4

The Escape technique works by requiring the user to slide in an indicated direction in order to make selections.

on the little green one. Next, he slides his finger in the indicated direction (3), and the object is selected (4). It's worth noting that traditional selection is also supported if there are no other objects nearby:

The downside of this technique is clear, in that touch targets in your UI must be labeled with a direction for sliding selection. But the advantage is also clear: The user sees the direction in advance so doesn't have to wait for a pop out or other method to make small selections.

Whether you use these techniques or others, they point the way towards fundamentally redesigning your user interface to account for fat fingers. Do not limit yourself to a classic selection model; think of redesigning your interface so that selection itself might not be necessary at all!

Must

- Ensure that users are able to precisely select objects in your UI. This can be done in a variety of ways, from adjusting the physical size of content to providing techniques that enable selection of smaller content.

Should

- Consider the *physical*, not pixel, size of content and ensure that targets the user will need to touch are no smaller than 1.6cm on large touchscreens and 0.9cm on small ones.

- Use iceberg targets to make actual selection areas larger than what you show to a user.

- Collect data correlating your users' perception of where they touch with the location collected by your device or platform, and consider adjusting to take into account these differences.

- Consider reducing the role of the land-on event in your system. Consider the techniques we have described above or your own techniques using different combinations of the finger/object interaction moments we described earlier.

Could

- Expand the region on which an object can be selected beyond its graphical representation, so that selecting a pixel or two above or below it still selects that object.

- If small targets are essential, such as for placing the cursor, consider using a technique such as cursor placement on the iPhone, where the user is given the ability to fine-tune their selection.

SUMMARY

Designing your UI in such a way that users can always reliably select content will ensure that they always feel successful, like natural users of your interface. Making content too small is frustrating, and providing mechanisms to overcome this small size is essential.

VOICES FROM THE FIELD: THE FAT FINGER PROBLEM

Patrick Baudisch

Hasso Plattner Institute, Potsdam, Germany

The designers of today's mobile touch devices face a difficult challenge: On the one hand, users want tiny devices for maximum mobility, which leaves space for only very small user interface elements. On the other hand, users demand interface elements large enough for easy operation. Can we achieve both objectives at the same time?

The targeting problem with small buttons is linked to a very specific scale. Targeting works fine down to buttons about the size of a fingertip. For buttons smaller than that, the users' fingers cover up the button entirely, so that users cannot see the visual confirmation the button might deliver to confirm successful acquisition (the so-called fat finger problem). Consequently, users have to target without visual control.

Without visual control, users need to remember where the target is located, but it is not the uncertainty about the target location that poses a problem for users; it is the uncertainty about the location of their own finger. How can this be a problem?

Today's touch devices compute the contact point as the center of the contact area between finger and screen. Just like the target is occluded by the user's finger, so is the contact area, so that users have no way to observe it directly. Users essentially have to guess the shape of the contact area—and our studies indicate that they guess incorrectly. While they expect the center of the contact area to be located comparably close to the fingertip, the contact area extends farther back along the finger than most users expect. This misconception causes the contact point to be located farther "back" along the finger, which manifests itself as targeting error.

Until recently the only way to prevent this type of error was to employ fingertip-sized buttons, as evidenced by many commercial designs, such as Apple's iPhone. Just recently, however, my team found a way to overcome the problem. We conducted additional studies that revealed that users' misconception about the contact area is systematic in nature, that is, that a given person (for a given finger posture) tends to err by roughly the same direction and distance. Based on this observation, we constructed an improved touch-sensing mechanism we call Ridgepad. The device identifies users and determines their finger posture based on their fingerprint, which it takes during every single touch interaction. By compensating for user-specific offsets, the device allows users to reliably acquire targets less than half the size supported by traditional touchscreens. A miniaturized version of such technology might one day provide the basis for mobile touch devices that are half the size of today's devices.

Author Biography

Patrick Baudisch is a professor in Computer Science at Hasso Plattner Institute in Berlin/Potsdam and chair of the Human Computer Interaction Lab. His research focuses on the miniaturization of mobile devices and touch input. Previously, Patrick Baudisch worked as a research scientist in the Adaptive Systems and Interaction Research Group at Microsoft Research and at Xerox PARC and served as an Affiliate Professor in Computer Science at the University of Washington. He holds a Ph.D. in Computer Science from Darmstadt University of Technology, Germany.

 ## FURTHER READING

Holz, C., and Baudisch, P. The Generalized Perceived Input Point Model and How to Double Touch Accuracy by Extracting Fingerprints. In *Proceedings of CHI 2010*, Atlanta, GA, April 10–15, 2009, pp. 581–590. In this project, Holz and Baudisch provide a model for making touch selections using a fingerprint scanner far more accurate. While the precision of a fingerprint scanner is beyond most modern touch devices, their methodology of collecting the difference between the user's and the device's understanding of the position of the touch point can be applied broadly to any device.

Yatani, K., Partridge, K., Bern, M., and Newman, M. W. Escape: A Target Selection Technique Using Visually-cued Gestures. In *Proceedings of the SIGCHI Conference on Human Factors in Computing Systems* (CHI 2008), pp. 285–294, April 2008. Yatani et al.'s technique uses sliding direction to allow users to precisely select very small targets among a large number of dense targets.

No Touch Left Behind: Feedback Is Essential

14

Whenever we present a state of affairs which is known to be reinforcing at a given drive, we must suppose that conditioning takes place, even though we have paid no attention to the behavior of the organism in making the presentation.
—**B. F. Skinner explaining superstitious behavior,**
Journal of Experimental Psychology (1947)

DESCRIPTION

Picture yourself using a traditional PC: you move the mouse pointer to an on-screen object, you click the mouse button—and nothing happens. What do you assume caused the failure? The overwhelming majority of users in this situation assume that they have clicked on something that is disabled, that something happened that they did not recognize, or that the software has crashed. Now picture yourself using exactly the same application with a touch device. You reach out, touch that same object—and nothing happens. What do you assume caused the failure? This time, the overwhelming majority of users assume that the hardware has failed in some way. They push harder, tap the display more vigorously or slowly, or otherwise change the way they are touching the screen. Why the difference?

As always, the user is left to interpret this response using the feedback that has been made available by the system. In the case of a mouse input, feedback provided by both the operating system and the hardware helps the user to quickly isolate the cause. Visual movement of the mouse pointer reassures the user that the system is still working, the physical activation of the mouse button affirms that the input was received, and the position of the mouse pointer makes it apparent where the input was delivered. In touch-based systems, this is typically not the case, and so it is left to the application to provide feedback for all of these potential causes of unexpected behavior. Table 14.1 describes various possible causes of unexpected behavior, as well as the source and type of feedback available to dispel that cause in both a mouse and a direct-touch system.

Table 14.1 Causes of unexpected responses to input and the feedback given by the hardware or OS in typical mouse and touch systems to each, or left to applications (app)

Cause of Unexpected Behavior	Feedback Refuting Cause	
	Mouse	Touch
System is nonresponsive	OS: Pointer movement	(app)
Hardware failed to detect input	HW: Activation of button	(app)
Input delivered to wrong location (fat fingers)	OS: Visible pointer	(app)
Input does not map to expected function	(app)	(app)
Accidental input (arm brushing)	N/A	(app)
Overconstrained (too many contacts)	N/A	(app)
Max size reached	OS: Pointer moves past edge	(app)
Stolen capture (second user captures control)	N/A	(app)

Most applications do not provide an explicit feedback mechanism that can help users to understand why their action was not successful, and the application feedback is typically constrained to responses designed to signal the execution of successful actions—a lack of success is visually identical to not having done anything at all. How the application reacts to the user's input determines how well the user will understand the reasons for the unexpected behavior. The result is applications that *respond* to touch input, but do not provide information about the *causes* of those responses.

That this happens is not overly surprising. Firms accustomed to designing web-based applications have had the luxury of the mouse pointer, and the feel of the mouse buttons, to rely on. These have become such an integral part of the experience that they are forgotten entirely by designers. When designing a touch and gestural experience, however, these luxuries disappear—and it's up to the designer to provide a replacement for the feedback that disappears with them.

APPLICATION TO NUI

Understanding the connection between cause and effect is a particular problem for touch and gestural applications, since, as we have seen, dispensing with traditional input devices and visualizations causes a misattribution of error to the input device.

As we described in Chapter 12, the mouse pointer serves as a proxy for the user. When using direct input, the user's finger can function as its own indicator for a well-calibrated system's understanding of the input location. Despite this, there are uses for a cursor. In devices that can sense location prior to the input event, a cursor can serve as an indicator of the precise location for contact. Further, iconic, such as a paintbrush or vertical bar for text entry, cursors serve as an indicator of state or mode. Finally, the presence of the cursor and its response to user input give feedback to the user that the system is active, tracking, and ready to receive commands. While we would not argue for putting a mouse cursor onto the screen of a touch or gestural system, it is critical to understand that your system *must* include a representation of the system's understanding of the user's input. Your task will be to design this feedback. Sadly, with the notable exception of the Microsoft Surface, few UI toolkits designed for touch include it, so even if you are simply designing an application to run on a device built by someone else, you'll need to do this part yourself—unlike mouse-based systems, where the physical feel of the mouse and visual feedback of the cursor can be assumed.

Echo Feedback vs. Semantic Feedback

Input devices process a stream of sensors to yield a logical result. The system's feedback can be either an echo of unprocessed sensor data back to the user (here's what the system sees) or a semantic representation of the user's state (here's what the system knows), like the cursor. Traditional systems have trended toward the latter—a mouse, for example, senses only movement, but the feedback given to the user is of a *cursor position*, which is a logical state maintained entirely for the benefit of the user. In point-based interactions, the alternative (echoing back movement without showing a cursor) makes little sense. Richer input streams, meanwhile, might tempt the designer to skew the feedback more toward the unprocessed data, since it may represent a richer visualization. While richer, such a representation offers less clear information to allow the user to understand cause and effect. Making clear connections between cause and effect is critical in making interactions feel natural—users can improve their input and learn to work with the system effectively.

This may be directly the opposite of what your intuition says. You might ask, "If our goal is a 'natural' interaction, and there are no cursors in the 'natural world,' why would we include them in a natural user interface?" We remind you of Chapter 2, where we explain that the goal of a NUI is not to *be* natural, but rather to *feel natural* to your users. This is rarely achieved through mimicry. We humans need constant feedback in order to accomplish even the most simple task. If you want your system to feel natural, feedback is essential. And, as we shall see, clearly unnatural feedback is essential in achieving this natural-feeling result.

LESSONS FROM THE PAST
Superstitious Behavior

The mythology of Newton's formalism of gravity is that an apple fell from a tree as he sat outside at Cambridge. Tellings of the story differ as to whether or not the apple actually landed on his head—as if physically driving the idea into his mind.

It was from an oddly parallel experience that the principle of "no touch left behind" came to be. Daniel's own experience:

At some point in every business traveler's life, there will come a time where they will spend a few hours on a tarmac in a takeoff queue at New York's LaGuardia airport. It was during such an experience, as I sat in my chair, that the teenaged boy behind me pressed away on the touchscreen built in to the back of my seat. Whenever an announcement of a further delay was made, his movie would stop, and the touchscreen would stop taking input. At this, the boy would begin to furiously punch the controls, still visible on his screen, in an attempt to resume his entertainment. Each vigorous press on the screen would drive my head forward, and my nerve closer to the edge.

This has become such a problem that flight attendants can now often be heard reminding passengers that presses to the touchscreens are telegraphed to the passenger in front of them through the rigid medium of the airplane seat.

We are driven to ask the question: Why did this obnoxious little twit believe that pressing harder on the screen would get him a different result than touching lightly? After careful consideration, it is clear: we have a feedback problem.

We are all hard-wired to believe *post hoc ergo proctor hoc*—after it, therefore because of it. B. F. Skinner's breakthrough work in operant conditioning taught the world that superstitious behavior is the result of an application of this logical fallacy. Among his many experiments, it became absolutely clear that creatures are in a constant quest to make connections between cause and effect. When the real cause is not apparent, they will make inaccurate associations. In his experiments, the results were pigeons that believed they had to perform ritualistic dances to receive food (when in truth, the food dispenser was simply on a timer, thus effectively depriving them of a pigeon-perceptible cause—this led them to attribute the output, occasional food, as a result of what they happened to be doing, moving around).

Startlingly, early implementations of touch and gestural systems have demonstrated significant failures to provide sufficient feedback to enable users to understand and make proper associations between their input action and the system's output consequence. We call this the *feedback ambiguity problem*. We'll now run through a list of possible sources of unexpected behavior and explain how a mouse-based system provides this feedback (if it does), and how and why touch systems must do this explicitly in the absence of the pointer and physical button provided by a GUI.

In the section that follows, we will describe the feedback mechanisms our team developed for Microsoft Surface to address all of these sources of ambiguity.

SOURCES OF ERROR

To understand the problem, we must first understand all of the sources of possible error that are leading to a given state. In this section, we enumerate the sources of such error, many of which are unique to a touch and gesture-based system. This list is a formalization and expansion of that shown in Table 14.1.

Activation Event

When interacting with a traditional mouse-based GUI system, users feel a physical click when they depress the mouse button. When working with a touchscreen, users feel the moment of contact with the display. However, depending on the particular hardware, the moment of activation can vary. With some vision-based systems, for example, activation occurs before the finger reaches the display, which might result in an initial position of the touch contact that differs from where the user thinks the contact occurred. With some resistive technologies, a degree of pressure is required for activation. There is no consistent physical sensation connected with this transition. A correct feedback should indicate the activation moment and help the user to be accurate in their touches. Another such problem is the fat finger problem.

Fat Fingers

There are two elements of the fat finger problem: occlusion of the screen by the finger and the reduction of the contact area to a single point causing users to "miss" targets they are physically touching. When the fat finger problem causes a missed target, the correct feedback must clarify that this failure was due to a miss and, ideally, demonstrate how to avoid missing in the future. Activation must also be made clear.

Activation

When a user's finger lands on the device, it is critical that the system provide immediate feedback as to whether the user has landed on an active element or one that will "ignore" their input. When using a trackpad on your laptop, if you tap the button below it, you feel that it has activated. If you instead miss and hit the chassis of the laptop, you know that you have missed because you can feel it. Touch systems must also provide feedback for both the "active" and "inert" touches. Whereas mouse-based systems can rely on the feel of the button to distinguish this, touch systems must do this in software. This is also true of nonresponsive content.

Nonresponsive Content

Invariably, applications will include elements that are not intended to respond to touch: deactivated controls, background images, etc. Although visual cues should afford inactivation to the user, this state nonetheless adds another source of error in which the user will receive no reaction, requiring correct feedback.

Accidental Activation

With a multi-touch system, "every touch counts." Accidental activations are common—users might brush the screen accidentally, or point at content during conversation. When this occurs, users are able to observe only the consequence to the application. Some accidental inputs are not noticed by the user, and so sudden changes in the state of the system cannot be properly linked to their cause. A meaningful feedback would make the causes of accidental activations clear to the user.

Multiple Capture States

In a WIMP-GUI system, UI controls have two capture states: captured (typically entered when the mouse is clicked on a control) and uncaptured. When working with controls on a multi-touch system, more than one contact can capture controls simultaneously. For example, selecting the thumb of a slider with two fingers can mean that it will not track directly under a single finger when moved.

When too many contacts have captured a control, its behavior can be well defined but inconsistent with the direct-touch paradigm, leading to confusion. We term this state *overcaptured*. To help the user understand overcapture, the contact visualization system must include a visual distinction between not only uncaptured and captured contacts, but also overcaptured ones.

Physical Manipulation Constraints

The direct-touch paradigm is also broken when movement constraints are reached. This can occur, for example, when attempting to move an object past the bounds of its container or to resize an object past its size limit.

Interaction at a Distance

Use of controls can extend beyond the bounds of those controls. For example, in a traditional GUI, the scrollbar can be captured by selecting it with the mouse. At that point, vertical movements of the mouse are applied to the position of the thumb, and horizontal movements are ignored. The result is that the mouse pointer can be moved away from the slider while still controlling it. This is equally necessary in a touch system, but mapping fingers to their controls is a potential source of confusion, with multiple touchpoints, controls, and users all interacting simultaneously.

Stolen Capture

In a traditional GUI, controls are captured by selecting them with the mouse pointer. In a multi-touch system, multiple fingers may attempt to capture a control simultaneously. How to deal with multiple, possibly contradictory touches to the same control is an issue decided by framework designers. In the DiamondSpin SDK, "click" events are generated every time a user taps a button, even if another finger is holding it down. In the Microsoft Surface SDK, "tap" events (equivalent to "click") are generated for buttons only when the last captured contact is lifted from the control. While both approaches have merit, a consequence of the latter is that buttons can be "held down" by a user. When twinned with the issue of *interaction at a distance*, it is possible that a button can be "held down" by a contact not actually touching that button. When a subsequent "tap" fails, the source of failure should be visualized.

Tabletop Debris

Users of tabletop systems have been observed to place objects on the surface of the screen. The table used in that study did not sense the presence of objects on its surface. This is not true, however, of all sensing technologies used in multi-touch systems. The result can be unexpected behavior when the system responds to these unintended inputs. In our own internal observations of users, we found that this was particularly problematic when an object would act as an additional contact for an object being manipulated by the user.

When scrolling a list, for example, the Microsoft Surface SDK uses the average distance traveled of all contacts on the list to compute its movement. Because it is interpreted as a stationary contact, a beverage placed on the surface of the table has the effect of halving the speed of scrolling a list. A visualization framework should visualize both when debris on the table is being interpreted as an input, and when stationary contacts are placing additional constraints on movement.

THE CONTACT VISUALIZER

In order to address feedback ambiguity, Microsoft Surface employs a Contact Visualizer, which provides visual states and transitions to provide clear indications of the system's current state, and the cause of that state (Figure 14.1).

This contact visualizer was found to reduce errors by over 50% and to lead users to describe the system as more responsive and better at understanding their intentions. Of course, we in the know understand that, in actuality, it is the user who better understands the system's responses.

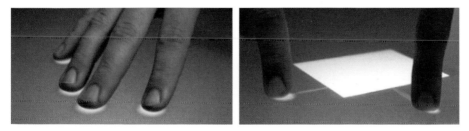

FIGURE 14.1

Each contact with the display is given a response and persistent visualization. Left: Photograph of the Contact Visualization system. Right: Tethers indicate that the fingers have slipped off the item because it reached maximum size.

DESIGN GUIDELINES

It is incumbent upon the designer to ensure that each and every source of error has a distinct response, ensuring that the user fully understands the link between the cause and effect of what they are seeing on the screen. This leads to the design goal of "no touch left behind"—ensure that every input to the system is meaningful and receives a clear response that allows users to link it back to their physical actions.

The Surface contact visualizer provides a layer of visualizations that is divorced from applications. When designing an application, you may prefer that the visual responses be more in keeping with your own design. Following the guidelines in this section will ensure that your system has sufficient feedback to allow users to understand their input and the consequences of that input.

Must

- It is essential that visual responses be provided to make clear the connection between cause and effect.

- For single-touch systems, we have developed a set of visual states and transitions that will ensure minimal coverage of the various error causes. Providing unique visuals for each of these states and transitions will provide a set of responses that is sufficient to disambiguate the various causes of unexpected behavior (Figure 14.2).

  State 0 cannot be visualized in most systems, as it precedes detection. The visualizations of transition A and state 1 address the problem of clearly indicating the *activation event*. They also help to note *accidental activations*, as unintended contacts receive an individual response, allowing the user to correct the posture. To help the user to differentiate between *fat fingers* and

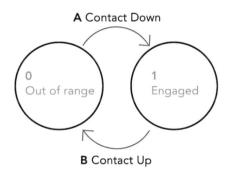

FIGURE 14.2

Touch visualization states and transitions. 0: not yet touching; 1: stationary contact; 2: moving contact.

nonresponsive content, and to visualize *selection*, the visual provided for transition A differentiates between contacts that have successfully captured an object, and those which have not (Figure 14.3).

To address *fat fingers*, we also included an animation for transition D (Figure 14.4). This animation emphasizes the hit testing point. To overcome occlusion, transition D delays its feedback subtly, so that it will continue to be visible for a moment after the user lifts her finger. Further, as the contact visualization disappears, it contracts to the hit test point, so that this point is the last thing seen by the user (Figure 14.4). Unlike previous work, the goal is not to assist the user in making the current selection, but rather to improve accuracy over time by helping the user to learn the point/finger mapping.

- In addition to the basic contact visualization, additional states were added to address issues that arise primarily with multi-touch systems. These issues are *multiple capture states*, *physical manipulation constraints*, *interaction at a distance*, and *stolen capture*. In examining these problems, we found that all could be addressed by adding just two states and their associated transitions. These are shown in Figure 14.5.

State 3 is described earlier as *overcaptured*: when the number of contacts captured to a control exceeds the available degrees of freedom of that control,

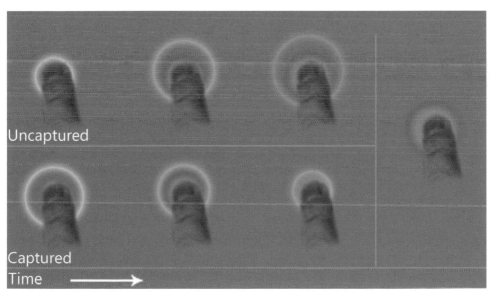

FIGURE 14.3

Left: Two animations are shown for transition A. If an object is captured, a circle shrinks around the contact. If not, it "splashes" outward. Right: State 1 is identical for both captured and uncaptured.

FIGURE 14.4

Transition D (see Figure 14.1): When contact is lifted, the visualization shrinks to the hit testing point.

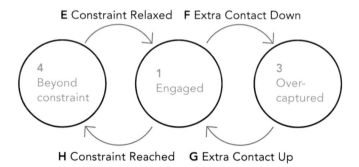

FIGURE 14.5

Additional visual states and transitions for multi-touch. 1: engaged (see Figure 14.1); 3: object is overcaptured; 4: contact operating beyond constraints.

necessitating breaking the direct-touch input paradigm. For example, overcapturing occurs if two fingers have captured the thumb of a slider, or if three have captured an object enabled for two-finger rotate/translate/scale. As in the basic contact visualizations, this difference is conveyed through the transitions. Transition F receives the same visual treatment as transition A for an uncaptured contact, and transition G the same as a captured contact. To differentiate these, however, transitions F and G are applied to *all contacts* captured to a control, clearly differentiating states 3 and 1.

State 4 is a condition under which the user has met a constraint on translation, scaling, or rotation of an object. In the Microsoft Surface SDK, these contacts remain captured to the object even though they are no longer touching it. An alternative capture model might cause the contact to lose capture of the object once the finger is no longer touching it. Whatever model is employed, it is critical that a visual be provided to explain why the object is no longer under the user's finger—this addresses the problems of *physical manipulation*

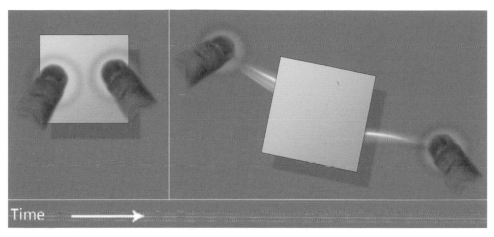

FIGURE 14.6

Tethers indicate that a size constraint has been reached on an item being scaled.

constraints and the *interaction at a distance*. To visualize these constraints, we employed a visualization similar to the trails seen in state 2 (see Figures 14.10 and 14.11). In state 4, the trails become "tethered" to the point at which the constraint was reached, illustrating that the contacts are now "slipping" from their last point of direct touch (Figure 14.6).

A purist's interpretation of state 4 would yield tethers when interacting with the majority of controls, since most map multiple degrees of freedom to a single dimension or cannot be moved. What we found, however, was that this could produce what we termed the *Freddy Krueger effect*, where tethers were appearing regularly all over the display. We reduced the frequency of the tethers to the minimal set needed to address specific as sources of error (see above).

The first such situation was the overconstrained scrolling of a list. It was determined through iterative design that, in most cases, the reaction of the list itself matched user intent and thus did not require visualization of constraints. The remaining case involves tabletop debris, which can cause slower than expected scrolling of a list. In this situation, determined by the presence of a stationary contact, tethers are rendered to demonstrate that the list is scrolling slowly because of that contact (Figure 14.7).

The final state 4 visualization visually tethers contacts that have slid off of, but are still captured to, controls. Again, to reduce unnecessary visuals, we split these into two classes. For controls that can be manipulated from a distance, the visualization is shown from the moment the contact slides off the control. For stationary controls, the tether is shown only when another contact attempts to actuate the control, addressing stolen capture (Figure 14.8).

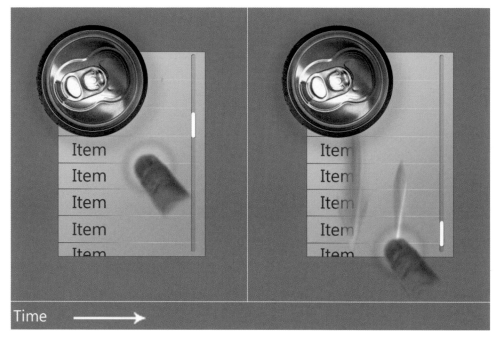

FIGURE 14.7

Tethers indicate that slow scrolling of the list is due to the presence of the stationary contact.

Should

- To properly achieve the goals of a NUI experience, we recommend that the visual states be integrated into the application. For example, rather than drawing tethers to show that the object has stopped growing, a visual "bounce" effect would provide the same results.

- Most touch hardware suffers from inevitable lag—an elapsed time between the instant the user does something and when the consequence of that action is rendered on the screen. A manifestation of this in a direct-touch system is that when dragging an object on the screen, it can "lag" behind the finger, so that the lag is actually visualized as physical distance between the finger and the object it is dragging.

  The faster the user moves, and the larger the screen, the more significant the problem. In a system that provides a visualization of where it "thinks" the user's fingers are, this problem could be exacerbated, since it will be rather blatantly pointing out that it is wrong (Figure 14.9)! To address this, you should consider adding an additional state to your visualization, so that it changes when moving. This change is a tacit acknowledgment of the lag and should give the appearance of it being "intentional" (Figure 14.10).

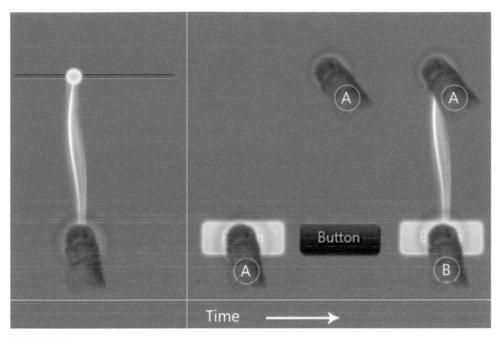

FIGURE 14.8

Left: Contact controlling the slider is visually tethered to it at all times. Right: For stationary controls, such as buttons, the tether is shown only when another contact attempts to actuate the control.

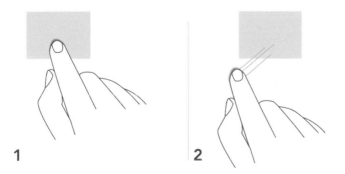

FIGURE 14.9

As a user drags a finger on the screen, the lag inherent in any interactive system manifests itself as a physical separation between where the finger actually is and where the system "thinks" it is at any given moment. Adding a visualization that tells the user "Here's where I think your finger is!" can exacerbate this lag.

Could

• Consider customizing for the particular input device on which the system will be running. As we have described elsewhere, touch software is typically built on top of a reduction that obfuscates the details of the sensors. While this makes development easier, it makes it less likely that software will take advantage of the unique attributes of its hardware. For example, consider displaying raw sensor output, such as shown in Figure 14.12.

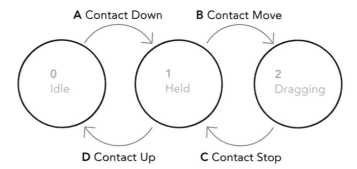

FIGURE 14.10

By adding a special state for objects when they are moving, any lag appears to be intentional.

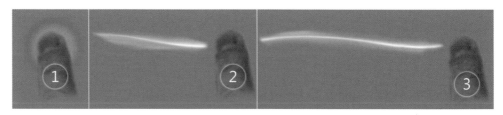

FIGURE 14.11

State 2 is shown as a trail, which reduces the perception of lag. 1: contact is static (state 1); 2: begins to move (transition B); 3: moving (state 2).

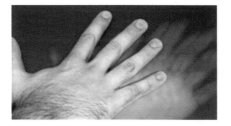

FIGURE 14.12

An early attempt to visualize input by displaying raw sensor data. This approach does not generalize across device types.

SUMMARY

While there are great advantages to direct-touch software, and there is a tendency to reduce abstraction and to allow direct interaction, as we have described in the early chapters, this does not alleviate the need for careful design of system responses. Indeed, the burden is actually increased: While designers of yesteryear were able to rely on the physical feel of the mouse and feedback of the pointer, touch application designers have no such luxury. The result is that they must spend more time carefully designing the array of responses to ensure that the user properly understands the various causes of the system responses they will see, lest they become a horde of dancing pigeons.

Touch versus In-Air Gestures

> *My fellow Americans, I'm pleased to tell you today that I've signed legislation that will outlaw Russia forever. We begin bombing in five minutes.*
>
> —Ronald Reagan

DESCRIPTION

As we have described in Chapter 3, technologies inhabit an ecological niche, in that each represents a set of potential uses and markets. Just as those who failed to understand the true utility of touch input predicted the death of the mouse and keyboard, new technologies, such as Xbox Kinect and the Sony EyeToy, that offer touchless gesture input might incorrectly be believed to be a replacement for touch and touch gestures. Certainly, devices that enable users to gesture in air open a seemingly all-new world of interaction potential—and perhaps new ecological niches as well. To the well-trained expert, however, it can be seen that in-air interactions share a great deal with those based on touch. This difference is easily expressed and understood using tools presented in this book, and will enable the quick and easy transfer of design knowledge from touch-based to touchless gesturing.

APPLICATION TO NUI

As we have seen, NUI is not a technology, but rather an experience that can be created using technology. Different sensing technologies are suited to different situations. As one rather well-known researcher is fond of saying, "Everything is best for something, and worst for something else." In-air gesturing, which can be sensed by devices like the Sony EyeToy and the Microsoft Kinect, is suitable in some circumstances where touch input is less so. In living rooms, with digital signage, and in other environments where walking over and touching a screen might detract from the experience, in-air gesturing helps close that gap.

LESSONS FROM THE PAST

The wrong way to think about in-air gesturing is "touch at a distance." The right way to think about it is as a unique input/output paradigm, which must be designed separately and differently from a touch one. That being said, many of the tools we have described elsewhere in this book are applicable to this input methodology as well as to touch input. We will focus on one particular differentiating element: that in-air gestures suffer from a "live mic," similar to the one that Ronald Reagan apocryphally encountered in the early 1980s when he delivered the quote that opens this chapter. In the case of in-air gesturing, this refers to the always-on nature of in-air gesturing and the need to "clutch"—to differentiate physical actions that are intended to drive the computing system from those that are not. In the case of touch computing, the clutch comes when the user lifts her hand from the digitizer. In most cases, when the hand is in the air, the system can't see it. This is true too of the mouse: Lifting your hand from the mouse (or lifting a mouse in the air) causes it to stop sending position change information to the system.

In Chapter 12, we described the state-transition model of input devices. Using this model, we explained that touch is fundamentally different from mouse input in one very important way: Typical touch input has no tracking state, or zone where the touch is registered by the system, but not yet engaged.

We pointed out that modern operating systems actually rely rather heavily on a tracking state and that designing well for touch input would mean designing an all-new UI that does not rely on the tracking state to provide a preview. If you thought that was hard, wait till you see this: in-air gesture systems are typically *one-state* input devices!

You can see now the challenge faced by those designing games and experiences for such input devices: There is no mechanism in the hardware that will differentiate between movements that are intended as gestures to the system and those that are not. When designing a touch application, there is little concern about this—if the user needs to cover his mouth to sneeze, scratch his head, gesture to another person in the room, wring his hands, stretch, or any other of a thousand different non-input actions, there is little worry that your sensor, the touchscreen, will send these to your app as "touches." You can simply assume that these will be filtered out by the simple fact that the user will stop touching the screen while doing them. This is not the case for in-air systems. The sensor will be buzzing away, like the camera and microphone pointed at President Reagan, happily sending all of these events to your application or platform.

This fact makes it easy to encounter errors in recognition of the types described in Chapter 28: where either the user does not intend to perform a gesture but the system recognizes one anyway (*false positive* errors), or the user believes she has performed a gesture but the system does not recognize it (*false negative* errors). These two problems can happen just as easily with touch as with in-air systems, but because of the "live mic" problem, they are likely to happen more often. To understand this, imagine the simple task of pushing a virtual button using both a touch

FIGURE 15.1

Selection using a pigtail gesture.

input and an in-air input device. In the touch case, this is relatively simple to accomplish: The user puts a finger on top of the button and lifts it within its bounds. In the in-air case, it is decidedly more complicated. The naive designer might say, "When the user points at the button, call it 'pushed.'" But this won't work—it's like aiming with a fully automatic rifle with the trigger stuck on "fire." As the user lifts a finger toward the screen, it is pointing the whole way and would be "pushing" every button as the finger is lifted. How then do we distinguish between aiming and firing in a one-state input device? Several approaches have been explored for in-air and other similar contexts that are worth examining.

Reserved Actions

The reserved-action approach takes a particular set of gestural actions and reserves them so that those actions are always designated as either navigation or commanding. For example, Ken Hinckley and his colleagues at Microsoft Research examined the problem of how to distinguish between strokes intended as commands and those intended as drawings in a pen interface. They reserved the "pigtail" gesture for issuing the "invoke menu" command (Figure 15.1).

This approach has the advantage of following an ink-based system without requiring a menu or mode. Want to draw a circle around something? Just go ahead and do it. Want to select something? Draw that same circle, but add a little pigtail to the end, and the system interprets it as a command. The disadvantage of this approach is also equally clear: The user of such a system could never draw a pigtail, because that is a reserved action. False positives are likely, since users of a drawing program are likely to draw strokes that cross themselves fairly often without intending them to invoke the command.

In-air gesturing has also been shown with reserved actions. Grossman and his colleagues invented *Hover Widgets*, a set of gestures performed by the user of a tablet PC with the stylus hovering in the air above the screen (Figure 15.2). Users could use the tracking state on the tablet PC as it was intended for a classic UI, as a preview for what would happen when they transitioned to engaged by touching the pen to the device. If they happened to move the pen in a particular pattern above the device, however, they would invoke commands.

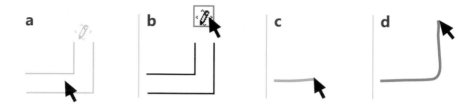

FIGURE 15.2

The Hover Widgets are invoked by moving the stylus in a particular pattern in the air above the device.

In this case, false negatives are more likely than false positives. This is because the "hover" zone above a tablet PC is rather small, and it is likely that the user will exit that zone during the gesture. However, the principle is sound: This reserved action is unlikely to be performed in the normal course of pointing, and is thus on the right track.

Reserving a Clutch

Similar to but different from a reserved action is a reserved clutch. This is a special class of action dedicated to creating a pseudo-tracking state. Similar to the clutch in a car, which connects or disconnects the engine from the wheels, a gestural clutch is an indicator that you want to start or stop recognition of the gesture. An obvious method for such a clutch would be an invisible plane in front of the user. When the user moves her hands in the air, they are tracked. To engage, they must push past that invisible plane.

The advantage of a clutch over a reserved action is immediately apparent: It provides an *a priori* indicator to the recognizer that the action to follow is either intended to be treated as a *gesture* or not. As we will learn in Chapter 18, the earlier your recognizer can differentiate gestures from non-gestures, the more accurate and positive your user experience will be. Another nice effect of a clutch is that it enables the complete gesture space to be used. In a system using Hover Widgets, for example, what if the user just happened to want to move the pen over the surface of the digitizer, but didn't want the Hover Widget action to happen? A clutch provides an obvious mechanism to differentiate the two situations, without having to set aside whole classes of actions.

Unfortunately, a virtual clutch may also cause errors. In the example of the invisible plane, if the plane is too close to the user, it's likely that he'll cross it unintentionally and frequently (false positive error). If the plane is too far away, it's likely that he'll fail to cross it when he intends to (false negative error). Unfortunately, there can be little doubt that these "too close" and "too far" zones will not border opposite sides of a "just right" zone, but rather that they will overlap and be different for different users, or even the same user over time.

A better example of a reserved clutch is the use of a "pinch." When the hand is in a regular pose, it is tracked. When the user pinches the finger and thumb together, it causes a transition to the engaged state. This approach is less likely to be subject to false positive errors, since this action is one that is unlikely to occur in the natural course. It is also less likely to be subject to false negative errors, since it is fairly easily detected and differentiated from other actions. It does, however, have the obvious disadvantage that you remove the pinch (or whichever gesture you choose) from the set of gestures you could otherwise use for other things in your system.

Despite the reduced probability of false negatives or positives, there may well be occasions in which a reserved action or clutch is not feasible. An alternative is to make use of multi-modal input.

Multi-Modal Input

Another solution to the live mic problem is multi-modal input. To understand this solution, we'll turn to the iPhone.

A question frequently asked of us by designers of touch applications is "Why does the iPhone have a button?" An engineer would point out that it allows the system to turn off the touch sensor, which saves power. Aside from this reason, there would still be a need for one that may now obvious to you in light of the live mic problem: without the button, how could the user be guaranteed to always be able to exit an application and return to the home screen? A reserved action might work (say, any time the user were to draw the Apple logo, or slide 5 fingers together on the screen, the application would exit and return to the home screen), but this would be problematic for the same reasons we have outlined above. Instead, multi-modal input is used: touch input is sent to the application, while hardware buttons control universal parameters (e.g., volume) and basic navigation (e.g., go home, open music controls).

Another example of multi-modal input commonly attempted with in-air gesture systems is to use speech input in combination with gesture. The "put that there" system was developed at MIT in the late 1970s and early 1980s. In it, the user could point at a screen, and the point was tracked. To transition between tracking and engaged states, the user issued speech commands. For example, to move an object from one place on the screen to another, the user would point at it, then say "Put that," which moved the system into "engaged." The user would then move her finger to point at the new location, and say "there." The advantage of multi-modal input is also obvious—it does not reduce the vocabulary of the primary modality the way that a reserved action or clutch do.

Another example of multi-modal input is the use of the keyboard to mode mouse clicks or drags. Drag an icon in windows and you will move it from one place to another. Hold down the CTRL key while you drag it, and it will make a copy instead of moving the original. Using input devices and methods in combination with one another may on its face seem more complex, but it can in actuality greatly simplify the problem of how to differentiate inputs and solve the live mic problem.

DESIGN GUIDELINES

Understand the live mic problem and how you will need to design for it. Consider the lessons of this chapter and the live mic problem. Aside from this, consider all of the lessons contained elsewhere in this book: for the most part, they apply equally well to both in-air gesturing and touch.

Must

- Understand the *live mic* problem as it applies to in-air gestures and design your system accordingly.

- Include mechanisms to differentiate between those actions that the system should recognize and those it should not.

Should

- Consider the solutions we have proposed here: reserving actions or clutches, or using multi-modal input to solve the live mic problem.

- Carefully consider and study your live mic solution. Do not assume that an action that you can perform easily will also be performed easily by your users.

- Consider the problems of both false positives and false negatives in defining your solution.

Could

- Design your system so that there is no need to solve the live mic problem by completely redesigning the UI from the ground up, and taking this issue into account.

SUMMARY

While touch and in-air gesturing may at first seem quite different from one another, there is only one significant subtlety that differentiates them: the live mic problem. Fully understanding and addressing it will allow you to apply the other lessons from this book to both touch and touchless gestural interaction.

FURTHER READING

Hinckley, K., Baudisch, P., Ramos, G., and Guimbretiere, F. Design and analysis of delimiters for selection-action pen gesture phrases in scriboli. In *Proceedings of the SIGCHI Conference on Human Factors in Computing Systems* (Portland, OR, April 2–7, 2005). CHI '05. ACM, New York, NY, pp. 451–460. DOI=http://doi.acm.org/10.1145/1054972.1055035. In this work, Hinckley and his colleagues examine various methods for telling the system "The stroke I just entered wasn't intended as ink, but rather as a command." They consider a variety of mechanisms, and conclude that the pigtail method is clearly superior.

Grossman, T., Hinckley, K., Baudisch, P., Agrawala, M., and Balakrishnan, R. Hover widgets: Using the tracking state to extend the capabilities of pen-operated devices. In *Proceedings of the SIGCHI Conference on Human Factors in Computing Systems* (Montréal, Québec, Canada, April 22–27, 2006). R. Grinter et al., eds. CHI '06. ACM, New York, NY, pp. 861–870. DOI=http://doi.acm.org/10.1145/1124772.1124898. In this work, Grossman and others at Microsoft Research build a set of simple hover-based gestures to complement those built-in to the tablet PC. The Hover Widget gestures differentiate themselves from other actions performed in the hover zone of the PC by reserving specific physical movements to invoke them. These are distinct from other types of in-air gestures in that they are meant to complement a pen input system, where touching the pen to the display performs other actions.

Creating an Interaction Language

Mechanics, Dynamics, and Aesthetics: The Application of MDA

16

It's not the meat; it's the motion.

—Maria Muldaur

DESCRIPTION

The mechanics of a product and the dynamics of use determine the aesthetics of the product experience.

Mechanics are the essence of any software product. Simply stated, the mechanics of a product are what it can do (functions) and what actions (behaviors) the user must perform to activate those functions and what goals are implied or promised by the product. One also might think of mechanics as the "objects" (virtual or real), the rules of operation, and the goals (end states) that are achievable with the product. For software products one can think of mechanics as what goes on the disk (or can be downloaded).

Hunicke, LeBlanc, and Zubek have applied the mechanics, dynamics, and aesthetics framework to game design. Consider a game like chess. In chess the objects are the pieces and the board. The rules of play define where pieces can move under what circumstances and how pieces are captured. The goal of the game is to capture the king. Together, the objects, rules, and goals are the "essence" of chess. The game can be rendered in various ways—simple portable plastic board and pieces, elaborate carved pieces and board, an electronic chess playing game—but they are all chess because of their identical mechanics. In effect, the definition of chess is embodied in how it is played. This way of defining words, that is, in terms of their use, has been elaborated on by Wittgenstein.

Extending the concept of mechanics to software products is illustrative. The objects are often virtual objects—text, graphics, formulas, avatars, targeting reticles, mini-maps, etc. In addition, other things that the user interacts with, menus, dialog boxes, rulers, and the like, are also objects. Some of these objects are primary (text, graphics, etc.); others are secondary (menus, dialog boxes, etc.). Creating or modifying primary objects is the reason for using the product. For example, I use an editor to create text objects. Secondary objects affect primary objects. Menus or dialog boxes change the rendition of text (its font, size, or style). We could also consider the physical input medium. In most cases this will be a pointing device (e.g., a mouse) and text input device (e.g., a keyboard).

In any meaningful system, objects have rules of operation. A primary object like text appears at the insertion point when a user types. The text that follows the text being typed moves to the right and down, provided the user is in insert mode. In overstrike mode, text replaces text to the right in a one-to-one correspondence. All secondary objects have rules of operation and rules that govern their effect of primary objects. Together, the primary and secondary object and their rules of operation constitute the means by which the "goals" of the product are met. Goals can be general—I want to make a document—or quite specific—I want to change this letter to the Trebuchet font.

When users engage a game or any product, their actions vis-à-vis the game or product constitute dynamics. For example, when players play chess, the movement of the pieces constitutes dynamics. While the mechanics of chess are fixed, the dynamics vary within a range. Players can make only "legal" moves. Conditions of victory are pre-set. However, the players' behavior is not completely determined. Players bring their own knowledge and individual motives to the game. Each particular game has a broader context, for example, it could take place in a park. These characteristics make each chess game unique and interesting. The social context also plays a role. The game may be between old friends, in which case the interaction between the players could be more important than who wins. Alternatively, the game could be in a tournament in which winning is key. In other words, dynamics are predictable (you must play by the rules) but never fully determined. Every chess game is unique, but all follow the same rules. Thus, chess fulfills the criteria for a good game: simple to learn but hard to fully master.

When software products and their supporting hardware are used by people, that interaction generates dynamics—user actions. Just like in a game, users bring their background knowledge and their own goals to the situation. The knowledge can be either "domain" knowledge (e.g., the author is a good writer) or "product" knowledge (e.g., the author knows how to use MS Word or LaTeX to create the document she wants). The goals are part of the context. Goals may change, but it's useful for the analyst or designer to be aware of them. Thus every interaction with a product is constrained by the objects, rules, and purpose of the product (mechanics), but every interaction will also have emergent properties determined by the user, her knowledge, her motives, situational factors (she must finish a five-page report by tomorrow), and possibly changing goals.

Finally, the dynamics of a game are the source of the aesthetics of the game. Drawing on the chess example again, a highly competitive game will elicit conclusions about the game and reactions to it. For example, an observer may conclude that it was a "good" game. Based on the actions during the game, the observer concludes that the opponents were evenly matched and the outcome was unpredictable. The players will have their own aesthetic conclusions. For example, one player may conclude that she played below her potential or that her opponent "cheated" by distracting her. The conclusions can take any form, for example, "chess is not for me." They could also be emotional, for example, "I feel angry and I won't play him again." These conclusions about the game—intellectual conclusions, personal conclusions, and emotional conclusions—are called aesthetics. They refer to the player's experiential conclusions about this game, chess in general, herself, or her opponent.

We apply this construct of aesthetics to any product. People draw conclusions from the use of the product. That product is hard (or easy) to use. The conclusions may be emotional and global: "I hate product X." Or they may be subtle and nuanced: "Don't use product Y if you have to produce a document with many tables, but product Y is great if you are writing a novel."

Figure 16.1 depicts the mechanics, dynamics, and aesthetics (MDA) framework.

This framework of mechanics, dynamics, and aesthetics was developed to analyze game design. It can be usefully applied to any product, but there are some important differences between products and games. In games like chess, the rules are well established, are extensively documented, and change very slowly. Once you learn the rules of the game you can play and gain experience. As you become better at it, you understand more "dynamic possibilities," for example, if I do X, that leads to condition Y, and my opponent is likely to do Z. Your aesthetic appreciation

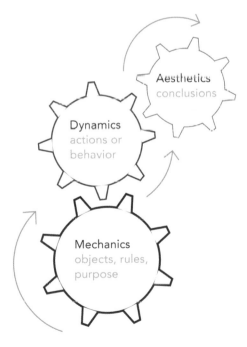

FIGURE 16.1

The MDA framework.

may change. For example, you may learn to appreciate getting beaten by a worthy opponent in a well-fought game. You may take away "learnings," for example, I'll try the end game on my next opponent.

Applying the MDA model to products helps us appreciate certain distinctions, and new possibilities emerge. For example, the mechanics of the primary objects in a product may facilitate or hinder its use in a given domain. An editor that used overstrike mode exclusively would not be well suited to free-form writing. Free-form writing often involves inserting text between already-written text, which is hard to do in overstrike. On the other hand, overstrike makes text replacement very easy (the deletion step is eliminated). It works well for replacing data in forms. Insert editors compensate for the difficulty of replacement by including an overstrike mode or by pending delete (select the text to be replaced and type).

Beyond the behavior of primary objects (e.g., text), game and product designers are faced with the challenge of the design of secondary objects. The behavior of these secondary objects imposes an additional burden on the user. They must not only learn the domain, but also learn how to use the "tool," that is, the secondary objects. Consider an electronic chess game. The user may type in commands to move pieces on a virtual board. The designer must aim to make this as easy to learn as possible since in and of itself it typing commands contributes nothing to the "joy of chess." The designer is aided by the fact that chess has a traditional notation system that many players are familiar with. The designer of electronic chess can simply implement that system.

In software products, design teams often face two challenges. The product must teach domain knowledge and must teach tool knowledge. Early users of modern editors had to learn about fonts and layout. These are part of the domain knowledge that was the traditional domain of printers. In addition, the designs had to teach tool knowledge—where and how the user can change the font of a word or a paragraph or a document. This problem was compounded by the fact that users want to learn by doing as compared to reading. As a result, design became not merely matching the actions of a domain but representing these to users so that they could understand (or learn) the domain and learn the tool. The design of the mechanics of a system can be very challenging.

Some exemplary products accomplish both these goals very well. Users become skilled practitioners, quickly learning both the domain and the tool. In some cases they even enjoy the process. Some products like games exist only for pleasure (by and large). Designers of games often strive to make this learning fun by eliminating unnecessary challenges and introducing challenges progressively, creating a gradual ramp for learning as you play. These "ramps" consist of well-designed steps in which both the domain knowledge and the tool knowledge are progressively introduced.

APPLICATION TO NUI

By definition a NUI offers an opportunity to introduce products where the mechanics are readily practiced. There is a high probability that the product works the way one expects it to work. These "intuitive" or natural mechanics should lead to highly effect dynamics. Use should be smooth and expert-like without long periods of training or practice. A user's progress will be more or less continuous, without regression or long plateaus. A motivated learner will develop deeper skills with each game. Her growth in skills will be about chess, not about the tool she might use to play it. The aesthetic result is that the device is experienced as delightful and fun to use. The user feels empowered by the technology rather than frustrated, enslaved, or ridiculed by it.

Consider a NUI version of chess. In that version one could move the pieces by touch, that is, touch the piece and move it to the destination square. NUI chess could also prevent illegal moves, such as moving bishops off the diagonal. In this way it aids the beginner in learning *in situ*. This example illustrates some of the essential elements of a NUI system. "Learning" focuses on primary objects—pieces, their movement, and conditions of success. The novice will learn the mechanics of chess relatively quickly and with pleasure. The transition to skilled player may be even more rapid than it would be with a traditional board and pieces, since illegal moves are precluded and valid moves may be highlighted. A second player is optional. The computer can play that role, and the difficulty level can set by the player to ensure the right level of challenge. Progress can be tracked and games can be stored and reviewed, with supplemental teaching. Playing will be more fun. Minor but burdensome tasks, such as picking up the game and finding lost pieces, are eliminated. NUI chess also eliminates the need for secondary objects. The player need not learn a notation system and enter codes to indicate which pieces move where.

Once the mechanics are mastered, a NUI version would aid the players in developing skill. It could do this in several ways. Games could be automatically replayed so that the novice can study how she won or lost. This uses technology as an aid and possibly substitutes for traditional instruction or informal discussion with other players after a game is over. The replay could be enhanced by explanatory text or by allowing the player to intervene at any time and play the game from that point, allowing one to practice mid-game or mating strategies.

One could also imagine a natural way of learning during play. Often novices at chess adopt an informal rule that a move is not complete until you remove your finger from the piece. This allows them to position a piece and study the board. One could easily imagine electronic chess allowing the same action but enhancing it by showing the novice what other pieces were a threat. Any number of mechanisms are possible. Threats could be shown after a delay (the computer is scanning for the novice) or on command.

The critical NUI elements of the development of expertise are that new information is introduced progressively, it occurs in a way that is consistent with the level of the novice and desired state of expertise being strived for, the learning takes place in the context of use, and the learning is perceived as fun.

Contrast this approach to the very traditional approach to learning chess. One typical element of traditional learning is studying books that describe typical patterns of movement. This often requires the learner to learn the notation of chess. While this may be valuable, it is not natural and can be a stumbling block.

The example captures the essence of a NUI. It is an interface that encourages rapid transition to skilled practice by removing nonessential objects and rules, enhancing the learning of essential rules, enabling the process of skill acquisition to be pleasurable, and offering technological enhancements that enrich the experience. Natural does not mean primitive, or even intuitive. To the non-player there is nothing intuitive about chess. But to the experienced player and the willing student, a natural interface to chess is the way to go. We could introduce our own "Turing test" for a natural user interface. It is one that will be chosen over others by the majority of both novices and experts. In other words, in most cases students of chess and accomplished players will choose it over playing chess with the traditional board and pieces.

Actually, designing a NUI system can be a quite subtle and difficult problem depending on the domain or task. There are no foolproof and simple heuristics one can follow to create a NUI. However, we can provide some guidance for how to approach designing a NUI system.

Removing intermediaries like the keyboard and a specialized pointing device, for example, the mouse, is a possible step to this more natural interface. By removing these "transducers," the user is able to interact directly with the objects that the computer system presents. However, such removal is not foolproof. It depends on the task and the current dominant practices. For example, replacing the keyboard for tasks that primarily involve text creation would be problematic given the evolved state of keyboard design and the skill level of the population. It will be a long time, if ever, until a virtual keyboard can match the performance of a regular keyboard. However, a sufficiently accurate and fast voice recognition system may become a contender at some point in the future. Even more subtle approaches may be more natural in some situations. For example, anticipating the word that user is typing by offering options, or a keyboard system that allows only valid entry by rendering "wrong" virtual keys inoperative (some auto navigation systems adopt that approach), may speed the user to skilled practice. Stretching the point, one could even see autocorrect in software systems as "natural" if the user gets to skilled practice more quickly and the results are better.

A NUI promises straightforward mechanics, smooth and flawless dynamics, and consequently positive aesthetics. Needless to say, this nirvana is not easily achieved. The development of new hardware capabilities offers the possibility that these NUIs may emerge, but only the possibility. In practice, designing and implementing such interfaces are extraordinarily difficult. The rest of this book will provide some insight into how such interfaces can be built.

LESSONS FROM THE PAST

With some justification, one can see the evolution of the human-computer interface as a slow but relentless progress toward a more NUI-like interface: one that enables skillful performance rapidly without diminishing the result, and perhaps enhancing it.

In this chapter we have taken a framework that has been useful in game design and applied it to the NUI. Like NUIs, games face the challenge of creating skilled practice without making the interaction trivial. They have adopted interesting ways of addressing that challenge. For example, game designers think in terms of the difficulty ramp of the game: How can we make each stage of learning the game just challenging enough to make it interesting, that is, not too trivial and not too insurmountable? They also think in terms of creating a lawful world where players can anticipate, plan, and strategize about their approach to winning. Some games face the additional challenge of representing in some way real-world environments. For example, driving games can simulate the physics of driving high-performance cars, or they can simplify the physics and provide some support. How much the physics are simplified and how much support is provided is a strategic decision.

DESIGN GUIDELINES

The MDA framework does not offer detailed design guidelines. Instead, it provides a framework for thinking about design. It also hints at pitfalls such as assuming that the mechanics are obvious or assuming that new capabilities will necessarily lead to delight. But by using MDA and our experience with games, we can offer some guidance to design teams.

- Begin with the fundamental mechanics of the interaction. If your understanding of those do not draw on the situated knowledge of skilled practitioners, it is unlikely that the implementation of the NUI will be successful.

- Do not draw inspiration from pre-existing interaction paradigms: beginning with a command system, a GUI, or a web interface almost certainly guarantees inconsistency and failure.

- Consider carefully what is skilled behavior in a domain and how the path to skilled behavior could be shortened without cheapening the skill.

- Remove secondary interface controls wherever possible.

- Do not consider how to use technology to enhance the interaction until you have designed the fundamental interaction and how to teach it quickly and easily. Only then consider the enhancements that technology can add. For example, design the chess game first and make the action of the pieces work smoothly and the pieces clearly differentiated. Only after that is working should you consider enhancements and then focus on those that enhance the progress to skilled performance. For instance, first make illegal moves impossible but in a fluid way, such as not allowing a piece to follow the user's finger to an illegal square, but allowing tracking to resume when the user moves the piece in a legal direction. Get that right before you consider such enhancements as auto replay and teaching.

- Finally, beware of creating plateaus. One pointed criticism of many modern so-called NUIs is that the user quickly develops skill to a certain level but will never progress beyond that level. The Wii is a good example. Wii tennis may be fun at parties. It may do great social good by allowing physically impaired folks to enjoy some tennis-like movements and thrills, for example, winning. But becoming an "expert" in Wii tennis is unlikely to be a path to becoming a tennis champion.

SUMMARY

In this chapter we explicated the MDA framework and applied it to the NUI. We distinguished between primary objects (those that are inherently part of the task) and secondary objects (interface controls). NUIs minimize the latter. We suggested a Turing-like test for the successful NUI: would skilled practitioners and eager learners prefer it to traditional training approaches. Finally, drawing from game design, we suggested some principles to guide the development of a NUI.

 ## FURTHER READING

Hunicke, R., LeBlanc, M., and Zubek, R. MDA: A Formal Approach to Game Design and Game Research, http://www.cs.northwestern.edu/~hunicke/MDA.pdf. The MDA framework has proven very useful for thinking about game design and improving games. While there are a number of classification systems for aesthetics, the value for our purposes is in the clear distinctions this framework makes between designing the "thing," using or playing with the "thing," and the users conclusions about the "thing." We have applied it to NUI because we think it helps advance the concept of NUI beyond the ideas of a set of primitive gestures. It has also served to shape the thinking of the Games User Research team at Microsoft Studios (http://mgsuserresearch.com/).

Wittgenstein, L. (1953) *Philosophical Investigations*, translated by G. E. M. Annscombe, Blackwell. We call out Wittgenstein here because of his analysis of language. Specifically, that the meaning of language is embodied in its use. This chess is not defined by a dictionary definition but by the cultural practice of the play of chess, that is, the mechanics. You don't really know what chess is until you learn to play it, and then your knowledge of it depends on your level of play (as untalented amateurs we are merely dilettantes who draw on chess for examples). However, Wittgenstein's discussion of the Martian who watches a chess game is instructive. Our hypothetical Martian watches a game of chess and then argues that the outcome is completely determined. The players are stunned. But the Martian was right; she was just focusing on the mechanics of chess. For the players the rules were in the background, and yes, they did determine the play, but the players were focused on the dynamics (their emergent play) and their aesthetics—how they interpreted the game. The greatest design occurs when the dynamics and aesthetics intended by the mechanics the designer created are matched by the dynamics and aesthetics of the player. That is, the product is used as intended and evokes the reactions the designer intended.

New Primitives

17

Even the literature of the Party will change. Even the slogans will change. How could you have a slogan like "freedom is slavery" when the concept of freedom has been abolished? The whole climate of thought will be different. In fact there will be no thought, as we understand it now. Orthodoxy means not thinking—not needing to think. Orthodoxy is unconsciousness.

—George Orwell, 1984

DESCRIPTION

Modern software design has been divided up into professions, often distinguished as information architecture (designing the layout and flow of an application or website), interaction design (assembling components of interaction, such as *links*, *buttons*, and so on), and visual design (deciding on the overall and specific look of an application or site). None of these operates at a sufficiently low level to create designs for new technologies. The vast majority of designers have never considered the fundamental mechanics of a link, or a *click*; this concept is so ingrained in their understanding of computers that they think of it as axiomatic. *Click* has become a part of the language spoken by users of interactive technologies. Ask someone to speak aloud as they browse the web on their touchscreen phone, and you will hear them tell you that they are "clicking links." The metaphor of the button has been so deeply engrained in the mechanics of interaction that one might fear there is no going back. As we will discuss in greater detail in Chapter 21, modern user interfaces grew in a tight coupling with the evolution of the mouse. As we move to new input devices, we will need new primitives.

The Ingsoc government of Orwell's Oceania sought to eliminate undesirable actions by first removing the building block used to form the intent: language. In the fragment above, we understand the power of the fundamentals of language as Ingsocs believed it to be: if there were no words to describe a thought, the mind would be unable to form it. While modern linguists might debate the efficacy of such a plan for spoken language, there is no denying that the basic building blocks **115** of the user experience form the foundation of its success. Shaking the mouse cursor on the screen does nothing in the Windows and Mac OS worlds, not because such an action *could not* be recognized by the system, but rather because the designers have chosen that this action *should not* do something. In the user interface world, there can be no denying the power of the basics of the interaction language: get them right, and your system could seem simple, even *natural* to use. Get them wrong, and your user experience has no chance of success, even before you have designed any of what is traditionally thought of as the user experience.

The building blocks of an interaction language are what we refer to as *primitives*. To understand their role, you might think of four levels of actions: (1) what is physically possible with the device (I can slide the mouse on a table, I can turn it upside down, I can juggle it…), (2) what is actually recognized and conveyed by the device (only movement on the table), (3) the even narrower subset of what is recognized to those things to which system responses are tied (movements of the mouse are recognized as a "drag," which allows the user to move on-screen objects from one place to another. However, the actual shape of the drag does not matter—all that matters in a drag is the start and end point. Dragging in a heart shape while dragging does nothing different than dragging directly between the two points.), and (4) the expansion of the primitives in the form of controls (e.g., clicking and dragging a slider changes a one-dimensional value, clicking and dragging on an ink canvas draws a two-dimensional stroke, clicking and dragging an icon moves it somewhere else).

Each of these levels is critical. What is physically possible is limited by the laws of physics and biomechanics. What is recognized is a function of your hardware—different hardware recognizes different things, and is the subject of Chapters 21 to 27.

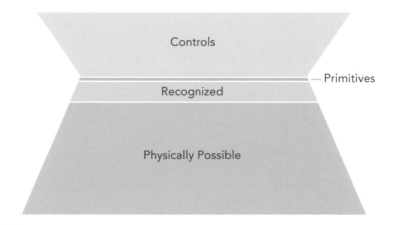

FIGURE 17.1

Each level is a subset of the one beneath until the primitives are reached. Those primitives are then composed into a larger set of controls. Keeping the set of primitives small makes the language easy to learn. For example, clicking and dragging a paint palette draws, clicking and dragging on a scroll-bar scrolls a page.

How you expand your primitives by building controls or gestures is the subject of Chapters 14 and 15. In this chapter, we will describe the development of the primitive actions: those physical actions which are detected by your sensors that you will select to be primary units of interaction of your system.

APPLICATION TO NUI

Not all applications written for a given platform will require new primitives. Indeed, the ideal would be for primitives to be more or less standardized across a platform, the same way they are now in Windows and Mac OS (those which are more or less standard across them: click, double-click, CTRL-click/right-click, etc). But we're not there yet—different touch platforms employ different primitives, and it's not uncommon for application writers of touch & gestural systems to build their own. This is largely due to the fact that very few toolkits have been released which provide a good and comprehensive set of primitives for the design of touch interaction. Instead, most are simply copies of mouse primitives. This is no doubt because we're simply too early in the process—the design work is yet to be done. We need an explosion of applications with different primitives to finally settle down through a darwinian process into a smaller set of primitives which will become a standard within each platform, and possibly, eventually, across platforms.

This can be seen as both opportunity and crisis. The burden for the designers of touch applications are much greater than for mouse-based systems, because you can't rely wholly on the toolkits you have to work with. At the same time, this gives designers far more freedom to experiment and to help shape the future of touch interaction.

LESSONS FROM THE PAST

Where most designers of touch systems err is in believing that the primitives provided for the mouse are also the right ones for touch systems. To understand why this is problematic, we'll now examine two input devices, the mouse and the pen, and explore how a failure to design new primitives led to the failure of pen-based systems.

What the Mouse is Good At

A mouse is designed to detect two physical actions well: travel from one point to another (*point*), and the pushing of buttons (*click*). In most mouse GUI toolkits, a *click* is registered if the pointer is positioned over an object, and the button is then depressed and released. If the cursor moves off of the object between the time the button is depressed and released, no *click* is generated. The requirement of no movement is to reduce situations where the user might click the wrong location or press the button by mistake (what we'll call a *false positive* in Chapter 20). It gives them an escape route: They can push down the mouse button, see that they have missed their intended target (or changed their mind), and then drag the mouse off of the on-screen control to safely release their button without triggering a click. For this to work well, there must also be a low risk of the system failing to detect a click when the user intends one (Chapter 20: *false negative*). The mouse is ideally suited to this in the case of *clicking*: Its large surface area provides sufficient static friction that it is unlikely to slip due to the force of the user pushing the button. As for the moving from one place to another, the mouse is also ideally suited to this – extensive, exhaustive studies over the years have shown the mouse to be faster than joysticks, pens, trackballs, you name it—the mouse is faster for pointing.

What the Mouse Is Bad At

It's essential to note the subtlety of the primitive of *pointing*: It's the movement *from one place to another*. This is distinctly different from following a path – the mouse provides terrible control for actually controlling the path of movement. Don't believe us? Open up a drawing program and try drawing a perfect (heck, even passable) circle. Now grab a pen and a piece of paper. Which one was faster, and which one looks better? A defender of the mouse might at this point pipe-up and say "there is no need to control the path of the mouse! The user needs only to move over a target and click – so who cares? If you want to draw, use a stylus." And of course, they'd be right, but they'd also be missing the point: the reason there is no need to control the path of the mouse is *because the UI has been designed that way*. The astute designer might note moments in operating systems where the path does matter – but these moments are examples of poor design. For example, navigating sub-menus: Slide too far outside the narrow path of the root of the menu, and the sub-menu disappears. No doubt this is why sub-menus have been all but eliminated from more modern software.

The job of a designer of primitives is to understand what your hardware is good at detecting, and what the applications will need. The mouse GUI was an example of where this has been done extremely well, through 40 years of innovation, failure, missteps, and corrections. An obvious example of where the software was not designed for the hardware was in the Tablet PC.

What a Pen Is Bad At

The early version of the Windows-based Tablet PCs were essentially operated by the pen emulating the mouse. As we will describe in Chapter 21, this sort of situation is largely due to the business decision of wanting to ensure old applications could be operated by the new system. Of course, a careful examination of the pen will reveal that it is *terrible* at one of the two things a mouse is best at: *clicking*. As the pen approaches the digitizer, the cursor jumps around with every small movement of the pen. Once the pen is touching, it is extremely easy to slip by some small amount, ensuring that no *click* is generated in the application (Chapter 20: false negative). It's even harder to perform a right-click, which typically requires the user to press a button on the barrel of the pen while they are trying to keep it still on the device (or hold it down in an awkward posture while they perform their *click*). As for *pointing*, the stylus is passable, but one must also consider the digitizer: Most digitizers detect the stylus only when it's within an inch or so of the digitizer. The consequence is that the user is usually doing most of the physical *pointing* movement with the pen out of range of the digitizer (what we called the "out of range" state in Chapter 13). This means that any controls which rely on knowing the movement during a *pointing* movement won't work correctly, or you will force the user to keep the stylus close to but not quite touching the digitizer, which can be a pain.

In truth, it's almost hard to imagine a worse device for controlling a WIMP GUI. It's no wonder that the Tablet PC never caught-on.

What a Pen Is Good At

Where the pen excels is in the area where the mouse does not: controlling the path of movement. Users can quickly sketch, write, and annotate. Detractors of the Tablet PC will often note that typing is much easier than hand-writing. And of course they're right. But that misses the point – if your application requires a lot of typing, it's not right for a pen-based system. But for all of these other tasks: active reading, sketching, brainstorming, entering mathematical equations, the pen wins by far. What has held back the user experience of pen-based devices is that they have relied on a user interface largely designed for the mouse. Imagine if the Tablet PC's software had been built completely from the ground up taking these simple facts into account.

Designing New Primitives

As you saw in Figure 17.1, the primitives used in a system are used in combination to form controls. Thus, this for-mouse design of the WIMP GUI lives in the controls themselves. Just as you would never try to push a physical button with a pen, nor does it make sense for the button to be the metaphor or interaction method for a pen in the virtual world. These controls, however, are formed as collections of the more fundamental primitives which are designed at a lower level. One can imagine a creating a user interface where clicking is never required. What if only *crossing* were recognized? To

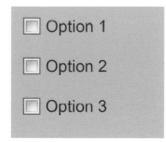

FIGURE 17.2

Traditional GUI checkboxes. These are activated by applying the *click* primitive to the white square. In most, but not all tookits, the user can also *click* the label.

understand what we mean, consider the traditional checkbox, as we see in Figure 17.2. These are activated by applying the *click* primitive. This is easily done with the mouse: the user *points* the pointer over the control, and *clicks* to toggle the state of the box. This simple control is perfectly designed for the mouse. But it is terribly designed for pen input, since a *click* is very hard to perform with the pen, for the reasons we described above.

Instead of *click*, a pen-based UI might employ *cross* as a primitive. What we mean by this is that the user would slide the tip of the pen over the control. It wouldn't matter where the stroke were initiated, or where it ended, but if it passed-over the control, it would toggle it. The users could stroke over the control, or they could choose to draw a little check-mark, whatever they wanted. Figures 17.3 and 17.4 show what that might look like.

In addition to being easier to perform than a click, another advantage of a crossing-based checkbox is that multiple boxes could be crossed with a single stroke, as we see in Figure 17.4.

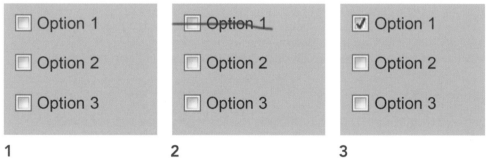

FIGURE 17.3

Hypothetical, *crossing*-based checkboxes: Stroking over them toggles their state. (1) the control. (2) ink showing the path of the user's pen stroke. (3) the checkbox shows the new state.

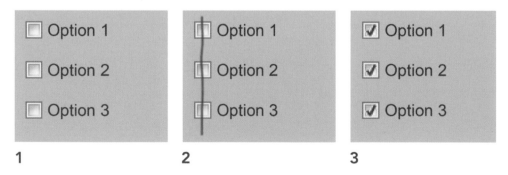

FIGURE 17.4

Crossing-based checkboxes: the user selects multiple boxes with a single stroke.

The disadvantage of a *crossing* primitive is that it might have a high degree of accidental detections if the user became a little sloppy (Chapter 20: false positives). An alternative would be an *escape* primitive, where the stroke must initiate within the bounds of the object, but end outside it. Or an *entry* primitive, where the stroke must initiate outside and terminate within the object. Each would have pros and cons, which you would need to evaluate. Once a decision was made on the primitives, it could then be extended to the controls. It is obvious how a radio button or button might work under any of these schemes. Of course, which controls you create depends more on the applications and context of use of your system. But they will all be composed of the primitives you build for your hardware. A critical mistake made by the designers of pen-based interfaces was starting with the controls, instead of with the primitives. As soon as they missed replacing the *click*, there really was no hope that they would build a for-pen user interface.

Hope of a for-pen user interface is not lost. An excellent design exercise was conducted by a group of researchers at the University of Maryland. *Crossy* was a drawing program, designed for use with a pen, which had all of its primitives replaced by *crossing*. It is a source of inspiration for how to define new primitives, and then design controls using those primitives.

DESIGN GUIDELINES

The unfortunate truth is that a definitive set of touch primitives has yet to be designed. A few have been seen on a bunch of systems: pinching to zoom in and out, sliding the finger up and down to scroll. Continuing to evolve these will be the task of designers of touch-based platforms and applications. There is a tendency with touch and gesture systems to believe that more actions can "naturally" be promoted to primitives. This seems intuitive, since we have such a large vocabulary of primitives when interacting with objects and with one another—we don't just point at ideas on a page, we say them, while using pointing gestures to aid in conversation. As we alluded to in Chapter 2 and will discuss in more detail in Chapter 30, the set of primitive actions which we all perform without prompting is incredibly small. Ask 10 people what the gesture should be for "turn that box red," and you'll get anywhere from 5 to 10 different gestures. The take-away, of course, is that you will *always* need to teach any new primitives and higher-order commands you introduce. How this is done is covered in great detail in Chapter 19, applying the principal of scaffolding we discussed in Chapter 12.

Overlap Primitive Sets for Novices and Experts

There is a tendency to optimize for quick learning. This can be accomplished by, among other things, having a very small set of primitives. This approach, of course, optimizes for novices and neglects the opportunity for users to learn and become experts. There is a lesson to be learned from the WIMP GUI, which has a rather large set of primitives for both mouse and keyboard. For the mouse, there are *click*, *double-click*, *right-click* (*function-click* for the Mac folks), *scroll*, and of course *point*. For the keyboard, these are roughly every key on the keyboard, with some combinations in the form of accelerator keys (e.g., *Apple+C* to copy, *CTRL+V* to paste). The beauty of this system is that the mouse and keyboard primitives actually co-exist entirely, without interference. A user could drive both *Windows 7* and *Mac-OSX* using only a keyboard or a mouse. The keyboard primitives (aside from text entry) exist as a set exclusively for the benefit of expert users. The beauty of their design is in how well these systems co-exist, and how well the users are supported in starting out with the mouse, and then gradually learning the more advanced primitives of the keyboard. As we describe in detail in Chapter 19, this is one of the few areas where the Windows UI unquestionably is better designed than OSX. Users of either operating system would be well served to use the Windows treatment of overlapping primitives as a study in how this can be done well, and consider how you might do so in your touch applications.

How Many is the Right Number of Primitives?

A critical issue to consider is the number of primitives. This is an area of potential trade-off of expert vs. novice use. If your system has very few primitives, they can be learned more quickly. If your system has a large number of primitives, it may take longer to learn them, but an expert can perform a single primitive more quickly than using primitives in combination. An obvious example of this trade-off is the scroll wheel added to the mouse, or two-finger scrolling on modern trackpads: in the olden days, "scroll" was not a primitive, it was enabled by controls that could be manipulated using *point* and *click* primitives (the scroll bar). But someone recognized that promoting that logical action to a primitive would enable faster expert use – now scrolling is as easy as pointing (to the window to be scrolled) and sliding the wheel or two fingers on the trackpad. The disadvantage is obvious: novices have more to learn. There is no hard and fast rule as to which is the right number. An oft misapplied number in design circles is the capacity of working memory (5–9 items). Since primitives are stored in long-term memory, this value does not apply.

Constructing and Evaluating Primitives

Another disadvantage of the mouse's *scroll* primitive vs. using *point* and *click* to manipulate a scroll bar is that it's harder to follow what someone else is doing when they use the scroll wheel while you are looking at their screen, since you lose the added information of seeing which end of the scroll bar they are *pointing* towards before they *click* and the window starts to scroll. This is an example of something that probably cameup (or should have) when hardware manufacturers and software designers were evaluating the *scroll* primitive. As a general methodology for designing and evaluating primitives, we have found great success in a two-pronged approach.

When engineers construct something, we have observed that they tend to like to work *bottom-up*. A bottom-up approach focuses on answering three questions: What can the hardware reliably detect? What can the users do in a physically comfortable way? What can the users understand and learn? In contrast, a *top-down* approach tends to be favored by designers. This approach also seeks to answer three questions: What will interaction with the overall system look like? What are the contexts of use and usage scenarios? What is the unifying theme to the interaction? Where we found great success after several false starts was in actually evaluating all of these at the *same time*, rather than favoring one approach over the other. This is because each tends to look out for pitfalls in the other. For example, designers tend to overlook the strict realities of the hardware, and engineers tend to drive towards experiences which optimize efficiency over a properly scaffolded experience. As we will discuss in more detail in Chapter 31, a multi-disciplinary team observing a Rapid-Iterative Test and Evaluation methodology has the best chance of creating a great set of primitives.

There are few hard and fast rules when it comes to primitive design, but those that we have found are enumerated below. Most of the chapters of this book have some element of good primitive design.

Must

- Take into account what the hardware is good at. Your primitives must be sensed reliably.

- Take into account what your hardware uniquely supports, and consider expanding your primitives to include these elements. This will help you to avoid generic design which does not differentiate your platform.

- Take into account the overarching questions: What does the user need to be able to do, and what do you want the expert user's behavior to look like? Building-out a few different elements of your design (or applications on your platform) will lead naturally to selecting primitives from the overlapping sets.

Should

- Avoid questions like "what feels natural to me?" As with any other element of a user experience, the designer is far from a typical user.

- Follow the RITE method, outlined in Chapter 31, to iterate on your primitives.

- Follow a simultaneous bottom-up and top-down design process. Chapters 3–12 focus on how to aid the top-down designer, while the remaining chapters focus on how to aid bottom-up design, or guide your process.

- Consider carefully the size of your set of primitives, and avoid erring by having too few, placing an upper-bound on performance, or having too many without a scaffolded (Chapter 12) self-revealing gesture language (Chapter 19).

Could

- An excellent approach to supporting both novices and experts is to have overlapping sets of primitives, one better suited to experts, one catering to novices. The lessons of Chapters 11 and 12 demonstrate how to start small and expand your set outwards.

SUMMARY

Primitives make up the basic language of your interaction. If you are building atop a platform, some of those primitives may have been defined already, but there is no rule that you must use them. In truth, most of the UI toolkits and platforms designed for touch either contain only a very small set of primitives, or they have the wrong ones. Free yourself to consider an even lower level of interaction than is typical in creating an application for the GUI. Because touch and gestural input is in its infancy, you have little other choice.

VOICES FROM THE FIELD: UI AS LANGUAGE

Kay Hofmeester

A user interface is the communication medium between human and computer. It requires a language in order for us to communicate our intent to computers. Touch is an enabler which requires a new language, framing input into the system. A computer replies using a language consisting of visuals and audio.

The touch language has gestures and compound manipulations. Gestures can be compared to phrases, compound gestures resemble sentences. For instance: Finger down can mean "this item." Tap (finger down and up) can mean "open this item." The system plays its part in the conversation: When the finger touches the screen, it should immediately react, telling the user it has registered the touch. Then it should highlight the item the finger is touching, confirming the selection. When the finger is lifted it should present an animation to indicate the item is being opened.

Users often try to use interface language conventions they know from systems they used previously when they encounter a new language. An example of the set of conventions that users will apply to touch languages is the GUI language of Windows/Icons/Menus/Pointer. The touch interface has to make clear that it refers to a different language. Our research has uncovered that to learn the new language, it is more effective to provide opportunities to use the new language than to teach it. Once open to learning, the user is likely to overcompensate for learning the new language. This means trying to apply the new rules and rejecting the old rules. We can make use of this state of learning by making exploration of the system and its language safe and rewarding.

Biography

Kay Hofmeester is User Experience Lead on the Microsoft Windows team, working on input languages for the next generation of Microsoft Windows. Kay previously managed the Surface design team and worked on Windows Phone. Before joining Microsoft, Kay was Creative Director at Agency.com and Design Manager for long-term European design research projects, focusing on future communication technologies. Previously he worked as Director of Interactive Design at a music e-commerce company and at Philips Design.

FURTHER READING

Apitz, G., & Guimbretière, F. 2004. CrossY: a crossing-based drawing application. In *Proceedings of the 17th Annual ACM Symposium on User interface Software and Technology* (Santa Fe, NM, USA, October 24–27, 2004). UIST '04. ACM, New York, NY, 3-12. DOI= http://doi.acm.org/10.1145/1029632.1029635

The Crossy project from the University of Maryland provides an example application build with a different primitive, *cross,* far better suited to pen input than *click* and *point.* Consider it as a case study in the creation of new primitives, in both bottom-up (crossing is better then clicking for a pen) and top-down (what should expert use of a pen-based drawing program look like?).

The Anatomy of a Gesture

18

Anatomy is destiny.

—Sigmund Freud

DESCRIPTION

According to Wu and his co-authors, a gesture consists of three stages (Figure 18.1). *Registration* is the moment that the type of action is set. Next is *continuation*, which adjusts the parameters of the gesture. Last comes *termination*, which is when the gesture ends. For the engineers, a gesture can be thought of as a function call: The user selects the function at the registration phase and specifies the parameters of the function during the continuation phase, and the function is executed at the termination phase (Table 18.1). In most touch systems, these phases correspond roughly to physical changes.

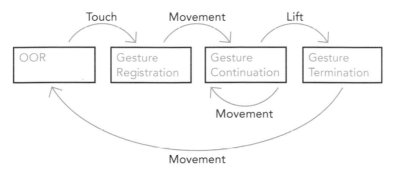

FIGURE 18.1

The three stages of gestural input and the physical actions that lead to them on a pen or touch system. OOR is "out of range" of the input device.

Table 18.1 Registration, continuation, termination

Registration	Continuation	Termination
Place two fingers on a piece of content.	Move the fingers around on the surface of the device: The changes in the length, center position, and orientation of the line segment connecting these points are applied 1:1 to scale (both height and width), center position, and orientation of the content.	Lift the fingers from the surface of the device.

APPLICATION TO NUI

To draw from an example you should now be familiar with, consider the two-finger diverge ("pinch") gesture that has come to mean *zoom in* or *zoom out*. This model of gestures allows for an abstract examination of the gesture language, as shown in Table 18.1. As we will see, multi-touch input provides significant advantages to gesture design. By deeply understanding a model for how gestures are designed, we will be better equipped to build not just individual gestures, but a *set* of gestures that are both consistent and error-free.

LESSONS FROM THE PAST: AMBIGUITY

There is a temptation among designers to try to make every registration and continuation action the same: put a single finger down on a piece of content and move it on the screen. While this might make for a simple UI, it severely limits the set of possible gestures and can lead to ambiguity. Let's build up a theoretical gesture language, beginning with a possible *delete* gesture: To delete something, we'll flick it to the left side of the screen (Table 18.2).

Two things are immediately apparent. The first is that there is no continuation phase of this gesture—the system doesn't know it's a *flick to the left* until the user has flicked, and there is no next step. This isn't surprising, since the delete command has no parameters—there isn't more than one possible way to delete something. The second striking thing is that the registration requires two steps. First, the user places her hand on an element, then she flicks to the left.

Requiring two steps to register a gesture is problematic. First, it increases the probability of an error, since the user must remember multiple steps. Second, error probability is also increased if the second step has too small a space relative to other gestures (e.g., if flicking in another direction leads to another action—or worse, if simply moving something, rather than flicking, is a gesture). Third, it requires an explicit mechanism to transition between registration and continuation phases: if flick right is "resize," how does the user then specify the size? Either it's a separate gesture, requiring a modal interface, or the user will keep her hand on the screen and require

Table 18.2 Stages of our theoretical delete flicking gesture

Registration	Continuation	Termination
1 Place finger on an item. **2** Flick to the left.	None	Lift the finger from the surface of the device.

Table 18.3 Stages of various theoretical gestures, plus the manipulation processor's one-finger move gesture

Gesture Name	Logical Action	Registration	Continuation	Termination
Rename	Enter the system into "rename" mode (the user then types the new name with the keyboard).	**1** Place finger on an item. **2** Flick the finger down and to the right.	None	Lift the finger from the surface of the device.
Copy	Create a copy of a file or object, immediately adjacent to the original.	**1** Place finger on an item. **2** Flick the finger up and to the left.	None	Lift the finger from the surface of the device.
Delete	Delete a file or element.	**1** Place finger on an item. **2** Flick the finger up and to the right.	None	Lift the finger from the surface of the device.
Move	Change the visual position of an object within its container.	**1** Place finger on an item. **2** Move the finger slowly enough to not register as a flick.	Move the finger around the surface of the device. Changes in the position of the finger are applied 1:1 as changes to the position of the object.	Lift the finger from the surface of the device.

a mechanism to say "I am now done registering; I would like to start the continuation phase." Last, the system cannot respond to the user's gesture in a meaningful way until the registration step is complete, and so this prolongs this feedback.

Let's consider a system that implements just four gestures: one for manipulation of an object (grab and move it), along with three for system actions (rename, copy, delete) using flick gestures (Table 18.3). We can see the flow of a user's contact in Figure 18.2. When the user first puts down his finger, the system doesn't know which of these four gestures the user will be doing, so it's in the state labeled "<ambiguous>." Once the user starts to move his finger around the table in a particular speed and direction ("flick left" vs. "flick right") or pattern ("slide" vs. "question mark"), the system can resolve that ambiguity, and the gesture moves into the registration phase.

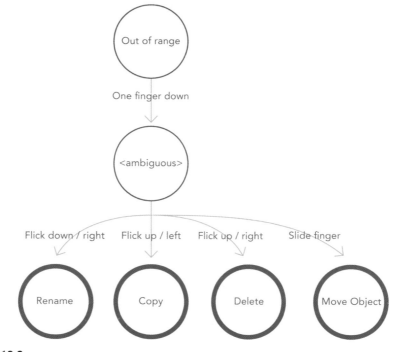

FIGURE 18.2

States of a hand gesture, up to and including the end of the registration phase. The continuation and termination phases are not shown.

Let's look first at how the system classifies the gestures: If the finger moves fast enough, it is a "flick," and the system goes into *rename*, *copy*, or *delete* mode based on the direction. Consider now what happens for the few frames of input while the system is testing to see if the user is executing a flick. Since it doesn't yet know that the user is not intending to simply move the object quickly, there is ambiguity with the "move object" gesture. The simplest approach is for the system to assume that each gesture is a "move" until it knows better. Consider the interaction sequence in Figure 18.3. Because, for the first few frames, the user's intention is unclear, the system designers have a choice. Figure 18.3 represents one option: Assume that the "move" gesture is being performed until another gesture is registered after analyzing a few frames of input. This is good, because the user gets immediate feedback. It's bad, however, because the feedback is wrong: the system is showing the feedback for the "move" gesture, but the user is actually performing a "rename" flick; the recognizer just hasn't tripped yet. The system has to undo the "move" at the time of registration of rename, and we get an ugly popping effect. This problem can be avoided by providing no response until the user's action is clear. This would correct the bad feedback in the "rename" case, but consider the consequence for the "move" case (Figure 18.4).

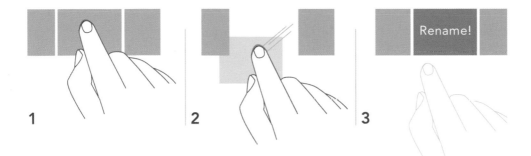

FIGURE 18.3

Interaction of a "rename" gesture. 1: user places finger on the object; 2: user has slid finger, with the object following along; 3: the "rename" gesture has registered, so the object pops back to its original location.

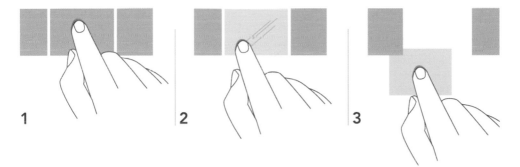

FIGURE 18.4

Interaction of a "move" gesture in a thresholded system. 1: user places finger on an object; 2: user slides finger along surface (the object does not move because the "flick" threshold is known to have not been met); 3: the system is confident that this is not a flick, so the object jumps to catch up to the user's finger.

Obviously, this too is a problem: The system does not provide the user with any feedback at all until it is certain that the user is not performing a flick. The problem is ambiguity: because we have overloaded one-finger sliding with a large number of possible gestures, the recognizer can't tell us quickly enough which one is being performed.

Solving Ambiguity

The goal, ultimately, is to avoid the time during which the user's intention is ambiguous. Aside from all of the reasons outlined above, this ambiguity also creates another bad situation in designing the recognizer: deciding quickly the recognizer should pick out a "flick" from a "move"? The user has put her finger down, and it has started moving—how soon does the recognizer click over to *delete* mode, versus waiting to give the user a chance to do something else? The sooner it makes the decision, the more likely there will be errors, since less data are available to make the right decision. The later it decides, the longer the user will get ambiguous, or worse, incorrect feedback. It's just a bad situation all around.

The solution is to tie the registration event to the finger-down event: As soon as the hand comes down on the display, the gesture is registered. The movement of the contacts on the display is used only for the *continuation* phase of the gesture (i.e., specifying the parameter). The problem, of course, is that we have a large number of operations that we might want to perform, but now a more limited number of possible gestures.

Multi-touch gives us a solution. By allowing us to move registration up to the moment of contact, we can explode the set of possible gestures, but without increasing the possibility of error. We do this by tying the registration to the number of fingers. Consider as an example two gestures from the iPhone gesture language: *move* and *zoom* (Table 18.4).

Applying the same type of diagram we used above, we see two detached trees (Figure 18.5).

The beauty of a multi-touch system is immediately apparent: The gestures are disambiguated not only by the movement of the contacts on the device, but also by the posture of the hand (in this case, how many fingers are touching). In so doing, we significantly reduce the possibility of accidentally tripping into the wrong gesture. There is no chance that the user will accidentally move when he intends to zoom—the number of fingers immediately tells the system which mode to go into, without any of the problems described above.

In addition to posture-based registration, we can also carefully expand the set of gestures for any one posture, so long as that set is easily and quickly disambiguated. Consider again the iPhone and the set of gestures supported by its lists: scroll, delete, and activate (Table 18.5).

Table 18.4 Two gestures from the iPhone gesture language: move and zoom

Gesture Name	Logical Action	Registration	Continuation	Termination
Move	Change the viewport onto an on-screen list.	Place one finger on an item.	Move the finger around the surface of the device. Changes in the position of the finger are applied 1:1 as changes to the position of the item.	Lift the finger from the surface of the device.
Zoom	Enlarge an object.	Place two fingers on an item.	Move the fingers around on the surface of the device. The changes in the length, center position, and orientation of the line segment connecting these points are applied 1:1 to scale (both height and width), center position, and orientation of the content.	Lift the fingers from the surface of the device.

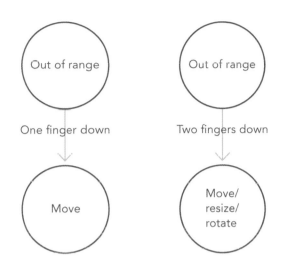

FIGURE 18.5

The this language has no branching, because the number of fingers on the device at the time of registration disambiguates the gesture a lack of branching means that registration is always happening at the earliest-possible phase.

Table 18.5 The iPhone set of gestures supported by its lists: scroll, delete, and activate

Gesture Name	Logical Action	Registration	Continuation	Termination
Scroll	Change the viewport of the list.	**1** Place one finger on a list item. **2** Move the finger in a straight line up or down.	Move the finger around on the surface of the device. Changes in the y position of the finger are applied 1:1 as changes to the position of the viewport. Changes in the x position are ignored.	Lift the finger from the surface of the device.
Delete	Show the delete button for an item in a list.	**1** Place a finger on an item. **2** Move the finger in a straight line to the right or left.	None	Lift the finger from the surface of the device.
Activate	Select the item in the list and activate it (e.g., "open this e-mail").	**1** Place a finger on an item. **2** Without moving the finger, lift it from the surface of the device.	None	None

This particular set does not take advantage of the posture-based disambiguation, although it could—there's no reason the makers of the iPhone couldn't have included a "zoom" gesture to enlarge individual list items, since placing two fingers on an item does not create ambiguity. What this approach does do, however, is reduce ambiguity in another way.

Note the improvement in the design of the "delete" and "scroll" gestures over the "flick" gestures we described above. In the previous example, flicking was registered after a certain time and distance. This is not so for the delete/scroll/activate decision: Because only direction matters, this decision can be made by the recognizer almost immediately, obviating the need for either lag or false feedback. If the user slides to the right even a little bit, it's a *delete*. If the user slides the list up or down, it's a *scroll*. If the user doesn't slide at all, it's an *activate* (Figure 18.6).

The key to unambiguous gesture design is to get the user through the registration step as quickly as possible. The faster this happens, the faster the system can give appropriate feedback, and the less likely the system will be to get the gesture wrong.

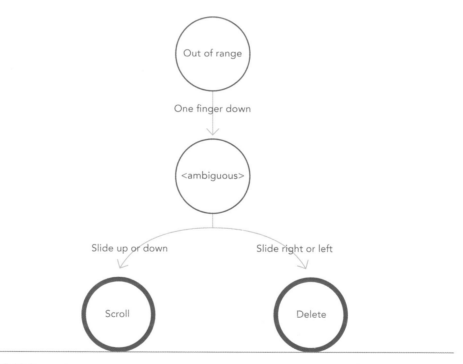

FIGURE 18.6

The anatomy of the iOS list gestures: When the finger is placed on the list, the mode is ambiguous. If the user slides parallel to the list, it scrolls. If the user slides horizontally, a "delete" button pops up. Differentiating gestures by direction is more reliable than doing it by speed, as is done in Windows.

DESIGN GUIDELINES

Must

- Minimize the number of steps the user must take before in order to register the gesture mode.

- Minimize overlap in the initial action—whatever action the user does first, make sure that as small a subset of your gestures as possible uses that same first action.

- Minimize the load required to transition between registration and continuation phases. It should be immediately clear to the user how to specify the command she wants to execute.

- Provide clear feedback for the user at each step, ensuring she understands when she has transitioned from registration to continuation, and how to terminate the gesture.

Should

- Map registration to the moment the user makes contact with the display. Thus, the location of the contact and its posture will determine which function will happen—after that, all movement simply adjusts the details of that function.

- Map termination to the moment the user breaks contact with the display. In so doing, you will be sure that there is always a clear moment where the user says "I'm done with this gesture."

Could

- Take this to a logical extreme, and register *only* based on the number of fingers. This approach is called a "chording gesture," similar to playing a piano.

SUMMARY

Gesture registration is perhaps *the* most important step to design. Overloading registration with possibly ambiguous or difficult to distinguish physical actions, such as flick and move, will create a system fraught with errors and without feedback. Two elements of gesture design can be used to overcome this. First, multi-touch input allows a broader range of possible initial postures, complicating the registration step. From this complication, however, we see an explosion of possibilities that allow us to separate out the gestures, so that each initial posture can map onto only one possible action or small set of actions. Second, when multiple gestures use the same posture, carefully designing them to reduce overlap of registration actions will reduce errors.

Properties of a Gesture Language

Personality is an unbroken series of successful gestures.

—F. Scott Fitzgerald

DESCRIPTION

A gesture language is a communication system. Its language depends on its fundamental clarity (each gesture is well-defined) and its overall coherence (the gestures make sense together). We can apply genetic epistemology of cognition to any gestural system. In doing so we are saying that a well-developed and easy-to-learn system will be one that operates logically in a way that is analogous to human reasoning.

Specifically, we apply Piaget's concept of the INRC group. The developmental stage of formal operations is characterized by the following four properties:

- Identity (I)
- Negation (N)
- Reciprocal (R)
- Commutative (identity of groups) (C)

In mathematics, identity means that an element is unchanged in a binary operation, for example, adding zero to a number, or multiplying a number by 1. Similarly, in cognition, an identity operation leaves the element unchanged. For example, if I change the shape of a lump of clay, its mass is still the same. In contrast, the negation of a number results in zero. In a sense, the number is "undone," becomes nothing. In cognition, negation is equivalent to "not," for example, "that is not true." Negating a lump of clay is a little harder to imagine, but imagine the clay being dissolved in water—it is negated. The negation operation may be reversible; for example, if I let the water evaporate, then the clay is left as a precipitate. In contrast to negation, the mathematical reciprocal is the inverse. For example, the reciprocal of 4 is 1/4 or 0.25. Reciprocal is different from negation in that a reciprocal results in identity $(4 \times ¼ = 1)$, while a negation results in zero $(4 \times 0 = 0)$. A direct physical **137** equivalent to reciprocal is harder to imagine. However, if we think of two physical dimensions it becomes easier. If you pour a liquid from a short container into a tall container a young child may believe there is "more" liquid. However, when children reach the stage of "formal operations" they "conserve" the volume of a liquid. In effect, they are treating two dimensions (the horizontal and vertical) as reciprocal to each other and thus can conserve the volume.

Commutative means that the sequence of operations does not matter. Addition is commutative; so is multiplication. However, when combined, the order of operation matters, that is, which operation is done when makes a difference in the result. The order of operations is assumed (multiplication first) or controlled with parentheses in the expression. Considering cognition, some operations are commutative; for example, suppose you reshape an object, divide it, recombine it, and shape it back to its original form. Regardless of order, the beginning and end state are equivalent.

APPLICATION TO NUI

By analogy, the INRC group in a gesture system means the following:

- Identity: when I perform equivalent actions, the system reliably does an equivalent action. To the user, it appears invariant.

- Negation: when I start an action, I can return to the previous state by doing the opposite action. To the user, the system appears forgiving.

- Reciprocal: there are actions that return some aspect of the system to its original state. This is not simple negation (i.e., undo); instead, it is a different action that returns an object to its previous state.

- Commutative: I can change the order of operations and the result is the same. Moving an object and then resizing it is the same as resizing the object and then moving it.

LESSONS FROM THE PAST

The greatest challenge in building a NUI system is making it learnable. To make a NUI learnable, it's best to consider the entire family of required operations (i.e., what you need to do in the entire system) and devise a system of gestures to support that set. A pitfall to avoid is trying to use a few gestures to support a large and complex set of operations. In our research for Surface we found that users would often try to complete a wide variety of tasks by tapping. Initially, tapping appears to show great promise because it's familiar to users, and even more deeply, it has a clear identity (i.e., it is seen as a unitary act). However, there are many problems with that approach. For example what is the negation of tap? In other words, how do you "untap"? What is the reciprocal of a tap? The GUI approach of treating tap as a simple selection depending on context (i.e., tap on the title bar and the window is selected and may pop to the top; tap inside a document and the document is selected and the cursor is inserted at the location of the tap) also leads users to try tapping on a NUI.

This is a transfer of learning problem. The tapping in the GUI was originally conceived as an accelerator. That is, you learned the system and then you learned that you could use tapping to perform the most common action in a given situation as a kind of default accelerator. Hence transfer of this kind of learning from the GUI makes NUIs seem hard and inconsistent. Rather than encouraging transfer from the GUI to the NUI, we should discourage such transfer. While this may seem counterintuitive, it makes sense. Consider the fact that many users familiar with command systems suggested making GUIs work like command systems so they could apply their knowledge. That would have been a serious mistake. Instead, the GUI altered some of the most fundamental aspects of command systems. For example, the syntax of most command systems was verb (command) followed by object. The GUI required selection followed by menu choice, in effect object then operation. This allowed the GUI to avoid "modes."

Let's consider how each of Piaget's four concepts applies to the NUI.

Identity

The starting point for a NUI is objects. These objects have identity and can be manipulated in various ways. But a NUI always begins with objects. Notice that this is not the starting point of a classic GUI, even though it may seem so. In fact, traditional GUIs begin with two fundamental constructs—objects (content) and applications (programs). This initial "schizophrenia" is hidden from most users. They simply "open" content and an application is "automagically" activated. However, there are breakdowns. When you are given content, for example, an email attachment, you may or may not have an associated application. The result is that you can't perform the typical action of opening the content. You get an error message and an invitation to associate this content with some application that exists on your computer, or you can find the appropriate application on the web. This is a perfectly adequate workaround. But it plunges novice (nontechnical) users into one of the most subtle aspects of the GUI—the distinction between content (objects/data) and applications (programs). It also requires the user to search for the "right" application to render and operate the content. That choice is not simple. Some applications will render content as gibberish. Other applications will render content but not provide the assumed operation. This challenge of matching application to content puts the user in an analogous position to the customer who goes to the hardware store knowing what she needs to do but not knowing which tool to ask for. In a well-designed NUI this would never happen. No content exits without the "right" application to render and operate on it. This implies that applications, as such, are invisible to the user. And they should be. Making both application and

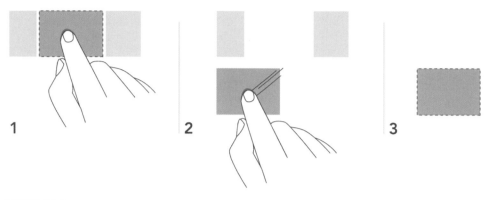

FIGURE 19.1

Identity—an object does not change.

objects visible is just a source of unnecessary confusion. Making applications visible to users is nonsense. New content should be created by simply accessing blank content. Applications that don't create content in the traditional sense, such as games, are accessible by dragging their environments from a holding area to the main work area. For example, to play chess you drag out a chess board (Figure 19.1).

Negation

Negation refers to an operation on objects and therefore is necessarily more complex than identity. To illustrate it in a NUI, we will consider opening an object that has been iconified and is located in a set of iconified objects. A tap could do that, and it's what most people try. But how would we get it back into the set of iconified objects? That is how would we "negate" our action. We could tap it again, but that might seem odd, particularly if there were multiple objects in the workspace or if we had performed other operations on those objects. Also, since a tap is actually a combination of three primitives (press down, very short hold, release), it's hard to undo mid-step. Instead, in the NUI, we could try dragging it out of the set. As we drag it past the boundary of the set of iconified objects, it enlarges slightly. If we continue hold down our finger and move it, the object tracks our movement. When we stop moving our finger, the object stays where we left it. When we let go of the object, it is ready to be acted upon—it has been moved out of a set of iconified objects, has increased in size by some reasonable amount, and is positioned where we lifted our finger. Notice that this suggests a way that we can easily "negate" this action. As the user begins to drag out the object and it enlarges, she is "notified" that it will be open if she releases it. Or she can move it back into the set, and as she does so, it will shrink. Releasing it in its original position returns it to an iconified state in the set of icons, that is, it is a negation (Figure 19.2).

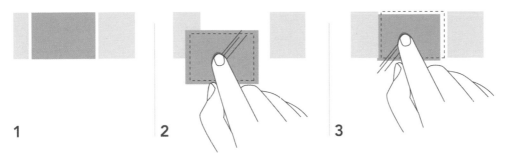

1   2   3

FIGURE 19.2

Reversibility—an operation can be reversed with no effect (the example I use is dragging an object out of a group and then returning it).

Reciprocal

Reciprocal is slightly more complex than negation. It is a different operation, and while it returns an object to a previous state, it may also have other effects. Let's consider a reciprocal operation in a hypothetical NUI system. If we stretch an object in the horizontal plane, we both increase its size and change its aspect ratio. If we then stretch the object vertically, we increase its size again, but if we stretch it the "right" amount we restore the original aspect ratio. Thus one aspect of the object—the "distortion" of a solely horizontal stretch—is undone, but another aspect of the object—its absolute width—is unchanged. A difference between negation and reciprocal action is that negation cancels an operation in progress, while a reciprocal action undoes an action after it is completed but may (or may not) leave some of the consequences of the action unchanged. The action that embodies a reciprocal operation may bear no physical resemblance to the original action that embodied a given operation. The action of vertical stretching is different from the action of horizontal stretching. In contrast, the negation operation is embodied by the opposite physical action. This illustrates one of the challenges of talking (and thinking) about a NUI. We often fail to distinguish our action from the system operation. We talk about "drag," but drag means that an object is "attached" to the movement of our finger. Drag is a system operation; movement is a physical action (Figure 19.3).

Commutative

Ironically, this most complex interaction is simple to understand. It simply means that the order of physical actions does not matter—the system will perform the same operations regardless of order. This is a common characteristic of many operations on several different types of systems: command, GUI, and NUI. For the most part, this is true of system operations. It is also true of many operations within an object. However,

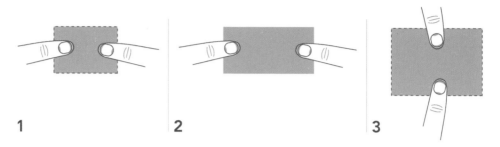

FIGURE 19.3

Negation—an operation undoes another operation—(the example I use is resizing past a limit results in the object being returned to the group; we could also illustrate this by stretching an object changes it aspect ratio and then a second stretch in the "other" direction restores the aspect ratio but does not undo/reverse the first stretch).

there may be exceptions. These exceptions depend on the object. For example, if we consider a chess game an object, then many operations may not be commutative since the data of the object (i.e., the game) changes over time. Moving your queen to a particular square may put her in danger of capture (or not), depending on the state of the board. Once she is captured, she's no longer available to be moved (Figure 19.4).

One of the greatest challenges of developing a NUI system is making the system coherent for the user, while making it relatively easy to master quickly. One way to do that is to consider these INRC characteristics. Consideration of the system as a whole in terms of these principles is particularly important if you are designing a system that does not draw on a well-understood and practiced set of conventions. For example, a game of checkers could be readily implemented using a NUI because it is familiar and the systematic rules of the action and interaction are well-defined. Building an entirely new system is much more difficult and is likely to be hard to learn if these principles are not considered in the early stages.

NUI designers should proceed cautiously. The initial questions to be considered are the following:

- What are the fundamental objects in the system?
- What operations do users expect to perform on these objects?
- What actions are most likely to occur to perform these operations?
- How are each of these actions reversed while they are being performed?
- What actions have reciprocal effects and what are these reciprocal effects?
- Which actions and operations are commutative?

This design of the entire system will require both feedback and feedforward. Affordances help the user to map the available actions to system operations. These operations and action pairs need to be systematically refined in user testing. It is particularly important to test them in combination.

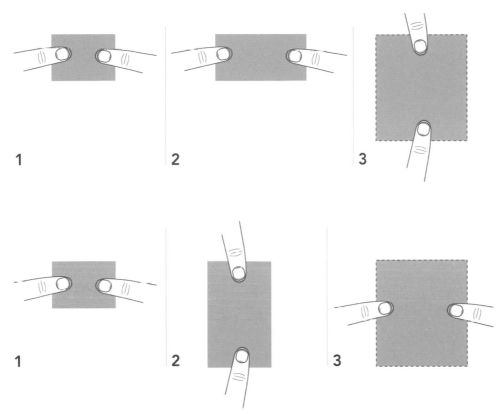

FIGURE 19.4

Commutativity—order of operations does not matter.

DESIGN GUIDELINES

Must

- As a starting point, all actions must follow the principles of identity, negation, inversion, and commutativity. Applying these principles helps make any system learnable and safe. Below, each principle is restated in terms of a touch NUI.

  - Identity: Objects are permanent unless explicitly deleted, and an action on a given object in a given context always yields the same result.

  - Negation: Any action can be reversed midcourse, and that reversal will return the system to its previous state.

  - Reciprocal: Once an action is completed, a side effect of that action can be undone by another action. For example, horizontal stretching of a graphic object will change its width and its aspect ratio. A subsequent vertical stretching of the same object will not undo the change in width but will restore the aspect ratio.

- Commutativity: Actions can be performed in any order and yield the same result.

Should

- Design teams should provide affordances and feedback, so that exploratory actions from the users will be elicited and can then be shaped by the system.

- The set of actions should constitute a coherent system before shortcuts are designed.

- The team should begin design with a clean slate and not draw from past metaphors.

Could

- Depicting the entire system, and the corresponding system states and feedback, can help a team see the overall system and help avoid inconsistencies.

SUMMARY

We have applied some of the concepts from Piaget's concepts of genetic epistomology to the design of a touch-based system. It seems logical to apply some well-accepted concepts from developmental psychology to understanding a system. In part, any NUI presents a new world for the user. It is natural, in the sense that it supports skilled and fluid practice and does not require that objects and operations be formalized into abstractions. However, that "naturalness" does not ensure that it is easy to learn, nor does it depend on transfer of habits from GUI experience. Instead, it presents a new, albeit more interesting and promising, set of challenges to the designer and the user.

FURTHER READING

Piaget's work created a new foundation for understanding the development of thinking in children. His over 50 years of writing are encyclopedic, profound, and insightful. These writings also show an evolution in thinking and are not always easily understood or interpreted. We have presented our interpretation—based in large part on the book *Genetic Epistemology*, translated by Elenore Duckworth and published by Norton in 1971. J. H. Flavell provides an excellent introduction to Piaget in *The Developmental Psychology of Jean Piaget*, Van Nostrand, 1963. A second excellent volume, *Piaget and Knowledge* by Hans Furth, was published by Prentice Hall in 1969.

Self-Revealing Gestures

The best way to teach somebody something is to have them think they're learning something else.

—Prof. Randy Pausch, "The Last Lecture"

DESCRIPTION

Self-revealing gestures are a philosophy for design of gestural interfaces that posits that the only way to see a behavior in your users is to induce it (*afford* it, for the Gibsonians among us). Users are presented with an interface to which their response is gestural input. This approach contradicts some designers' apparent assumption that a gesture is some kind of "shortcut" that is performed in some ephemeral layer hovering above the user interface. In reality, a successful development of a gestural system requires the development of a *gestural user interface*. Objects are shown on the screen to which the user reacts, instead of somehow intuiting their performance. The trick, of course, is to not overload the user with UI "chrome" that overly complicates the UI, but rather to afford as many suitable gestures as possible with a minimum of extra on-screen graphics. To the user, she is simply operating your UI, when in reality, she is learning a gesture language.

APPLICATION TO NUI

A common immediate reaction to a high-bandwidth, multi-finger input device is to imagine it as a gestural input device. Those of us in the business of multi-touch interface design are often confronted with comparisons between our interfaces and the big-screen version of MIT student John Underkoffler's Ph.D. work: Minority Report. The comparison is fun, but it certainly creates a challenge—how do we design an interface that is as high-bandwidth as has been promised by John and others, but that users are able to immediately walk up to and use? The approach taken by many designers is to try to map a system's functionality onto the set of gestures

145

a user is likely to find intuitive. Of course, the problem with such an approach is immediately apparent: The complexity and vocabulary of the input language are bounded by your least imaginative user.

At a more fundamental level, the goal of providing natural and intuitive gestures that are simultaneously complex and rich seems to contain an inherent contradiction. How can something complex be intuitive? What we have found in practice is that to achieve our goal of an interface that feels natural to its users, we must actually provide them with a UI. The trick, of course, is to do so in a way that is minimally intrusive and that makes it seem to the user as if she is "discovering" the gestures. To this, we will apply many of our design principles, the most salient of which we described in Chapter 10: we will scaffold our user experience.

LESSONS FROM THE PAST: CONTROL VS. ALT HOTKEYS

For a little fun (and perhaps some disillusionment), make an appointment at your local Genius Bar at an Apple store and bring along your OSX-based computer. When it's your turn, kindly ask the genius, "I can't figure out how to use this computer—can you please show me the basics?" As they reach for the trackpad, gently correct them—"Sorry, I meant how to use it using only the keyboard."

It is interesting how devotees to one OS or the other can take on a religious zeal about their choice. In truth, there are very few instances where someone with HCI training can point to a clear winner in the Mac OS vs. Windows debate. Different elements of each have merit. But one instance where Windows is the clear, indisputable winner is in the way hotkeys are designed and taught. In this lesson from the past, we will examine the Windows approach to hotkeys and take away a clear understanding of the merits of the approach.

Many users never notice that, in Microsoft Windows, there are two completely redundant hotkey languages. These languages can be broadly categorized as the *Control* and *Alt* languages. It is from comparing and contrasting these two hotkey languages that we draw some of the most important lessons necessary for self-revealing gestures.

Control Hotkeys and the Gulf of Competence

We consider first the most-used hotkey language: the *Control* language. Although the particular hotkeys are not the same on all operating systems, the notion of the control hotkeys is standard across many operating systems: we assign some modifier key (Function, Control, Apple, Windows), putting the rest of the keyboard into a mode. The user then presses a second (and possibly third) key to execute a function. Many users know a couple of these hotkeys—such as CTRL + X to cut and CTRL + C to copy (APPLE + X on a Mac, but recall we're talking about Windows here). What interests us is how a user learns this key combination.

Control hotkeys generally rely on two mechanisms to allow users to learn them. First, the keyboard keys assigned to their functions are often lexically

FIGURE 20.1

The Control hotkeys are shown in the File menu in Notepad. Note that the key choices are selected to be intuitive (by matching the first letter of the function name).

intuitive: CTRL + P = print, CTRL + S = save, and so on. Figure 20.1 shows some hotkeys from the Notepad application.

Relying on intuitiveness works well *for a small number of keys*, but it breaks down quickly—if CTRL + C means "copy," then what is the hotkey for "center"? This is roughly parallel to the naïve designer's notion of gesture mappings: we map the physical action to some property in its function (if we want "help," draw a question mark!). However, we quickly learn that this approach does not scale: Frequently used functions may overlap (consider "copy" and "cut"). This gives rise to shortcuts such as CTRL + H for "find next" (CTRL + R is "center", in case you were racking your brain). We also note the use of function keys as CTRL shortcuts—even though they don't actually use the CTRL key, they are still notionally CTRL shortcuts, as we shall see.

Because intuitive mappings can take us only so far, the menu provides the second mechanism for hotkey *learning*: the functions in the menu system are labeled with their hotkey invocation. This approach is a reasonable one. We provide users with an in-place help system labeling functions with a more efficient means of executing them. However, a sophisticated designer must ask themselves, "What does the transition from novice to expert look like?"

In the case of Control shortcuts, the novice-to-expert transition requires a leap on the part of the user: we ask her to first learn the application using the mouse, pointing at menus and selecting functions spatially. To become a power user, she must then make the conscious decision to stop using the menu system and begin to use hotkeys. When the user makes this decision, it will at first come at the cost of a loss of efficiency, as she moves from being an expert in one system, the mouse-based menus, to being a novice in the hotkey system. We term this cost the *gulf of competence*. The graph in Figure 20.3 demonstrates this idea—at the time that the user tries to switch from mouse to keyboard, she slows down.

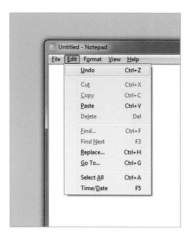

FIGURE 20.2

The Control hotkeys are shown in the Edit menu in Notepad. The first-letter mapping is lost in favor of physical convenience (CTRL + V for paste) or name collisions (F3 for find next—yes, F3 *is* a Control hotkey under our definition, which will be more clear soon).

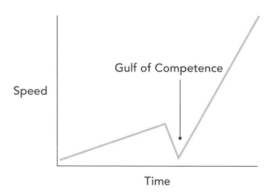

FIGURE 20.3

The learning curve of Control hotkeys: The user first learns to use the system with the mouse. They he must consciously decide to stop using the mouse and begin to use shortcut keys. This decision comes at a cost in efficiency as he begins to learn an all-new system. This cost is the "gulf of competence."

The gulf of competence is easily anticipated by the user: He may know that hotkeys are more efficient, but they will take time to learn. We are asking a busy user to take the time to learn the interface. The gulf of competence is a chasm too far for most users. Only a small set ever progress beyond the most basic control hotkeys, forever doomed to the inefficient world of the WIMP. Thankfully, we have a hotkey system that is far easier to learn: the Alt hotkeys.

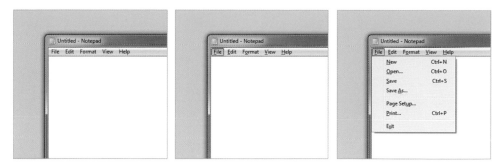

FIGURE 20.4

A novice Alt hotkey user's actions are exactly the same as an expert's: no gulf of competence. On-screen graphics guide the novice user in performing an Alt hotkey operation. Left: The menu system. Center: The user has pressed "Alt." Right: The user has pressed "F" to select the menu.

Alt Hotkeys and the Seamless Novice-to-Expert Transition

While the Control hotkeys rely on either intuition or the willingness to jump the gulf of competence, a far more learnable hotkey system exists in parallel that addresses both of these limitations: the Alt hotkey system. Like any hotkey system, the Alt approach modes the keyboard to provide a hotkey. Unlike the Control keys, however, on-screen graphics guide the user in performing the key combination (Figure 20.4).

Because the Alt hotkeys guide the novice user, there is no need for the user to make an input device change: He doesn't need to navigate menus first with the mouse, then switch to using the keyboard once he has memorized the hotkeys. Nor do we rely on user intuition to help them to "guess" Alt hotkeys.

The Alt hotkey system is a self-revealing interface, because there is no need for a help system or instructions—the actions are simply shown and followed. Better yet, the physical actions of the user are the same as the physical actions of an expert user—both press ALT + F + O to open a file. There is no gulf of competence. In applying this lesson to the gesture space, there is a highly relevant piece of work that should be examined in detail: marking menus.

Marking Menus: The First Self-Revealing Gestures

Marking "menu" is a bit of misnomer—it's not actually a menu system at all. In truth, the marking menu is a system for teaching pen gestures. For those not familiar with them, marking menus are intended to allow users to make gestural "marks" in a pen-based system. The pattern of these marks corresponds to a particular function. For example, the gesture shown in Figure 20.5 (right) leads to an "undo" command. The system does not rely at all on making the marks *intuitive*. Instead, marking menus provide a hierarchical menu system (left in Figure 20.5). Users navigate this menu system by drawing through the selections with the pen.

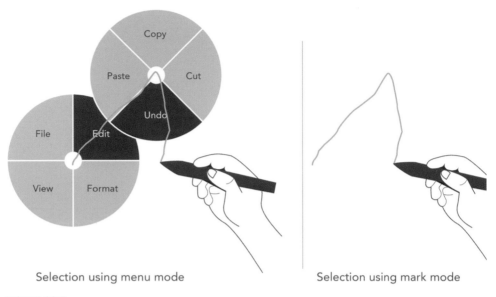

Selection using menu mode   Selection using mark mode

FIGURE 20.5

The marking menu system (left) teaches users to make pen-based gestures (right).

As they become more experienced, users do not rely on visual feedback, and eventually transition to interacting with the system through gestures, and not through the menu. It's important to understand that there is no difference in the software between novice and expert "modes"—the user simply uses the system faster and faster. Because there is a 200 ms delay between the time the pen comes down and when the menu becomes visible, novices declare themselves by doing exactly what comes naturally—hesitating.

Just like the Alt menu system, the physical actions of the novice user are physically identical to those of the expert. There is no gulf of competence, because there is no point where the user must change modalities and throw away all his prior learning. So how can we apply this to multi-touch gestures?

DESIGN GUIDELINES
Self-Revealing Multi-Touch Gestures

So it seems someone else has already done some heavy lifting regarding the creation of a self-revealing gesture system. Why not use that system and call it a day? Well, if we were willing to have users behave with their fingers the way they do with a pen, we'd be done. But the promise of multi-touch is more than a single finger drawing single lines on the screen. For all of the reasons we described in Chapter 18 and

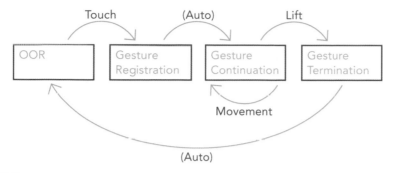

FIGURE 20.6

The three stages of gestural input and the physical actions that lead to them on a pen or touch system, as we described in Chapter 18. OOR is "out of range" of the input device.

throughout the book, we need to do better. We must consider: what would a multi-touch self-revealing gesture system look like?

First, we should recall from Chapter 18 the stages of a gesture. A gesture consists of three stages: *registration*, which sets the type of gesture to be performed, *continuation*, which adjusts the parameters of the gesture, and *termination*, which is when the gesture ends (Figure 20.6).

In the case of pen marks, registration is the moment the pen hits the tablet, continuation happens as the user makes the marks for the menu, and termination occurs when the user lifts the pen off the tablet. Seems simple enough. When working with a pen, the registration action is always the same: the pen comes down on the tablet. The marking menu system kicks in at this point, and guides the user's continuation of the gesture—and that's it. The trick in applying this technique to a multi-touch system is that the registration action varies: it's almost always the hand coming down on the screen, but the posture of that hand is what registers the gesture. On Microsoft Surface, these postures can be any configuration of the hand. Putting a hand down in a Vulcan salute could map to a different function than putting down three fingertips, which is different again from a closed fist. On less-enabled hardware, such as that supported by Windows 7 or the iOS, the variation is limited to some combination of the relative position of multiple fingertip positions. Chapter 25 describes this in detail. Nonetheless, the problem is the same. We now need to provide a self-revealing mechanism to afford a particular initial posture for the gesture, because this initial posture is the registration action that modes the rest of the gesture. Those marking menu guys had it easy, eh?

But wait—it gets even trickier.

In the case of marking menus, the on-screen affordance was needed only for the continuation phase, and it would pop up around the pen following registration. On a multi-touch system, because we have to give affordances before the registration phase, we need to tell the user which posture to go into *before the user touches the screen*. With nearly all of the multi-touch hardware on the market today, the hand is out of range right up until it touches the screen (see Chapter 15).

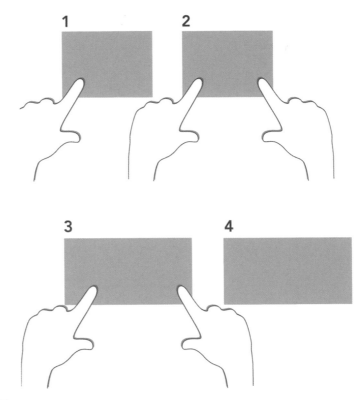

FIGURE 20.7

A theoretical gesture sequence for resizing a photo: Touch with one finger, then add another at the border, pull them apart, and lift.

One must consider affording each of the registration and continuation phases (the termination phase, which is almost always lifting the hand from the device, more or less affords itself). As you will learn in Chapter 27, there is no such thing as a "natural gesture," with the exception of moving things from one place to another, or "direct manipulation." A successful self-revealing gesture system will utilize this to afford actions, similar to the marking menu. Users of marking menus don't need tutorials. It was obvious: select things by tracing over them with the pen. Similarly, physical metaphors (things that slide, things that can be dragged, rolled, etc.) all afford movement.

An approach we advocate is one that we have dubbed "just-in-time chrome," which we present publicly here for the first time. To understand it, let's begin by proposing a gesture to stretch a photo in one of its dimensions. It goes like this: touch the photo with one hand, then touch the border of the photo with a second hand, stretch the hands apart, and lift (Figure 20.7).

This gesture is almost impossible to guess (we tested it with dozens of users). Many had experience enlarging pictures on iPhones, but the idea that they needed to put

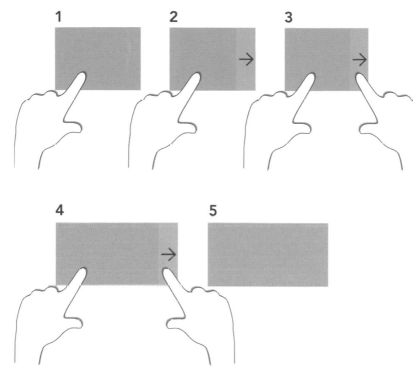

FIGURE 20.8

The same gesture sequence as above, this time with just-in-time chrome to help the user along.

their fingers in a particular location to stretch the photo horizontally wasn't guessed. But if we add just-in-time chrome, the sequence looks like that shown in Figure 20.8.

This gesture, in contrast, is incredibly easy to guess. The participants in our experiments got it right away, almost every time.

Just-in-time chrome begins with the assumption that there is an action that the user can perform that will tell the system where and what she wants to engage with. In the case above, the UI is shown only when the user touches the photo. To avoid the gulf of competence, the gesture must therefore also begin with a single finger touching the photo. The basic intuition here is to let the user touch the screen to tell us where it is she wants to perform the gesture. Next, show on-screen affordances for the available postures and their functions, and allow the user to register the gesture with a second posture, in approximately the same place as the first. From there, have the user perform manipulation gestures with the on-screen graphics, since, as we learned oh-so-many paragraphs ago, manipulation gestures are the only ones that users can learn to use quickly and are the only ones that we have found to be truly "natural."

These affordances are obvious for the continuation phase, but less so for registration. To address registration affordances, we recommend using the hover state of

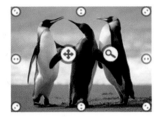

FIGURE 20.9

UI affordances are shown on tap. The user is told to put down one finger to resize the photo or two fingers to scroll or zoom. Whatever mechanism you use, applying the principle of scaffolding and the lessons of these earlier attempts at self-revealing user interfaces will lead you to far more successful multi-touch and gesture UI's.

your hardware (see Chapter 15), if you've got one. If you don't, then reserve a one-finger tap as a "I need more information" gesture. Thanks to decades of mouse use, this is the first action that users always take when they are trying to figure out what to do. An example of this is shown in Figure 20.9.

Just-in-time chrome is just one method of making your gestural interface self-revealing. The key is to consider affording registration actions as well as continuation actions. An alternative approach was investigated by Freeman and his colleagues at Microsoft: putting a layer of help on top of your application to afford both registration and continuation. While we don't particularly advocate for this approach in general, it is worth considering for certain applications.

Must

- Never rely on an action being "natural" (a.k.a. "guessable"). It's not.

- The only exception to the above is "direct manipulation"—users can and will guess to grab something and move it somewhere else.

- For gestures, present objects on-screen to which users respond.

- Utilize direct manipulation as an on-screen affordance in all cases. Want to afford the user putting their hand down in a Vulcan salute? Put a Vulcan-salute shaped button on the device for them to touch.

Should

- Re-use similar visual affordances to afford the same gestures over and over again. This is commonly known as a "user interface."

- Consider affording both registration and continuation phases of the gesture. This is a "should" only because your gesture system may have only one registration action, such as landing a single finger on the device.

Could

- Use hover capabilities of your input device (if present) to preview available actions before the user actually comes in contact with the display.

- Think about teaching more gestures over time. Consider how to layer your user interface in the same way game designers layer functionality over time.

SUMMARY

The biggest problem with making your gestures self-revealing is getting over the idea that gestures are somehow natural or intuitive. We have seen over and over again that users cannot and will not guess your gesture language. To overcome this, put UI affordances on the screen to which they can react.

UNNATURAL USER INTERFACES

Gord Kurtenbach

Autodesk

I often give a lecture entitled "un-natural user interfaces." This particular title is a setup to make people think I'm going to speak about examples of bad, "unnatural" user interfaces and how we need to design them to be more natural and intuitive. However, the surprise and hopefully entertaining twist of the lecture is that I claim there is no such thing as natural or intuitive interfaces. Effective user interface design is very carefully controlled skill transfer—we design interfaces so users can take their skills from one situation and re-apply them to a new situation. The classic example is the computer desktop. Users who are new to computers transfer their existing skills with the manipulation of real physical files and folders to the computer realm. It can be argued that moving around physical files is "natural," but that too is a learned skill—remember playing with blocks as a child? Consider another more "unnatural" example: Suppose we have software A, which new users find very difficult and unintuitive to learn, but it has been learned and is used by a large population of users. Software B copies A's interface style, hotkeys, etc. The result is that users of A can easily learn to operate B because the interface is familiar. In other words, they transfer their skills with A over to B. Learning software A from scratch did not feel natural or intuitive, but once learned, transferring those skills makes learning B "natural and intuitive." Nice trick!

This chapter describes how this fundamental and powerful concept of skill transfer applies to gesture input. Gesture input holds the potential of being vastly expressive, especially combined with multi-touch. However, without some sort of mechanism to help users learn these complex interactions, these interactions become as difficult as learning a sign language. The authors reveal the secret to successful interface design with gestures: A mechanism must be provided so users can easily learn the gesture set. To accomplish this, skill transfer is used in a powerful way. For example, an interaction technique called "marking menus" is described, where a user's skills with a graphical menu can used to magically teach a vocabulary of arbitrary "zig-zag" gestures. In similar fashion, with a method called "just-in-time chrome," users' skills with interpreting feedback and direct manipulation transfer directly into a rich vocabulary of multi-touch gestures.

Understanding the concept of self-revealing gestures is absolutely critical for the successful use of gestures in a user interface. Simply ask the following question for each gesture in your interface: How will the user learn it? Some gestures reveal themselves because we see others use them, like the ubiquitous "page-turn stroke" and "pinch-zoom." However, to harness the potential of richer, larger gesture sets the concepts introduced in this chapter are paramount.

Author Biography

Dr. Gordon Kurtenbach is the Director of Research at Autodesk (www .autodeskresearch.com), where he oversees a large range of research including human-computer interaction, graphics and simulation, environment and ergonomics, high-performance computing, and CAD for nanotechnology. Dr. Kurtenbach has published numerous research papers and holds over 40 patents in the field of human-computer interaction. His work on gesture-based interfaces, specifically "marking menus," has been highly influential in HCI research and practice. In 2005, he received the UIST Lasting Impact Award for his early work on the fundamental issues combining gestures and manipulation.

 ## FURTHER READING

Grossman, T., Dragicevic, P., and Balakrishnan, R. Strategies for accelerating on-line learning of hotkeys, *Proceedings of CHI*, 2007, 1591–1600. In this work, Grossman et al. study various methods for teaching accelerator keys.

Kurtenbach, G. *The Design and Evaluation of Marking Menus*, Ph.D. Thesis. Gord Kurtenbach, working with his advisor, Bill Buxton, at the University of Toronto, developed the marking menu. A series of publications describes the original concept, stages of learning, and how they can be integrated into interfaces. While each was published separately, it is his Ph.D. thesis that describes them all together in great detail.

Freeman, D., Benko, H., Morris, M., and Wigdor, D. ShadowGuides: Visualizations for in-Situ Learning of Multi-Touch and Whole-Hand Gestures, *Proceedings of ACM Tabletop*, 2009. In this work, Freeman and his colleagues make two major contributions. The first is a set of representative gestures that spans the space of possible gestural input to a surface-like device. The second is a teaching method they dub "ShadowGuides," for teaching gestures with on-screen affordances. In this chapter, we have emphasized that UIs built in to the experience should afford gestures. ShadowGuides, in contrast, provide a visualization that sits on top of the UI. While we don't recommend this approach in general (it represents earlier thinking in our work), it does nicely break down the idea of providing on-screen affordances for each of the registration, continuation, and termination phases of the gestures they teach.

A Model of the Mode and Flow of a Gesture System

I'm just preparing my impromptu remarks.

—Winston Churchill

DESCRIPTION

Building a gestural system requires the development and refinement of a language. That language must be simple to understand, internally consistent, and predictable. In previous chapters, we described the state model of input devices and the stages of a gesture. Like Sir Winston's "impromptu" remarks, the goal is, in essence, to not feel designed. In this chapter, we describe a method of representing a gestural language that combines these two ideas. We introduce the *mode and flow* model of a gesture language. This model allows for both a quick glance at and a deep examination of a gesture language, enabling teams to formalize their language for better coordination and iterative design. We were using this model in Chapter 18; here we will define it and demonstrate its use to dissect and represent a gesture language. Central to applying this model is the concept that gestures always put systems into a mode, in the same sense that UI designers use the term. We saw this in Chapter 18: Once the registration action has been taken, the system is then in that mode for subsequent actions. A simplification that allowed us to explain the concepts in Chapter 18 was that once a system was in a particular mode, it could not be changed—only terminated by lifting the fingers from the device. In this chapter, we will expand on this and demonstrate how users can *flow* from one mode to another, and how to use this tool to design those modes and flows.

APPLICATION TO NUI

As we described in our definiton of NUI in Chapter 2, the goal is to produce a system that allows the user to feel like a natural. This is best achieved through deep, rapid, iterative design of the system, as we will describe in Chapter 29. In order **157** to undergo such a process, a model of the thing being designed must exist. This model can be used for specs, for brainstorming, and for formalization of the language. In short, this model will enable the process and allow teams to speak with sophistication about their language. Countless times, we have been asked to consult on a gestural application or platform that just "wasn't working", because it seemed confusing or inconsistent. Our first step is always to lead the designers to model their language using this tool—as soon as this is done, the vast majority of problems become immediately apparent to everyone in the room.

LESSONS FROM THE PAST

In order to explain our model of gestures, we will examine in detail the gestures of the Safari browser on the iPhone. If you own an iPhone, iPad, or iPod touch, it might be helpful to pull it out of your pocket and use it to follow along.

The Safari browser accomplishes something that's actually quite impressive: It allows both "point and click" gestures and manipulation gestures to coexist on the same screen. The manipulation gestures on the device are highly refined, tweaked (it is safe to assume) through significant iterative design. Applying our model to this gesture language will allow us to uncover precisely how these subtleties were achieved.

Recall from Chapter 18 that gesture registration occurs when the system has decided definitively which gesture the user has initiated. In that chapter, we argued that this is best achieved with a minimum of ambiguity, which in turn is best achieved by mapping different gestures to different numbers of fingers or other differences in posture that can be immediately recognized by the system. The Safari gesture language does just this. Figure 21.1 is a simple representation of the mode and flow of the gestures on the browser.

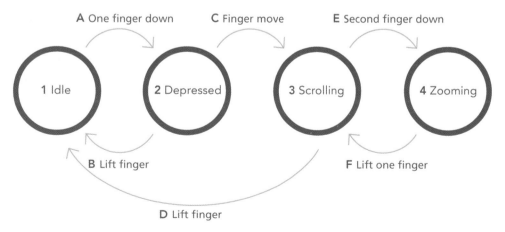

FIGURE 21.1

A simplified mode and flow model of the Safari gesture language.

From this model, we can see that the Safari browser has four gesture modes. It is always idling, depressing, scrolling, or zooming. The way the user transitions between these modes (the "flow") is shown with the arrows. You can understand this intuitively by following along with the sequence: open up a browser, and put your finger down on it. Before you start scrolling, the viewer is "depressed." In this state, you have not yet told the system whether you are going to scroll or just lift your finger back up. If you then start to slide your finger, you put the system into *scrolling* mode. If you then add a second finger to the display, you put the system into *zooming* mode, where you can enlarge or reduce the size of the content by spreading your fingers apart or moving them together. When you lift your fingers off the device, you put the canvas back into *idle* mode.

It's worth noting that there is no way to flow from scrolling mode back into idle—just stopping moving doesn't do it. There's a pretty good reason for this that will make more sense in a moment.

If you play with this a bit more, you'll realize that we made one simplification: You can actually flow directly from idle or depressed into the zooming mode by adding a second finger—you don't need to first scroll the canvas before you zoom. Figure 21.2 shows a slightly more accurate model.

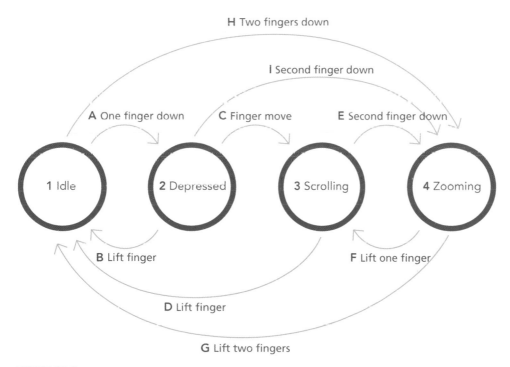

FIGURE 21.2

A more complete mode and flow model of the Safari gesture language.

Each of the modes in the system maps onto an action the user might want to perform. In the zooming state, the user is able to zoom in and out. In the scrolling state, she can scroll the page. In the depressed state, she can push a button. In the idle state, the system is waiting patiently for her to flow into another mode. It is immediately obvious that you will need to carefully design the modes of your gesture language. One of the beauties of the mode and flow model is that it makes it equally apparent that you will need to design the flow of the language just as, if not more, carefully than the modes.

Adding and Removing Flow Options

Looking at the above model, one might ask, "Why are there instances where there is no arrow pointing from one mode to another?" For example, why is it that, once in scrolling or zooming modes, the user can't get back to depressed mode? This is because the flow between modes is what generates events. The *tap* event, for example, is used to press a button in a browser. Someone might naively describe tapping as the following: "Putting your finger down on a control, then lifting it back up again." This is not an accurate description, however. In Safari, the tap event is triggered only when the flow of input follows the sequence "A, B"—that is, the user puts her finger down on the screen (neither moves it nor adds a second finger) and then lifts it. It was probably explored at some point to allow also "A, I, G" to trigger taps (that is, put down one finger, add a second finger, then lift both), or "H, G" (that is, put down two fingers, lift two fingers) to generate two taps. But these were disallowed. Why? We weren't there, but one can imagine that it was because tapping two different places at the same time would break a lot of websites, and sending the two taps sequentially could cause concurrency problems.

This was an important design decision, one that the mode and flow makes it immediately apparent must be made. Yet another example of the sophistication of the language is that "A, C, D" does not generate a *tap* event. It could—the user puts a finger down on a button, scrolls the page down a bit, then releases the finger—so why shouldn't it cause the button to activate? This was likely because of a high false-positive rate: if the user slides her finger, she wants to scroll, not activate a button. It also gives a handy mechanism for "canceling" if the user realizes she's about to make a mistake—she puts her finger on the button, it can then respond to show her what will happen, and she can then cancel by sliding her finger around. This design illustrates an important principle of the NUI, providing the user with both feedback about the current state and a way to cancel or complete the operation.

Yet again, the mode and flow model makes it immediately apparent that this design decision had to be made. As you develop your model, these design decisions become apparent when you ask "Which flows through the model should generate events?" You can enumerate all of the possible flows, and then ask "Does it make sense to have this generate an event?" If the answer is "I don't know," then that's a great question for a RITE study (see Chapter 29 on that topic). If the answer is an immediate "Yes" or "No," then you should probably still do a RITE study on it (because you are definitely not a typical user)—again, see the later chapter.

Splitting and Combining Modes

An additional step that should be taken when building your language is considering splitting and combining your modes. Combining modes effectively reduces the number of modes, and most designers understand intuitively that this simplifies the user's task of understanding your system. What may be counterintuitive to some designers is that adding modes by splitting existing ones can also improve and simplify the user's experience.

We can continue to dissect the Safari gesture language to reveal that even the model shown in Figure 21.2 is still a simplification. To see what we mean, open a web page and zoom in such that you could scroll vertically or horizontally. Now, start to scroll the page vertically; then, without lifting your finger, slide it horizontally. The page doesn't scroll horizontally—it has locked in to a vertical scroll. The same thing is true if you start out with a horizontal scroll; you can't then switch to vertical. The only way you can keep from locking into a particular axis is by starting out the scroll with a diagonal movement, at which point, you can scroll vertically, horizontally, or both at the same time, but you can't then lock in to scrolling just one or the other. We can model these subtleties with a mode and flow diagram. We realize that, while similar, these aren't three variations on the same mode—they are three different modes! The mode that we have called *scrolling* is actually three different modes: scrolling X/Y, scrolling vertical, and scrolling horizontal (Figure 21.3).

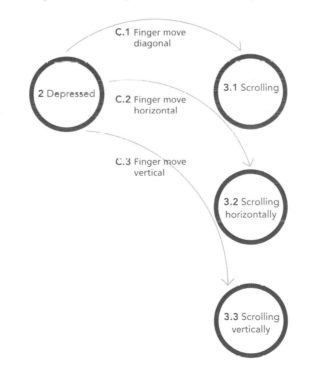

FIGURE 21.3

The *scrolling* mode is actually three different modes. The rest of the model still applies, but is omitted to simplify the figure.

Why this is done in Safari is simple. Consider how a user holds the phone in her hand and uses her thumb to scroll. When she starts out, the direction she wants is carefully mapped onto the movement of her thumb. As the motion continues, however, the thumb begins to arc, simply because of the physiology of the hand (try it yourself and watch the tip of your thumb—for further evidence, load a paint app onto the device and try again; you'll see the arc). By splitting *scrolling* into three different modes, the system is able to lock in on the user's intention and actually simplify the interaction.

So, the old adage that reducing modes leads to simplicity is not actually true in detailed gestures. A great way to iterate on your gesture language is to consider splitting or combining existing modes.

It's interesting to note that in the above model there is no way to flow between any of the three scrolling modes—the user has to lift her finger off the device and start over. In truth, there is a very subtle difference in the Safari gesture language between the horizontal scroll mode and vertical scroll mode: the user can flow from horizontal to vertical if she does it quickly enough, but there is no way to flow from vertical to horizontal. So the scrolling modes and flows actually looks like that shown in Figure 21.4.

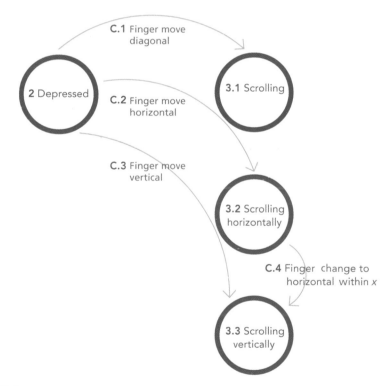

FIGURE 21.4

Flow C.4 is an extremely subtle element of the Safari gesture language. That there is no complementary flow between modes 3.1, 3.2, or 3.3 is noteworthy.

Since the goal in having three different scroll modes is to better lock-in on user intention, it makes sense that there is no way to switch between them. How often will a user really want to scroll in one direction and then the other? Certainly not as often as she'll want to do just one of the two, and so a trade-off was made in the design. The presence of flow C.4 (Figure 21.4) is likely the result of a subtlety of human dexterity: When scrolling down with the thumb, the point actually moves a little to the side before it moves down. Again, try loading a drawing app and viewing the trace for yourself.

The last design decision you will need to make will be to carefully tweak the physical action that leads to each step in the flow—how exactly the user moves between the modes.

Tweaking Flow Actions

We have seen that there is not one, but actually three scrolling modes in Safari. At some point in the process, the exact physical action needed to enter any one of them was tweaked, likely through rapid iterative design and evaluation (see Chapter 29). While that method will help find the answer, let's first understand the question. In the case of scrolling in Safari, the question is: what movements precisely differentiate diagonal, horizontal, and vertical scrolling?

It is well and good to say, "If the user's finger is moving horizontally, flow is from 'depressed' into 'scrolling horizontally' mode." Immediate follow-up questions would arise, however: "How close to horizontal does the movement have to be?" and "What angle exactly do we consider to be diagonal?" The difference between requiring absolute horizontality and allowing a little bit of give will make the difference between a gesture set that feels natural and one that is frustrating and finicky. Users aren't able to make a perfectly horizontal line with their thumb—so don't make them. Exactly how much give and take will exist in your language will be the final design decision you need to make, and it will take extensive user testing to nail the right response. An easy trap to fall into is to not bring in users and do testing. Because physical actions are highly variant across users, and because every time the developer tries the system they are training themselves to use it better, it is *essential* that fresh users be brought in for each round of testing. We have met dozens of graduate students and developers who have very cool gesture recognizers that only work for themselves!

DESIGN GUIDELINES

Effectively applying the mode and flow model of gestural interaction will simplify your task of building an effective gesture language.

Must

- Model your system using the mode and flow model.
- Consider all flows through your system, and consider which should generate events.

- Consider the three design decisions we have described above: adding and removing flow, splitting and combining gestures, and tweaking flow actions.

Should

- Carefully consider combining different modes to simplify the user's task of understanding your system.

- Carefully consider splitting an existing mode if it will help to better match user intent.

- Carefully consider each step of flow in your system—does it make sense to flow between these two modes? Is it likely to lead to errors?

- Spend time tweaking the physical actions required to flow between different modes in your system.

Could

- Use the RITE method, described in Chapter 29, to adjust each of these issues.

SUMMARY

Designing a gesture language that feels natural is an incredibly difficult thing to do. The mode and flow model of gesture languages will help you to do this better. The three design issues we have outlined, adding and removing flow, splitting and combining modes, and tweaking physical actions, require careful consideration, and this model will help you to understand exactly what to ask. The answers come from the lessons elsewhere in this book, in particular the RITE method of rapidly iterating, testing, and evaluating different options.

No Such Thing as Touch

Know Your Platform

The dynamic element in my philosophy, taken as a whole, can be seen as an obstinate and untiring battle against the spirit of abstraction.

—Gabriel Marcel

DESCRIPTION

The traditional mouse-based user interface, the WIMP (Windows Icons Menus Pointers), has as perhaps its most essential component an abstraction of the logical target of user actions. This abstraction has gone by many names. The inventors of the mouse, Engelbart and English, named it the *bug*, but later referred to it as the *telepointer*. In Windows, it is the *pointer*. In OSX, it is the alternately the *pointer* and the *cursor*. But by whatever name, it remains a focal point for user-generated events in the system. A funny thing has happened with the pointer: a kind of abstraction has grown-up around it, where a plethora of hardware can control it, and it is the movement of the pointer, rather than the hardware, to which application designers create their experiences. In our experience, this has led to widespread misunderstanding that the design of the GUI itself is abstract. It's not. It has been designed over more than 40 years of iteration to be highly optimized for a particular piece of hardware.

On the Lenovo laptop sitting here on the desk in front of us, we can control the position of the pointer using a trackpad, a thumb stick, and a touch screen. We also happen to have a mouse plugged-in, as well as a trackball and a pen tablet (yeah, we're cool like that). Six input devices, each of which possessing uniquely different physical characteristics, all drive the same experience: they move the mouse pointer around the screen. A reasonable question to ask is, which of them is best at controlling a WIMP interface? We may all have our own preferences, but put them to the test, and the mouse will come out on top every time. It's not a mystery why that is: it's because the people designing WIMP interfaces at PARC, Apple, Microsoft, DEC, and elsewhere all were designing and optimizing their software for **167** the mouse. Sure, each of these other devices has their place. Two finger scrolling on a trackpad is pretty handy, and the pen tablet is a lot better for drawing. But the mechanics of the WIMP, pointing and clicking, are designed for the mouse.

Give a smart group of folks the task of designing a user interface optimized for different hardware, and they can do it. A highly influential paper by Apitz and Guimbretière did just that: they created a set of controls entirely for the pen, to support a drawing application. Obviously, the drawing part was already better done with a pen than with a mouse—they redesigned the rest of the UI to be better suited to the pen (***FURTHER READING***). The biggest challenge for a designer of a NUI is to understand that the abstraction that WIMP GUI designers have been operating under is a lie. The GUI is designed for the mouse. And your job will be to design for other input devices. The goal of this chapter and the next few chapters is to give you a more sophisticated understanding of the hardware that will be available to you. There is not yet any equivalent of the pointer for touch computing folks—you need to design your user interface specifically and without abstraction for the hardware on which it will be running. This will be hard—but the tools of this chapter will help you to do it.

In this chapter, we provide a framework to categorize various input and display capabilities. In the subsequent chapters, we provide more details about specific elements of this framework. The goal is that you will begin to apply this framework in one (or possibly both) of two ways. First, to have awareness of on which platforms your designed software might be run. Second, to target your software to those platforms, to create what is truly a Natural User Interface.

APPLICATION TO NUI

The WIMP interface has led to complacency among designers. Fundamental elements of interaction are the same everywhere—a single point, moving around the screen, poking at controls and content. About this pointer, we know its location (x and y), and the state of its buttons. That's it. Input devices layered on top of the WIMP are all reduced to this small amount of information—the stylus of a tablet, standard resistive touch screens, trackballs, eye-trackers, voice-control, mice—all are reduced by the WIMP to exactly the same data: x, y, and button state. It's as if all literature must be expressed in limmerick, or all calculus in dance. The result is that all input devices, with their rich and divergent capabilities, are reduced to emulating the mouse. Simply put, this emulation makes lives easier, because designers of software need to design only for one input device, and all others are shoehorned into its capabilities. But the result is that controlling the WIMP with any input device other than the mouse can be painful. Don't believe us? Try using the a voice control system to navigate your computer, and you will see very quickly that you are essentially emulating the mouse using your voice. It is painful!

NUI is different in two ways. First, new technologies lend themselves to the creation of a more natural user interface. These technologies are excited precisely because they give us more information about the user's state. Paradoxically to some, this means that designing for them is much harder. A simple (x, y) coordinate is not enough. While any sort of reduction might seem to make your software suited to many different devices, it will fail to take full advantage of those technologies that provide more information. The pressure of the stylus, the hovering distance of a finger, the tone of a voice—all are fodder for creating designs that, to the user, feel natural. This leads us to the second problem: by doing away with this reduction, we expose ourselves to great difficulty: we no longer have a standard that we can use to design one-size fits all applications.

In this chapter, we will learn two lessons. First, the danger of one-size fits all design, and second, the various parameters which differentiate touch and gestural input technologies now and for the forseeable future. How to design for those parameters is the subject of subsequent chapters—here, we will concentrate on understanding them.

LESSONS FROM THE PAST

Nintendo is a company known for taking risks in user interaction. Its latest console, the Wii, has been a wild success, in part due to its leveraging of simple infrared cameras and accelerometers to enable a magical user experience. The success of the Wii has led many to forget several failed bets the company has made in the past with innovative user interface technology. But it is in the long history of those failed bets that we find a stellar example of the failure of a business, and its designers, to take advantage of a cutting-edge input device. To those familiar with the history, it will come as no suprise that we refer to the *Nintendo Power Glove*.

The Power Glove is worn by the user, and provides several degrees of freedom of movement. Its position in three dimensions is tracked, as are its roll, pitch, and yaw. Further, the degree to which each finger is "curled" is delivered to the game. Its marketing promised to usher in a new era of interaction with games. Freed from the tyranny of the controller, gamers would experience a magical world in which simple, intuitive, natural gestures replaced clunky, artificial game controllers. If not for the leather jacket and haircut on the gamer wearing the glove in its most famous ad, one might be forgiven for mistaking it for a modern-day spot describing a contemporary product. The Power Glove, it turns out, was roughly two decades ahead of its time.

The Power Glove was a total failure. While there were issues with the technology, that is not where the device failed. The Wii has found success following almost an identical technological path as the Power Glove—leveraging cutting-edge sensors capable of transforming the way players interact with their games. A question worth asking is: Why was the Wii a success, where the Power Glove was a failure?

One fundamental advantage the Wii has is that it was a *new platform*. Games designed for the Wii are designed for interaction with the Wiimotes and other specialized hardware. The Power Glove, in contrast, made the farcical attempt to enable control of *old games*, designed for the Nintendo controller. For the vast majority of the user's experience, using the Power Glove was essentially emulating the controller they previously used to play their games. Designers of the experience were retroactively disempowered, in that they had no opportunity to design, build, or test their game designs for use with the Power Glove. Truly, it defies common sense that a game well designed for a controller could ever be driven well with a hand gestures. Reviewers and gamers alike agreed that the experience was terrible.

But it wasn't because of the technology—it was because of how the technology interacted with the software, and simply put, that this software communicated with its user via an abstraction; in this case, not an *x, y* location, but rather the state of the eight buttons of a classic Nintendo Entertainment System controller (*UP, DOWN, LEFT, RIGHT, B, A, SELECT, and START*). Yes, all the magical input channels of the power glove were reduced to emulating presses of eight buttons. Gaming companies could have designed custom games for the Power Glove that took advantage of its unique characteristics, but they didn't. Why bother if they could just design for the controller, and know that the glove could drive those games, too?

A key takeaway from this lesson is that the controller was functionally complete for playing those games. The answer to the question "Name one thing you can do with the power glove that you can't with the controller" is—nothing! It is not in producing new functionality that a new technology excels. Rather, it is in producing a new *method* of interaction.

Further, we learn from this experience that a "lowest common denominator," in this case, the data generated by the controller, cannot provide a natural user experience for a more capable input device. One must resist the urge to survey available technologies, look for their common properties, and design for those experiences. Instead, one must design software experience in a tailored way, considering the unique physical characteristics of the technologies.

This lesson teaches an important design lesson, but it is just as important as a business lesson: natural user interfaces can only be achieved through tight coupling of the experience to their hardware.

DESIGN GUIDELINES

When creating NUI experiences, a thoughtful designer must consider carefully how to create experiences for the technologies that will be driving that experience. Even though our focus is on touch and gestural interfaces, the designer will still encounter a wide array of sensing and display capabilities. Figure 22.1 shows the data available to users of some of the most popular touch technologies.

To understand the scope of such a problem, let's consider an example. Let's say that a team develops an application on a 30" display running at 1280 × 720 (a 720 p HD monitor) to sell on the web. Let's further say that the team follows the rule of making touch targets at least 7 mm (which translates to 13 pixels on their display) wide. So far, so good. Consider now what happens if a customer installs

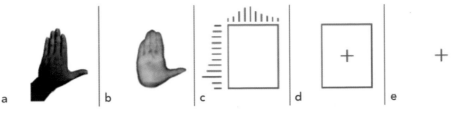

FIGURE 22.1

Various commercial devices' sensing of the same contact. (a) The user's hand on the device, (b) Microsoft Surface, (c) Circle Twelve DiamondTouch shows activation strength for each individual antenna, (d) a standard Windows 7 touch device provides a touch point and a bounding rectangle, (e) an Apple touch device, like the iPad, provides only an x/y point.

the application on a 13" laptop running at 1280 × 1024. All of a sudden, what was a perfectly reasonable button is now only 2.6 mm wide, and the application is totally unusable. This doesn't matter with traditional input devices—the scale of the device doesn't matter, because the physical mouse remains a comfortable size. It does matter with touch, where the size of a fingertip never scales. Designing well for new technologies requires actually designing for those technologies.

To help understand the differences among touch and gestural devices, we will review a list of parameters that differentiate them. In subsequent chapters, we will dive into deeper detail about many of these parameters and how to design software for each of the capabilities described.

Capability vs. Quality

It should be clearly noted here that this chapter is about capabilities, not quality. Technologies can be differentiated along many lines. This chapter describes a set of enablers of experiences and scenarios. As such, issues of reliability, sensitivity, or other such measures of quality are not discussed. Instead, we will focus on sensing technologies in terms of the user experiences they enable.

Demonstrated vs. As-Yet-Undemonstrated

We will now examine several input capabilities, and discuss how they have been demonstrated to be useful in enabling certain types of interaction. For each, we will describe what the capabilities are and mention a few uses that have been shown to enhance a user's experience. Keep in mind, while reading this, that the majority of uses of these sensing capabilities have yet to be demonstrated. As we have seen with the development of the modern mouse-based GUI, some of the best innovations, such as tooltips and numeric spinners, took decades to arrive on the scene. Thus, you should regard these descriptions not as prescriptive, but rather as inspirational.

Sensed Objects

The types of objects that can be sensed by a surface computer have perhaps the most immediately apparent effect on the user's experience. We define three types of objects, and various sensing capabilities associated with each. It is important to distinguish body parts, such as fingers ("touch"), from physical objects. Physical objects provide a means to communicate with the system. The objects can act as tools—especially a stylus, which we differentiate from other objects.

Touch

Touch is the number of contact points detected and tracked by the device. The number of simultaneous contacts has a significant effect on two elements: the gestures any one user can perform and the number of simultaneous users of the system (Figure 22.2).

Objects

The system is able to detect objects. These objects can be used as tools in the system or can serve as a means of perceived communication between the display and another device.

Stylus

The system is able to detect a stylus and distinguish it from any other type of contact. We distinguish between a stylus and other types of objects for two reasons: first, because a large number of commercially available surface computing devices are able to sense a stylus, but not other objects, and second, a significant field of research has been conducted focusing on interaction with a stylus, differentiating it from other objects. A stylus is more precise, allows for written input, and can be useful in distinguishing input by type (e.g., touches manipulate; a stylus writes).

Sensed Information

The ideal surface computer can track various physical properties of objects and body parts and their interaction with the screen. Here, we review the high-level categories of this information. We will provide more detail of each of the types in subsequent chapters.

Contact Differentiation

Systems with contact differentiation are able to identify the sources of contacts, so that a touch from one user is distinguished from the touch of another, as is the touch of an index finger from a ring finger. This is probably the most important of all parameters—if, for example, a system cannot differentiate between users, one cannot use toolbars in an application!

Hover

The system is able to detect contacts *before* they touch the display and is able to *distinguish* between hovering and touching contacts. This allows for improvements to user accuracy in selection and can be used to enable "previews" of actions that will occur at the moment of touch (e.g., "tool tips").

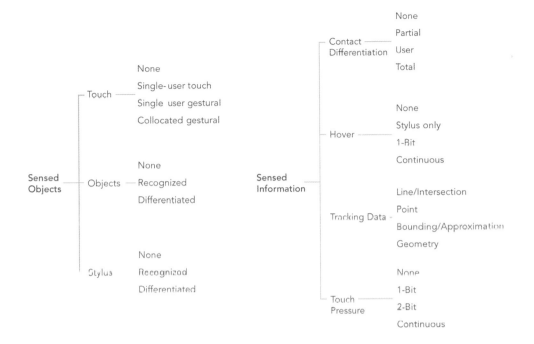

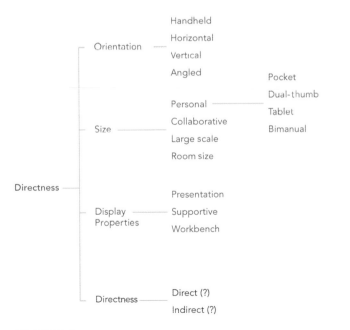

FIGURE 22.2

Our taxonomy of surface computing sensing properties.

Tracking Data

How much information about each contact is detected by the system. Examples of different levels of this taxonomy are shown in Figure 22.1. Whether we know only an *x/y* coordinate or we also know shape, orientation, etc., dramatically affects the gestures that can be included in your application.

Touch Pressure

The system is able to detect the force with which the contact is touching the display. This data can be used to differentiate input events (e.g., touching lightly equates to drawing a rectangle, touching more forcefully to placing the rectangle down on the canvas), as well as to vary continuous input (e.g., control the size of the brush in a paint application).

Display Properties

Properties of the display will ultimately lead to significant differences in your design.

Orientation

Will your device be a horizontal computer, requiring UI elements to be capable of facing each side? A vertical screen, mounted on a wall? Mobile, so that the UI needs to be used while being held? These considerations have significant impact on the design of various elements of your system.

Size

The size of the display of your target device is especially important for touch computing. Applications written for devices that fit in one hand will clearly require different design than those on wall-sized computers, since target distances on a large display might mean having to walk across the room. Further, information shown on a large display might not be visible all at once by any one user.

DPI

The resolution of the display, the actual number of pixels, is relevant but less important than the density of those dots on the screen, usually measured in dots per inch (DPI). This is, of course, distinct from display "resolution," which is a measure of how many pixels the display has—a 20" HD TV has the same resolution as a 60" HD TV but has very different DPI. In the example that opened the chapter, we saw the implications of an application being moved from a large TV-sized display to a higher-DPI laptop display—the application became unusable. We learn from this that applications' visual style and behavior must be differentiated based on the pixel density of the display, rather than simply by the number of pixels.

Direct vs. Indirect Touch

Researchers have described a variety of techniques that differentiate direct touch, in which touch and display devices are overlaid, from indirect touch, in which they are separated. The experience of touching a device without a display should be differentiated from that when the content is shown in a display beneath the finger.

While there are a number of reasons for this, the fat finger problem described earlier in this book (Chapter 13) is a clear example.

Summing Up

From this list of capabilities, we see that, plainly, not all touch devices are created equal. It is incredibly important that one avoid a "lowest common denominator" approach to the design of software. While tempting, this will, every time, fail to achieve a natural user interface. Instead, one must tailor the design to the input and display capabilities that the user will actually be experiencing.

Must

- Determine which sensing capabilities and display properties your application will have access to, and design for those capabilities.

Should

- Consider which elements of this list are not actually relevant to the experience that you are creating. Object interaction, for example, might not be suitable to your particular needs. Consider, however, how your application will co-exist with others that will be running on an object-enabled platform. This is true of all other capabilities. While there are old-fashioned controllers available for the Wii, a user is much less likely to buy a game that requires one. The Wii has a set of *de facto* standards for games running on its platform. Consider these on the platform for which you are building.

Could

- Design your application *first*, taking note of these capability requirements. Then, find the platform that will enable its use. This approach is obviously a more dangerous one, since you risk not taking advantage of capabilities on the ultimately chosen platform and also limiting the market potential of your application. It is an approach sometimes favored by designers who wish to avoid the confines of limited thinking imposed by considering hardware capabilities too early. As should now be abundantly clear, this is not the approach we favor.

SUMMARY

Good design is specific, not generic. The various parameters we have described in this chapter delineate the platforms on which your software may be run. Consider them carefully, taking into account the lessons described in the subsequent chapters, in which we describe how to design for and take advantage of these capabilities.

RISING ABOVE: THE LOWEST COMMON DENOMINATOR

Johnny Chung Lee
Microsoft Applied Sciences

It is often appealing, from a business and engineering standpoint, to reuse a working system as much as possible. It saves on development costs and minimizes risk. In many cases it is arguably the most efficient way to accomplish a task with the smallest amount of resources. As a result, there should be no surprise that there exists a push toward making as many components be as general purpose as possible, and a push toward becoming device- and platform-agnostic in order to maximize return on investment as well as maintain flexibility to unforeseen changes in the technology market. Specialization to a particular platform in software systems is frequently viewed as a bad thing, and in some cases is highly discouraged. The end result of practicing this particular philosophy is the "lowest common denominator" approach to design.

Since specialized capabilities are not guaranteed to exist on every target device, developers and designers are often encouraged to focus the intersection subset of target capabilities. As a result, there should be no surprise as to why the majority of consumer products today have a "lowest common denominator" feel, especially when it comes to the user interface design. They may be functional, but inelegant and undesirable. Yet, there have been several clear examples of highly successful well-known products that have demonstrated that when the user experience is a core differentiator for the product, specialization in the interface design isn't just one possible option, it is the only sensible option.

Every form of input technology, be it a mouse, a keyboard, a touchscreen, a stylus, speech input, a motion sensor, or a steering wheel, can be thought of as a different tool in a workshop. Each has their strengths and weaknesses. Each is ideal for some tasks and absurd for others. If you tried to use a screwdriver to cut a piece of wood and a hacksaw to tighten some screws, your colleagues might express some concern for your mental well-being. The same degree of concern should be expressed when witnessing someone attempting to use a touch system to emulate a mouse, or trying to use gesture input to operate a pull-down menu. Trying to design a user interface that works with multiple forms of input technology may achieve the minimum bar of functionality, but it will not provide a good user experience.

As advances in silicon fabrication continue to provide a reduction in the costs of computing, it becomes increasingly economical to manufacture highly specialized devices that serve smaller and smaller needs. The concept of owning a single general-purpose computer is diminishing. For some time now, we have been transitioning to owning a multitude of specialized computers, such as a laptop, mobile phone, video game system, television, music player, digital camera, navigation system, car keys, and our credit/debit cards. This diversity will only increase, and with it the way we interact with them, and with that, the types of interface technology we will use and the form factors of the device. The process of designing user interfaces moving forward must embrace specialization to specific devices. Continuing to hold on to an engineering tradition of reuse and generalization across multiple forms of interface technology is a guaranteed way to provide an underwhelming user experience and a guaranteed way to get left behind.

Author Biography

Johnny Chung Lee has a Ph.D. in human-computer interaction from Carnegie Mellon University and is a researcher at Microsoft Applied Sciences. His research work spans a variety of topics including projection technology, multi-touch input, augmented reality, brain-computer interfaces, and haptics. Lee is best known for his video tutorials on using the Nintendo Wii remote to create low-cost whiteboards and virtual reality displays, which have garnered over 15 million views. He was a key contributor to the tracking algorithms behind Xbox Kinect. In 2008, he was named to MIT Technology Review's prestigious list of top researchers under the age of 35.

The Fundamentals Have to Work

The woods are lovely, dark, and deep,
But I have promises to keep,
And miles to go before I sleep,
And miles to go before I sleep.
—**Robert Frost, "Stopping by the Woods on a Snowy Evening"**

DESCRIPTION

Every new interface paradigm begins with a promise to its potential users. The promise may morph from the time that it is in the minds of the visionaries who first proposed the paradigm to when it's adopted by those who instantiate that vision in products. The promise as understood by the user and as understood by the designer may be different. Finally, the promise itself is a source of risk for every product team that adopts it. The world is full of products and systems that never delivered on their promise and are long forgotten or cursed by their unfortunate users.

APPLICATION TO NUI

The NUI promises much. The promises are subject to misinterpretation. A team developing a NUI may incorrectly assume that a new input medium (touch, voice, gesture) makes their product natural. Rightfully, the user will expect more from an interface that calls itself natural.

LESSONS FROM THE PAST

The graphical user interface (GUI) is a good example of a promise that morphed over time. Doug Englebart is often called the inventor of the mouse, and he is, but the mouse was just a means to an end. The end, the goal of Engelbart's vision, was to augment the human intellect. Over time and in the hands of others, the promise of GUI morphed into making tasks easier and broadening the market for computing technology. In many ways this latter promise was realized. Fifty-odd years since Englebart's original paper, a vast domain of new capabilities has been extended to a wide range of people. Today, typical users compose typeset documents, create complex financial models, and access vast quantities of information (and misinformation) with relative ease. While cumbersome interfaces stubbornly persist and are constantly created anew, the ubiquity of technology is a testament to a lowering of barriers (i.e., the increased ease of use) for these new capabilities. The question of whether the individual's, the collective, or the average "intellect" is augmented by this growth in technology is highly debatable, and we have no desire to address that question in this book.

The *de facto* promise of the GUI, to make tasks using a computer easier, raises the bar for every product that adopts a GUI. The users expect more than functionality: They expect that the promised functionality will be easy to use. For example, introducing a new mark-up language with the promise of some new exciting features, then expecting that to create a new mass market product would be absurd to the point of delusional. The promise of easier access to capabilities is already thoroughly infused in users' expectations as they use a product. Parts of the product that fail to meet these expectations will go unused. It is not uncommon to discover users asking for functionality that already exists in a product. This perpetuating irony is driven in part by a lack of transparent ease of use in esoteric elements of the product. The tragedy of unused functionality is painfully acute because the development team has gone to the trouble and expense of building capabilities. These capabilities match users' needs, and "only" the interface got in the way. These are truly missed opportunities.

Implicit in the promise of each new paradigm are pitfalls for the development team. The first pitfall is that the development team may assume that simple adoption of the trappings of the interface ensures delivery on the promise. This was evident in many early GUI designs. They did include pull-down menus, dialog boxes, and a screen that showed what you were working on and would "get," yet they were unusable. The terms used in the menus were opaque to the intended users. The organization of the interface elements did not support expected task flow. The elements created on the screen seemed unrelated to the constructs that users employed in their work. The path to an intended result was totally unclear. In other words, while the GUI removed the syntactic demands and the memory requirements of a command system, it replaced those with a thicket of incomprehensible choices unrelated to the users' knowledge of the task domain. An even deeper and rare misunderstanding occasionally occurred. In these cases, the team failed to grasp some of the fundamental principles of the interface paradigm and adopted only the trappings. I have seen systems that ignored the object-operation syntax (select an object first, and choose the verb as a menu item) of the GUI and required the user to select an operation first and then the relevant objects would be highlighted. It was so contrary to expectations, it took some time to even grasp what was happening.

DESIGN GUIDELINES

The lessons from the unfulfilled promises of the GUI itself and the missteps of early development teams can provide us with some guidance to creating a successful NUI.

Must

- Start from scratch. Beginning with a successful GUI or web interface and simply translating it into a NUI is likely to fail. It would be like translating command language into a GUI paradigm.

- Consider the environment and the goal of the application. Each environmental goal of the application creates a "niche" in which an application and the way it is rendered will thrive or die. Some extreme examples make this obvious. Using touch for an interface in which the users' vision and hands are occupied would be highly counterproductive—even dangerous. Typing on a handheld device while driving is unnatural. Speaking commands makes much more sense in this context, provided the cognitive load is not too high.

- A NUI makes two promises. The first is that skilled use is obtainable very quickly. The second is that the interaction itself will feel enjoyable. In order to fulfill these promises, any NUI must be both efficient to learn and fun to use. Its feedback and feed-forward will lead the user to success without being oppressive. The actions themselves will be smooth and fluid.

- Pay attention to the underlying infrastructure that enables any application. The infrastructure of the GUI is well understood and works (for the most part). The mouse is used to control cursor movement; the keyboard is used to input text or input a command via accelerators. For the most part, these are dependable. The same cannot be said for the evolving platforms of NUIs. The hardware's reading of touch points is often unreliable. On one system we tried we were advised to "wet your finger" in order to help the system read your touch. This was on a bar table with a touch interface. Even then, contact was often lost. Regardless of what else such a system promised, that lack of reliability (let alone hygiene) on the fundamentals yielded it unusable.

Should

- A development team would be wise to start with an application that is both simple and different from existing applications on the GUI or the web. Simple games are often a good starting point for a team to learn how to design and implement a NUI.

- Get the mechanics right first. If the mechanics of the interaction, the gestures with their feedback, are not fluid and enjoyable, the system will fail. This has been understood in game design for years. The Mario Brothers franchise would not have been as successful if the mechanics of jumping were not fun.

Could

- It is wise to look at other NUI applications that are in the same domain. It will give the team insight on what works and does not.

SUMMARY

Building a NUI is not a royal road to fame and fortune. In fact, it contains more risk for a team because the user expectations will be higher. The development team may use well-worn skills and implicit assumptions from previous efforts that used other paradigms. This is likely to fail. The NUI requires not only that expert performance be obtained quickly with few false starts, but also that using the system while learning be fun. None of these challenges are insurmountable. The success of any NUI application depends on going the miles needed to keep the promise.

FURTHER READING

If anyone could be called the father of the GUI, it would be Douglas Englebart. The concepts that he pioneered in his Augment system underlie much of design we take for granted in the GUI. These concepts were well described in the in his paper prepared at SRI. This paper is available on the Internet. SRI Summary Report AFOSR-3223. Prepared for: Director of Information Sciences, Air Force Office of Scientific Research, Washington 25, DC, Contract AF 49(638)-1024• SRI Project No. 3578 (AUGMENT, 3906). http://www.dougengelbart.org/pubs/augment-3906.html

Number of Contacts

That's what an army is—a mob; they don't fight with courage that's born in them, but with courage that's borrowed from their mass.

—**Mark Twain**

DESCRIPTION

The number of simultaneous points of contact tracked by the input device will define the domain of the gesture language that can be developed. Classic hardware for enabling touch allowed one point of contact to be sensed—touching with multiple fingers would yield unpredictable results.

At the dawn of the age of commercial multi-touch, the number of contacts detected by hardware is highly variable. The Windows 7 gesture language, and hardware certification, is written to require only two points of contact. The iPhone gesture language is limited to two points of simultaneous contact, despite the hardware supporting more. Other hardware enables detection of far more, for a variety of reasons.

APPLICATION TO NUI

As discussed in Chapter 22, the hardware platform will greatly influence the gestural user experience built upon it , and Chapter 18 described the advantages of differentiating gestures based on the number of contacts. We classify three types of touch devices based on the number of contacts it is able to sense and report simultaneously:

Single-User Manipulation: Senses sufficient point of contact for a simple manipulation style gesture language: dragging, zooming, etc., such as on the iPhone. This language requires two points of contact, to enable the "zoom" gesture.

Single-User Gestural: A small number of contacts that allows a single user to perform gestures requiring multiple points of contact. The actual number of points depends on the gesture language. If enabling a piano, for example, this would be ten contacts.

181

Multi-User Gestural: A larger number of contacts that allow for multiple users to be engaged in multi-touch gestures simultaneously. The actual number of contacts depends on the number of touches that make up the gesture language being used on the system. A multi-user gestural system would support multiple users making gestural input simultaneously. This would be essential for a large conference table or vertical display.

LESSONS FROM THE PAST

Two elements are differentiated by the number of contacts a language supports: the nature of the gestures and the number of users.

Accelerators and Modifiers

Inputs to the modern WIMP GUI often require multiple fingers to engage at the same time. Inputting a capital letter, for example, requires pressing both SHIFT and the associated key. Copying an item requires holding the CTRL key while dragging it with the mouse. Most, if not all, multi-finger actions in a modern WIMP can be classified as either a "modifier" or an "accelerator."

The distinction between a modifier and an accelerator is subtle but important. A modifier is a key that, when pressed in combination with another action, alters that action—ideally, in a predictable way. For example, the CTRL key is a modifier, in that it alters the function of the other keys on the keyboard. Turn the mouse wheel key without the modifier, and it scrolls up and down. Turn it while holding the CTRL modifier, and it zooms in and out. An accelerator, in contrast, is a series of keystrokes that will lead to something happening more quickly than otherwise, such as "APPLE + C" to copy the selected item in the Mac OS.

Modifiers and accelerators have both been shown to be incredibly successful. Interfaces universally include them, from games to productivity software. Perhaps one of the most successful multi-finger interfaces is Adobe Photoshop.

Photoshop relies heavily on both modifiers and accelerators. It is not often that you see a more impressive display of expert computer use than an experienced graphic designer wrangling Photoshop. Their fingers fly across the keyboard, while the display changes constantly in, to the observer, unpredictable and nearly always incomprehensible ways.

One of Photoshop's most commonly used modifiers is the space bar. When clicking and dragging on the document without the space bar, the currently selected tool is applied to that part of the document. Holding the space bar, however, places the system into "hand tool" mode, such that when the user clicks and drags, the document pans. This simple modifier is incredibly powerful: it allows the user to operate at a high zoom level and apply a tool repeatedly without having to manually scroll or switch tools.

Photoshop's use of accelerators is also extensive. Pressing CTRL + SPACE zooms in, while pressing ALT + SPACE zooms out. A little searching online will lead you to a complete list of the accelerators and modifiers in Photoshop—the dense list we found is four pages long, listing hundreds of key combinations.

Of course, the point here is not that your application's functionality should be buried in obscure combinations of finger presses. However, the effective use of combinations of fingers has been shown, in this instance, to be effective in creating an incredibly powerful tool for experts. The trick lies in leading your novice users to become experts quickly, without having to read an instruction manual—as described in Chapters 10 and 20.

Design for Touch with a Second Finger

The addition of the second touch has enabled an expansion of the traditional set of actions in a GUI. User interfaces built with the certainty of the availability of this second point of contact can provide exciting accelerations and intuitive interactions.

A now-classic example of the use of a second contact point is to enhance one-finger panning and zooming by adding the ability to rotate and resize by dragging two fingers on the device. One of the earlier (though not first) examples of the use of this gesture is in MIT's metaDESK system. In this case, two models of buildings from MIT's campus are placed on the device. The map of Cambridge, MA, moves, rotates, and resizes to ensure that these buildings are placed at their geographically correct location. This system uses physical objects, rather than touches, but it established the standard for what interaction all multi-touch systems must have: Two fingers expand, rotate, and move content (Figure 24.1).

This interaction gets people excited. It also points to some of the power of differentiating gestures by number of contacts: there is no need to provide a pair of buttons to zoom in and out of the UI. Nor is there a need to provide a zoom mode in the traditional sense, differentiating input depending on whether the user has selected this or a "pan" mode. Instead, we simply teach the user that two fingers means zoom—and

FIGURE 24.1

The metaDESK system displayed virtual maps beneath physical objects. Moving an object would move and rotate the map to ensure that it was geographically correct. Adding a second model would cause the map to scale to ensure that the buildings were in the right virtual place.

they use it. This is one of the key ideas in the reduction of visual clutter that typify a NUI: we get rid of buttons by requiring the user to input in more than one way, differentiated by the number of fingers.

Another example of multi-finger gestures is the language of accelerators used on the MacBook trackpad. Just like the above example, input to the system is differentiated by the number of fingers. Sliding one finger vertically on the pad moves the mouse cursor up and down. Place two fingers on the pad, however, and perform the same action, and the current window scrolls up and down. Three fingers pages through a document, as we see in Figure 24.2.

Like the zoom gesture, the multi-finger differentiation of the trackpad input has also proven successful, in that users are able to quickly learn the gestures and perform them. They also provide mechanisms to rapidly differentiate input from the user, without having to use the GUI to select a mode.

An excellent example of a natural mapping of multiple fingers that users can immediately understand was shown by Igarashi and his colleagues. In their system, users could place multiple fingers on cartoon characters and bend and twist them to produce animations. The response of the characters followed an intuitive, physics-like manipulation pattern.

An interesting element we observed in the construction of our gesture languages is that it is actually rather difficult for users to intuit, or remember, that the number of fingers matters in differentiating modes. This seemed to cut directly across another of the elements of the hardware parameters we discussed in Chapter 22: directness. Even when expert users of multi-touch trackpad gestures, such as the ones shown above, were moved to a direct-touch system, any notion of being careful of the number of fingers they were using to manipulate an object went out the door. Participants in user studies would tell us they understood, and then proceed to forget within a minute or so, even after being reminded again and again. It seems that there is some quality of direct touch that is different from indirect touch in this way.

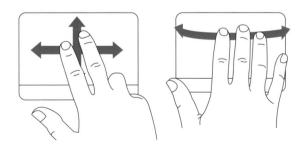

FIGURE 24.2

Images from http://support.apple.com/kb/HT1115.

Designing for One User vs. Multiple Users

Large multi-touch devices have the potential of enabling multiple users to interact with a system simultaneously. Multi-user interaction with software has been a household phenomenon for decades, mostly in the form of video games. What may not be immediately obvious, however, is that designing for one user does not scale up to designs for multiple users. To illustrate the point, consider the relatively simple interaction used to select a color in a paint application (Figure 24.3).

This now classic control is such a fundamental control for a GUI that it is very easy to miss a simple fact: this will not work for multiple users. As soon as the second user touches the control panel, she will change the color for *all* users, not just herself. There is no way to specify which color goes with which contact point (Figure 24.4).

One could easily write an entire book on the design of NUIs for multiple users. Suffice it to say for now, however, that very simple things break when moving from a single-user model to a multi-user one—especially if your system lacks user differentiation, discussed elsewhere. And the number of contacts that can be detected in your platform may be the best indicator of whether you will be designing a system for a single user or multiple users.

DESIGN GUIDELINES

Must

- Determine the number of contacts supported by your platform. Build your gesture language around this number.
- Ensure that, as early as possible in a gesture, the system knows which action the user intends to perform. Use the number of fingers the user puts down on the display to perform this identification.
- For direct-touch systems, be careful about differentiating modes by the number of fingers beyond some small set, or beyond what is immediately apparent by the graphics the user is touching.

Should

- Differentiate system gestures based on the number of fingers. Provide a clear and consistent mapping of what one finger does versus multiple fingers, and how users can remember the association and apply it consistently.
- Strive for consistency with other gesture languages, while simultaneously seeking to fully leverage the number of contacts detectable by your system.

Could

- Design your system for multiple users, considering carefully to ensure that such designs are successful.

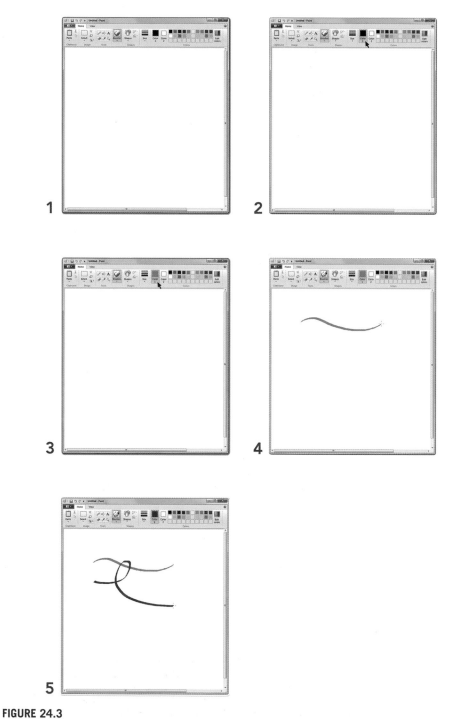

FIGURE 24.3

The use of a toolbar to select a color. This interaction does not work on a multi-user system.

FIGURE 24.4

Two users cannot use a classic toolbar model to paint in two different colors at the same time.

SUMMARY

We advocate the use of the number of contacts as one of the parameters allowing for instant identification of the user's intention, to reduce or eliminate any point in the interaction in which those intentions are unknown to the system and thus without feedback to the user. Further, it is clear that differentiating gestures by the number of fingers being used can be successful in creating a rich gesture language. Finally, we note that a large number of contacts detectable by a system can mean that multiple users will need to be supported simultaneously. Designing a multi-user system requires a fundamental rethinking of all elements of interaction and should be undertaken with due consideration.

FURTHER READING

Igarashi, T., Moscovich, T., and Hughes, J. F. 2005. As-rigid-as-possible shape manipulation. *ACM Trans. Graph.* 24(3), 1134–1141. DOI = http://doi.acm.org/10.1145/1073204.1073323. In this work, Tomer Moscovich and colleagues at Brown University allow users to grab, bend, and twist cartoon characters. The mapping between gesture and consequence of that gesture is immediate and intuitive. Users can learn it easily, and anticipate the effect of adding another finger to the interface.

Contact Data: Shape, Pressure, and Hover

25

> *To them, I said, the truth would be literally nothing but the shadows of the images.*
>
> —**Plato, the Allegory of the Cave, *The Republic***

DESCRIPTION

In *The Republic*, Plato describes a group of people shackled from birth such that they can see only the wall of a cave, on which the shadows of the world behind them dance in firelight. The prisoners, he argued, would develop and understanding that these flickering shadows *are* reality. By consequence, they might never develop an understanding of the full 3-D world from which those shadows are projected.

The shadows on the cave wall in Plato's allegory provide to the viewer an abstraction of reality. In the same way that someone trapped in this cave would understand only a portion of the reality an uncaptured person would experience, software on a touch device experiences only a slice of the reality of the user's actual physical interaction. This abstraction is useful, in that it is easier to program against—applications driven by a mouse need only care about the position of the pointer and the state of the mouse buttons. Other details are thrown away: the orientation of the mouse, the user's posture on the mouse, which hand he's using, how hard he is pressing the buttons—none of this is available to the application. While useful in the sense that this makes application development easier, this lost detail reduces the bandwidth of communication from the user to the device. An application *can't* find them out, even if it wants to.

APPLICATION TO NUI

NUI hardware is different. It detects more information about each element of the interaction, and these elements can be used to subtly adjust the experience in an intuitive and natural way.

Several variations in hardware exist, as described in Chapter 22. These variations influence both the detail and the type of information that is presented about each contact point. A designer must take care to ensure that they squeeze every last drop of expressivity out of the hardware their system will be using. Most important is to avoid the pitfall of determining a lowest common denominator across hardware, and designing your system to respond only to those signals commensurate with that lowest common denominator.

Instead, investigate deeply the capabilities of your hardware in terms of the detail it can detect. Take, for example, the difference between a full-touch and a multi-touch system (Figure 25.1).

Intuitively, we can see immediately the kinds of gestures that are possible with a full-touch system that are not with a multi-touch one, such as cupping an area of the screen or even a variation of American Sign Language.

The same is equally true of pressure: A system that detects pressure can respond in all manner of ways, varying intensity of system response proportionally to the intensity of the user's input.

Hover is a different beast. Hover, unlike the others, is not a parameter of the touch itself, but rather the ability of the hardware to detect hands *before* they come in contact with the input device. We described earlier the state-transition model of input devices, which points out that moving from mouse input to touch gives away a valuable preview state. Hover has the potential to bring back this state. It can be used to preview the effects of contacts, such as by indicating what the effect of a contact will be or suggesting alternative gestures.

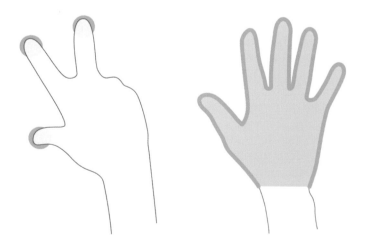

FIGURE 25.1

On the left, we see what a multi-touch system is able to determine about those fingers: namely, just the position of each of the fingertips. On the right, we see what a full-touch system is able to detect—the exact contour and shape of the area of the hand in contact with the device.

LESSONS FROM THE PAST

A friend of ours, Paul Dietz, likes to point to the evolution of musical instruments as a long series of experiments to perfect the user interface for creating music. For example, the harpsichord, a predecessor to the piano, helpfully illustrates how changes to a user interface can inspire people to push the limits of a particular field or discipline (Figure 25.2).

Each key on a harpsichord controls a mechanism that plucks a string. The plucking of the string is independent of how hard or fast someone presses the key. As such, harpsichord music relies on playing more notes to achieve the effect of greater loudness, which creates a significant shortcoming. The desire to be able to play softly ("piano" is the musical term) or loudly ("forte") led to the development of an alternative mechanism: the hammer. By striking the key harder, the hammer strikes the strings harder, and produces a louder sound. This new instrument was known by its signature feature, "pianoforte," because it could be played softly or loudly. Thus, the piano was born.

With the advent of an interface that allowed for dynamics (the variation of loudness in a piece), players and composers began to explore the possibilities. Piano music was more than just harpsichord music with dynamics; the new expressive capabilities allowed for a fundamental change in the type of music that could be

FIGURE 25.2

A harpsichord, which lacks the degrees of freedom of input offered by a piano.

played. Baroque harpsichord music is intricate: the artistry is often found in very fast, complex patterns of notes. By comparison, piano music has a much greater expressive range, from delicate to soulful. The not-so-subtle point here is that while adding degrees of freedom to an interface may at first appear to offer limited benefits, this addition can fundamentally change the capabilities of the device and also affect what you wish to achieve with it.

The advent of electronic musical keyboards has followed a similar, albeit shorter, path. Early keyboards used simple on/off switches. But this design lacked the expressiveness of the mechanical piano. Over time, extra degrees of freedom have been added. Now, all but the cheapest toy keyboards can sense "velocity." To detect velocity, many keyboards use two switches that trigger at different key positions. By measuring the time between the two activations, the keyboard can translate the velocity of the key strike in a way that allows it to mimic the pianoforte capabilities of a real piano.

Still, the evolution continues. An unfortunate limitation of most keyboard instruments is that once a note is struck, there is little one can do to vary the note's characteristics. To add even greater control, many keyboards have a pitch wheel—a separate control typically used to bend the pitch of all of the depressed notes while they are sounding. This functionality comes at the price of having to dedicate a hand to this function. A more powerful solution used on expensive keyboards is a feature called "after touch," which is a pressure sensor that detects how hard a key is being pressed as it is held down. Some keyboards have a single sensor for all of the keys, which adds a single degree of freedom. The most sophisticated keyboards have a pressure sensor for each key, which allows talented musicians to add effects to individual notes as they play. These additions are too new to judge whether they will change the direction of music.

The lessons we have learned from looking at musical instruments include the following:

1. Input technologies slowly evolve to become more expressive.
2. As they evolve, the devices that use the interfaces take advantage of the expanded capabilities in fundamentally different ways.
3. One-bit on/off can be evolved through multi-bit velocity/pressure.

DESIGN GUIDELINES
Contact Data

Contact data vary widely across devices. The least expressive is a simple x/y coordinate of a contact. The most expressive is a detailed contour of the contact area. In between, bounding boxes and other types of data can be obtained.

Contact data can be used to abstract to an "orientation" of a contact, or more directly by allowing shaped gestures, such as cupping in a physics simulation. Just how expressive your system will be depends both on its needs and on its context of use. Orientation, for example, can be used to make simple gestures more expressive—moving a photo across the screen with one finger is fine, but allowing the user to rotate it by twisting the finger adds more control.

Hover

Hover can best be used to regain the lost state described in Chapter 12 as the state-transition model of input devices. In traditional WIMPs, this state is used to preview. First, the action is previewed just by the fact that the mouse pointer indicates what object will be impacted by a click. Next, in most modern WIMP implementations, hovering over an object with the mouse pointer gives an additional preview. Sometimes this is the form of a textual description of the function (a "tool tip"); sometimes this is a more subtle highlighting of the object under the mouse).

When using the hover state, we must distinguish between two types of hover.

Continuous vs. Discrete Hover

Discrete hover sensors tell you simply whether the object is physically touching the device or is somewhere above it. In contrast, a continuous hover sensor gives you a z value, an actual physical distance between the object and the display.

Discrete hover can always be simulated by a system that provides continuous hover. Obviously, continuous hover is the most expressive.

Both discrete and continuous hover can be used to offer a preview of the effect that actually touching the screen will have. Naturally, the inputs during hover and those during touch can be divorced completely, and research systems have shown this approach. What we have found, however, is that this divorcing is not actually the most valuable use of this state. Instead, continuous hover can offer a continuously changing preview, such as providing a lens effect where targets grow as the finger approaches.

Pressure

Pressure as a NUI Enabler: Why Bother Sensing Pressure?

At first glance, pressure is a tempting target as an enabler for natural input. While you'll never catch us broadly classifying modalities on an imagined spectrum of naturalness, let us point out that pressure is hard to control. As such, it requires significant feedback and learning over time. The purpose of what follows is not to make an argument for pressure as an input to touch, but rather to point out a few things that we already know about the use of pressure in a touch system.

Precise Pressure vs. Pressure Proxies

Pressure is the force with which users touch the display. Sensing this force directly is one way of detecting pressure. Alternatively, a device might sense secondary indicators of this force. Examples include changes in contact area, or shape changes of a contact. This technique is called the "SimPress" (or "simulated press") technique, as we see in the figure shown in Figure 25.3.

Absolute vs. Relative Pressure

Whether sensed directly or indirectly, the output from the device might provide absolute pressure so that the same force always yields the same value. Alternatively, the process might produce relative pressure, or pressure changes for a particular contact. Note that the capabilities of such sensors vary: The former would allow you to build a scale, while the latter would not.

FIGURE 25.3

The SimPress technique allows pressure sensing on devices that can't actually sense it, like Microsoft Surface. Instead of measuring force, the device measures change in contact area when the user presses down.

Localized vs. Pad-Wide Pressure

Whether a device senses pressure locally for each contact or for the pad as a whole does not matter for a single-touch device. For multi-touch devices, however, the type of pressure sensing makes a great deal of difference. Earlier, we described keyboards that can sense pressure for one key or for multiple keys; the same principle applies to touch. Note that Apple trackpads can detect pressure on the whole pad, but not for individual contacts.

Continuous vs. Discrete Pressure

Pressure can be sensed continuously or discretized into levels. Like anything else, the application dictates the most appropriate mode of detection. One of the more promising uses of continuous pressure was shown to allow users to tilt and quickly adjust the z ordering of objects—to move something down in z order, simply push on it harder than on the object you would like higher up in the order.

Discrete pressure, in contrast, is used to target particular values. Unlike continuous pressure, users can consistently target particular levels, as long as those levels are appropriately selected.

One-Bit vs. Three-Bit Discrete Pressure

Pressure can be discretized in any number of ways. Two of the most interesting ways are one-bit and three-bit pressure.

One-bit pressure creates two pressure levels: light and heavy. This approach enables techniques like the SimPress, where the user touches on the display for one activity, and then presses down to engage. Similar to a key on a keyboard, resting your finger on a key has one effect, while pressing down has another. Using one-bit pressure in this way is very useful because it allows a preview followed by an "engaged" state—just like a mouse pointer, the user can specify the location and then press down.

One-bit pressure is used in the same way on trackpads, such as those in Apple laptops: Touching lightly moves the pointer around the screen, and pressing hard sends a click event to the targeted pixel.

Three-bit pressure is interesting because it maps onto humans' perceptual capabilities. Ramos et al. tried varying levels of discretization and ultimately found that their participants could consistently select from among seven levels of pressure. Anything greater than seven, and users couldn't target it accurately. They then built a set of "pressure widgets" that used those seven levels in creative ways to allow users to give varying levels of input. Note that the feedback includes the continuous pressure values, which then get mapped onto one of seven levels. The key element here is that three-bit pressure is not a reduced sensing capability over continuous pressure; rather, it's an intentional bucketing of pressure values to make it useful to the user.

Bringing It All Together

Contact data, hover, and pressure can each add both expressiveness and complexity. A key concern is the scope of the release of your application. As we have seen, the notion of "touch input" is a myth— actually there are a myriad of devices with extremely variable capabilities, each of which can lay rightful, if ambiguous claim to the term "touch".

Must

- Determine which type of hover, contact data, and pressure your hardware is capable of, and design for that type.

- Use pressure to adjust subtleties and parameters of input, rather than as a primary indicator.

- Use hover to preview the effect of making contact.

- Use contact data to provide a more expressive interface.

- Use no more than seven levels of pressure if you want the user to be able to target it precisely.

Should

- Consider the use of relative, rather than absolute, pressure. Controlling absolutely the force with which one hits something is a skill that takes time to master. In contrast, giving the user feedback on the initial touch, and allowing the user to adjust up or down relative to that level, is much easier.

- Provide highly expressive feedback to the user, even if your interface does not require it. For example, simply pressing a button requires no pressure or hover. While you could still use a button, consider having the feedback vary by the values of these inputs.

Could

- Use pressure in one of the particular ways that we have shown above.

SUMMARY

Hardware is highly variable regarding what it can detect from a point of contact, in terms of shapes, pressure, and hover. The best systems will seek to maximize their expressivity by pushing the boundaries of parameters they detect. If you are responsible for the hardware, push the limits! If you are not, sit down with the person who is, and understand exactly what your sensors can provide your software. The more you can get, the more expressive your system will be, and the more delightful and natural it will lead your user to feel.

VOICES FROM THE FIELD: MULTI-TOUCH AS MULTI-CURSOR

Andy Wilson

Microsoft Research

Here is a basic question for any multi-touch sensor: if multiple contacts are allowed, precisely how many contacts are there? Consider the first figure in this chapter: On the left, there are three contacts. This is obvious enough. But consider as the hand moves to the pose on the right. We might say there is one contact at the end (the whole hand), but what about all the moments in between? If your answer is "I don't know," consider that the computer probably doesn't either. Furthermore, if your answer is "I don't care," consider that contact tracking is likely to "hallucinate" the movement of multiple unorganized contacts, perhaps resulting in erratic motion in your application. As with many idealized models (and perhaps life in general), it's the interstitial cases that get you.

I argue that the notion of a set of discrete contacts is borne out of our experience with cursors, and bears little resemblance with the way the real world works. Imagine grasping a coffee cup. Do the physical processes of friction and gravity that lead to the coffee cup rising to your lips rely on some mysterious process that counts the number of "contacts"?

The list of discrete contacts that systems pass to applications is a convenient and potentially limiting view of touch input. This is particularly evident as the fidelity of our sensing systems increases and we are tempted to model more sophisticated kinds of input. Are there practical alternatives to the view of multi-touch as multi-cursor? As the coffee cup example suggests, we can think of touch as impacting a simulated world of physical objects through collisions and tiny bits of friction forces. In our research, we have used physics engines of the sort used in video games to simulate these effects directly, achieve more realistic manipulation of objects, and completely avoid the notion of a discrete contact.

Even if you don't go so far as to embed your application in a physics engine, it is good to be aware of the consequences of assuming the seemingly innocuous idea of the "contact."

Andy Wilson is a Senior Researcher at Microsoft Research. There he has been applying sensing technologies to enable new modes of human-computer interaction. His interests include gesture-based interfaces, computer vision, inertial sensing, display technologies, and machine learning. In 2002 he helped found the Surface Computing group at Microsoft. Before joining Microsoft, Andy obtained his BA at Cornell University in 1993, and Ph.D. at the MIT Media Laboratory in 2000. Publications and videos of his work are located at http://research.microsoft.com/~awilson.

FURTHER READING

Cao, X., Wilson, A., Balakrishnan, R., Hinckley, K., and Hudson, S.E. ShapeTouch: Leveraging contact shape on interactive surfaces. *Proceedings of TABLETOP 2008, IEEE International Workshop on Tabletops and Interactive Surfaces,* 139–146. Xiang Cao and his colleagues at Microsoft Research explore the use of postures for gestural input into a system. For example, a user can close a window only by touching the corner with an "L" shape of their hand. ShapeTouch increases expressive power, enabling interactions like this that avoid accidents without useless dialog confirmations.

Grossman, T., Hinckley, K., Baudisch, P., Agrawala, M., and Balakrishnan, R. Hover Widgets: Using the tracking state to extend the capabilities of pen-operated devices. *Proceedings of CHI 2006,* Montreal, Canada, April 2006, pp. 861–870. Tovi Grossman and his collaborators demonstrate the use of the hover state to differentiate gestures. In this case, a set of gestures is presented that can be activated *only* while hovering.

Ramos, G. "Pressure Sensitive Pen Interactions," https://tspace.library.utoronto.ca/bitstream/1807/11121/2/Ramos_Gonzalo_A_200801_PhD_thesis.pdf, a thesis submitted in conformity with the requirements for the degree of Doctor of Philosophy. Gonzalo Ramos performs an exhaustive review of the capabilities of uses of pressure in a pen-based system. This review includes work both in human capabilities and in uses for those capabilities. An example is a set of "Pressure Widgets," controls that are manipulated by touching them with various levels of pressure.

Vertical, Horizontal, and Mobile

26

> *What does mysticism really mean? It means the way to attain knowledge. It's close to philosophy except in philosophy you go horizontally while in mysticism you go vertically.*
>
> **—Elie Wiesel**

DESCRIPTION

We have reviewed some of the important characteristics of a touch system. We've stressed that it be learnable and that it be suited to its environment. We have discussed how to achieve those goals and also offered a framework understanding gestures. In this chapter we discuss the effects of input device orientation and size on the design of interactive systems.

Multi-touch interaction with a phone is conducted with thumbs and while holding the device. Multi-touch interaction with wall-mounted displays is conducted with fingertips and arms extended. The physicality of the interaction is clearly different, as is the context of use and also the tasks that the user is likely to want to perform. Handhelds, e-readers, tablets, booklets, slates, desktops, tabletops, laptops, and wall-mounted displays each have their own unique affordances, and thus their own ecological niches. Correspondingly, software designed for such devices will need to be further tailored to account for these factors. A detailed review of all of these differences would require a book unto itself. Instead, in this chapter, we will do the next best thing: we will provide an overview of the issues, and point the way toward solutions.

APPLICATION TO NUI

We have described in Chapter 2 that the goal of a NUI is to make its user feel like a natural. It should be obvious that the orientation and size of the display will have **199** an impact on the user's task, and thus they will have a differentiating impact on the user's goals and expectations of how the device will function. This also serves to illustrate the point made so explicitly in Chapter 22, that the best software is tailored software. Clearly, a screen that is wide will require a different user interface than one that is tall—even more clear is that such screens are likely to be used in different contexts, and so require designs that suit their ecological niches, as we discussed in Chapter 3.

LESSONS FROM THE PAST

The degree and extent of the work to be done are masked by prior experience with the mouse. The cursor-controlled desktop metaphor was well-suited to scaling to different screen sizes and to different (though similar) input devices. Both 8" netbooks and 30" desktop displays could be controlled with equal prowess using the separated input and display devices and the pointer's abstract input representation of the user's position. What should be abundantly clear to you now is that, with touch input, this is simply not the case. We have voluntarily foregone this convenient separation of input from display, and thus we must design the software accordingly. In practice, this means understanding important issues of biomechanics, interaction areas, windowing, and chassis gestures, which we will discuss in detail in the design guidelines.

DESIGN GUIDELINES

Biomechanics and Contact Shape

The area with which the user touches the device is dependent on the angle and orientation of the user's finger. The difference in this area for mobile and larger screens is rather obvious: mobile devices are typically held in the hands, with the thumb being used to touch the screen. Less intuitive is that there is also a difference in contact area for vertical and horizontal displays, as we see in Figure 26.1.

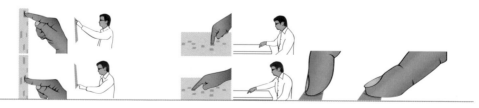

FIGURE 26.1

Left: Wherever the user touches a vertical screen, the contact area of the finger is more or less constant. Right: On a horizontal screen, targets closer to the user receive a very different contact area than targets that are farther away. Contact areas also vary for mobile devices where users interact with thumbs and fingers, each with a different contact area.

This difference in contact area (side of thumb, tip of finger, pad of finger) will dramatically affect the targeting accuracy of your device. As such, the screen and digitizer should be carefully calibrated to take into account these differences.

Also intuitively varying with screen size are the shape and nature of gestures that can be comfortably performed. Touching targets on opposite sides of a handheld screen means moving the thumb. Doing this with a large display may mean walking from one end of the screen to the other. Further, touching objects at the top of the screen is more physically tiring than touching those at the bottom. To the point of physical comfort, you should also consider how the user can comfortably interact with your software: on horizontal screens, the user is likely to rest her arm on the device itself, meaning that false touches may show up in your data stream. With mobile devices, she will hold the device in such a way that she can rest her arm on her body or surrounding objects. With vertical screens, resting is less convenient, requiring the user to return her hands to a desk or to the sides of her body between touches.

Interaction Areas and Privacy

Also clearly different are the nature of the display and how the user will interact with it. A small, mobile device may be intended for interaction primarily by a single individual, held between the hands. As the screen size changes, however, so too does the number of users who might be interacting with it. In designing your software, consider whether the information is private or public: will multiple viewers share the display, or can you assume the individual will use it alone? Take, for example, the design of a poker game. For a small, mobile device, one could assume that the user's cards could be shown on screen when it is his turn. For a vertically mounted screen, however, the cards should be shown only when other users aren't looking. Of course, a horizontal, tabletop-like screen offers the best of both worlds, if you include a gesture that the user can use to hide his cards from other users (e.g., the cards are shown only when the user's hand is sensed in a "karate chop" shape above them, which would serve as a natural blind to other users).

Portable screens that can be vertical or horizontal are particularly interesting. Ask yourself the question, In what ways should your application behave differently if it senses the user has placed the device flat on a table?

Windowed and Non-Windowed

Perhaps the most obvious difference between mobile devices and other display types is whether the content should fill the screen or whether it will be windowed. One luxury for iOS designers is that they did not have to deal with the issue of hierarchy: should a drag scroll the content of a window, or should it move the window? This issue of hierarchy is perhaps the single greatest issue that affected the design of the gesture language for the Microsoft Surface project—and a satisfactory design was never developed.

Chassis vs. Touch Gestures

Mobile devices may not concern themselves with windowed content, but they do introduce a whole new class of gestures: chassis gestures. This is the name we have given to gestures detected with sensors such as accelerometers, magnetometers, and gyroscopes. In the iOS, this is limited to two gestures. The first is simply reorienting the device and having it respond by rotating content. What is interesting about the iOS is where it *forces* the user to perform this gesture. On the iPhone, if the user is browsing the web with the phone held vertically, when they play a video, it automatically starts playing horizontally: the user is forced to turn the device. When we stop to consider it, this is a rather bold design—it forces the user to change her posture to better suit the content. The second chassis gesture is one that is far less often detected: shake to undo. Try typing some text. Made a mistake? Shake the device and it will offer you the option of deleting it. This shake to undo applies to a rather small set of actions in the operating system (one can't, for example, shake the device to undo deleting an application), so it fails to apply the lessons of Chapter 19. Further, there is no mechanism to reveal it to the user, missing out on the lessons of Chapters 10 and 20. Nonetheless, it is an example of a class of gestures not possible on a nonmobile device.

Must

- Consider the primary purpose of the system. The interaction and visual design follow from that purpose.

- If the system is extended to other environments, avoid altering its primitives. If the new environment is incompatible with the fundamental aspects of the design, then consider designing a new system.

Should

- Be willing to alter parameters of the system to improve its functioning in new environments. While the primitives may not change, other elements may. For example, if a system was designed on a large system and is now being implemented on a smaller system, consider giving feedback when users approach boundaries.

- Avoid blending designs that were intended for different environments. A blended design often presents an incoherent learning environment for users. To them, the system will at best appear inconsistent; at worst, it will seem random, or they will assume that it is not working at all when they try something that worked in a different context but is unavailable now.

- If you must combine different systems, make the modes clear to users.

Could

- Consider how your application should behave differently if it senses the user has placed the device flat on a table.

SUMMARY

The form factor of the display is important in that it suggests two very different elements that should be considered for design. The first is the ecological niche in which the device will be operating (Chapter 3). The second is how the physicality of the device changes the user's interaction with it, in the same way that other properties affect the tailoring of software to hardware (Chapter 22).

Process: How Do You Get There?

VI

The User-Derived Interface (UDI)

27

> *The best argument against democracy is a five-minute conversation with the average voter.*
> *It has been said that democracy is the worst form of government except all the others that have been tried.*
>
> **—Winston Churchill**

DESCRIPTION

One seemingly simple approach to creating a "natural" user interface would be a democratic one, that is, let the users "define" it. A method of accomplishing this would be to show users the various end states that the system offers (i.e., its functionality). We could then show the system in its initial state and ask the user, "What would you do to create the end state given this start state?" Distilling the actions from many users for each end state, and combining those synthesized actions into a complete system, would seem to ensure the creation of a natural user interface. This approach of creating a context for users to act and then generating an interface based on their actions has been called the user-derived (or designed) interface (UDI). In a gestural-based system, there is a place for UDI, or, as some have called it, User-Defined Gestures. It turns out, however, that the scope and applicability of this tool is smaller than one might expect.

APPLICATION TO NUI

The UDI approach has been shown to be useful in creating successful interfaces that required little or no training. For example, in command systems when users were given the task "See that Bill gets the message about the keyboard study from Bob," they would use a small subset of words to achieve that state. Typically, their **207** responses were "Send this to Bill," "Mail message 9 to Bill," and the like. By itera-tively modifying the command parser, we were able to create an interface that sup-ported simple mailing tasks (e.g., print, send, forward, delete, file, find). The parser included elements such as synonym support and pronoun disambiguation. The com-bination of these features created a robust system, handling over three-quarters of the commands typed spontaneously by users.

This approach would seem a sensible way to create a natural user interface. If we could create a successful command system by simply building on what users did spontaneously, why not apply the same approach to creating a NUI system? So we and others tried it.

LESSONS FROM THE PAST

Wobbrock and his colleagues from Microsoft Research chose the various com-mands that can be performed with a mouse and keyboard in windows. These included moving objects, copying objects, switching windows, and any number of other actions. As we described the UDI method, they users images of the inter-face before, and after the action was performed. They then asked the participant what gesture they would use to transit the interface from the before to the after state. What they found is surprising to some, but hopefully not to readers of this book: there was almost no action that yielded the same gesture in each case. What's worse, users would perform precisely the same gesture in more than one situation, and not notice the conflict. The one gesture they did find to be consistently applied was *manipulation*: moving an object a short distance from one place on the screen to the other. Users would universally touch the object with one or more fingers, and slide their hand along the table. For any other action, at all—the participant responses were not the same as one another.

It seems ironic that a UDI method would work well for an abstract command sys-tem but fail when applied to a NUI system. There are several possible explanations. In a command system we made use of a well-practiced skill—typing commands. In the NUI the only well-practiced skills that are readily extrapolated from "naive phys-ics" are actions like moving and rotating. For other actions there is no commonal-ity. Second, in a command system we could build the commonality incrementally over time by modifying the parser. In a gestural system the initial diversity was too great. Third (and perhaps most ironic), the fundamental action of a command sys-tem, typing words, is well understood prior to coming to a new system, and the system automatically provides good feedback, that is, characters appear as they are typed. In contrast, the primitive actions for a gestural or touch-based system require constant feedback. One needs to know that the system is responding as one expects it to. After all, the real world works that way. For example, if you stretch a rubber band, the band provides continuous feedback. In contrast, the test bed for the NUI necessarily provided no feedback while the gesture was being executed. We have taken the failure of the UDI method to produce a natural set of gestures to mean we simply applied the methodology to the wrong question. It did give us the incredibly valuable result that there is no such thing as a 'natural gesture'. Beyond this, it is clear that later in the process, when the user is presented with a user interface, this method can be used to test and iterate on affordances of the design.

A gross overgeneralization would be to conclude that testing users is not a productive way to design a NUI system. In fact, testing the system with the intended user base is essential. The testing simply needs to be the right sort of testing, combined with the right questions. Ultimately, creating a NUI is not the place for "projective methods" like UDI or for participatory design approaches. As an entirely new way of interacting, elements of the NUI such as affordances and feedback need to be carefully designed and rigorously tested. While the UDI was not the right approach to defining the NUI, the RITE method worked well. We describe that approach in Chapter 29.

DESIGN GUIDELINES

Must

- Understand that there is no such thing as a 'natural gesture'—you need to design the set of gestures in your system.

- Design teams need to create an overall and detailed vision for the interactive system before they begin representing and testing it.

- Design teams should test that vision with prototypes of varying degrees of fidelity.

Should

- When doing such testing, the team should pay more attention to user behavior than user evaluation. Users will often suggest elements of systems they are familiar with, such as GUI elements. The temptation to take their words at face value should be resisted. Their behavior shows what users need to and can do.

SUMMARY

Creating a NUI requires feedback from users, but the methods need to be carefully chosen, and the evaluation of that feedback should be done with care and perspective. The UDI method that had worked well to define a command system did not work well for the NUI. On the other hand, carefully planned RITE testing did work well.

FURTHER READING

For a discussion of the UDI philosophy, method, and application to command languages, see Good, M. D., Whiteside, J. A., Wixon, D. R., and Jones, S. J. Building a user-derived interface. *Communications of the ACM,* 1984, 27(10), 1032–1043, available through the ACM digital library: http://portal.acm.org/citation.cfm?id=358274.358284&coll=ACM&dl=ACM&CFID=10 3583941&CFTOKEN=45376533. For a discussion of the UDI as applied to gestural systems, take a look at Friebrink, R. D., and Morris, M. M. Dynamic mapping of physical controls for table-top groupware. CHI 2009, Boston, MA, 471–480. Available from the ACM Digital Library: http://delivery.acm.org/10.1145/1520000/1518778/p471-fiebrink.pdf?key1=1518778&key2=5241883 821&coll=ACM&dl=ACM&CFID=103583941&CFTOKEN=45376533.

Jacob O. Wobbrock, Meredith Ringel Morris, and Andrew D. Wilson. 2009. User-defined gestures for surface computing. In *Proceedings of the 27th international conference on Human factors in computing systems* (CHI '09). ACM, New York, NY, USA, 1083-1092. DOI=10.1145/1518701.1518866 http://doi.acm.org/10.1145/1518701.1518866

Lessons in False-Gesture Recognition

---

28

*Abbott: Well, let's see, we have on the bags, Who's on first, What's on second,
I Don't Know is on third...*
Costello: You don't know the fellows' names?
...
Costello: Well then who's on first?
Abbott: Yes.
Costello: I mean the fellow's name.
Abbott: Who.
Costello: The guy on first.
Abbott: Who.
Costello: The first baseman.
Abbott: Who.
Costello: The guy playing...
Abbott: Who is on first!

DESCRIPTION

Recognition errors are instances where your software will trigger recognition of a gesture where none was intended (which we term *false-positive* errors), or where the user intends to perform a gesture but it is not recognized (which we term *false-negative* errors). Creating a gesture language with a high rate of false positives is the first mistake made by rookie gesture designers. Here's an example straight from a recent meeting discussing in-air gestures:

"When a user wants to delete something, they should just be able to shake it, and it will disappear. That's obviously the most natural thing."

There are two obvious problems here. The first and most apparent to the now-informed reader (of Chapter 2 especially) is the misunderstanding of the term "natural" in NUI—it's not about what's guessable or what mimics some other experience, but rather what makes the user feel like Michael Jordan while using your system. Nothing makes the user feel less like a natural than a false-positive recognition of a gesture. This leads us to the second problem: The shaking gesture is likely to have a pretty high false-positive recognition rate.

APPLICATION TO NUI

Designing your application/device/platform so that both novices and experts feel like naturals when they use your gesture-based system is the goal of a natural user interface. As we saw in earlier chapters, this relies on strong affordances (Chapter 20) and feedback (Chapter 14) to allow the user to learn a language of gestures (Chapter 19). This chapter will discuss a key consideration in building your gesture language: reducing false-positive and false-negative recognition of your gestures. In so doing, you will ensure that users are successful in conveying their intended actions to the system and that the system's response is as the users expect. To accomplish this, you will need to do a great deal of tweaking of your gesture language, as well as of your affordances and feedback. Recognizing false positives and false negatives will be a key tool in conducting RITE studies to quickly iterate on and improve your language (Chapter 29). Our work in this area has been influenced by *signal detection theory*, an area of psychology. Here, we distill its essential elements and demonstrate how these are applied to building a NUI.

LESSONS FROM THE PAST
False-Positive Recognition

The high false-positive rate for a shaking gesture might seem obvious. It's pretty likely that someone at some point will shake an object simply to draw attention to it, or move it and then realize they want to change direction, and trigger a false-positive recognition. But it's also likely to be done at other times. Think about the first thing that you would do if the system didn't respond the way you expected. As we discussed in Chapter 14, with a touch system, users press harder and repeatedly on the device. Guess what—when you add manipulations to the system, they start shaking objects on the screen. Consider, therefore, the user experience proposed here: the user has just had something happen that she didn't expect in her application—maybe there was a glitch, maybe a moment of a frozen display—but she thinks that she's not being "seen" properly. So she shakes the object. The system's response? It deletes the object that the user was trying to operate on. That'll teach 'em.

The last source of false-positive activations is in failures of the gesture recognition system. The user may be performing what she believes is the correct gesture.

Another person watching her do it might also conclude that she is performing the correct gesture. But, for whatever reason, the recognizer does not detect it as the correct gesture. An astute designer might ask, "What are the other gestures in the system, and how likely is it that another of these might get confused for a 'shake' by the recognizer?" Understanding that gesture recognition systems are far from perfect will help you to better design your experience. The notion that designers can live in an abstraction created by the platform may have been true in the mouse world, but it simply isn't in the world of touch and gestures: you will have to get down and dirty with your recognizer, and manually tweak your gestures using the tools and methods we have described.

False-Negative Recognition

All of this worry about false positives might lead you to conclude that you should obfuscate your gestures by avoiding those actions that users are likely to take accidentally or are likely to trip the recognizer. "Want to delete an object? Hold an object in one hand while tapping out the words to the Canadian national anthem in Morse code with the other." This leads us to the complementary next problem: false negatives.

False negatives occur when the user thinks that he has performed a gesture correctly, but the system does not recognize it. Note a subtle distinction here: we're not only describing about instances where the user actually *has* performed a gesture correctly, but rather where he *believes* he has performed it correctly. This can be caused by problems with the recognizer, but in our experience, it is far more likely to be caused by a user misunderstanding regarding how, when, or where to perform a gesture. And it's the designer's job to make sure the user knows how, when, and where gestures are properly performed.

Tweaking to Balance Recognition

The example of our extreme delete gesture is an obvious case of overcompensation for false-positive recognition. More subtle examples of tweaking to get it right also exist. For example, consider carefully the way scrolling works on the Safari browser on the iPhone, as we discussed in Chapter 21: if the user starts scrolling vertically, the system locks in to vertical scrolling, so that as the user's thumb arcs during the drag it won't trigger horizontal scrolling (try scrolling up with your thumb on an iPhone—notice how at the end of the gesture your thumb is moving almost completely horizontally? The gesture recognizer is compensating for that). The same is true of horizontal scrolling. Start out scrolling diagonally, however, and the gesture will not be recognized as either a vertical or a horizontal scroll, and so is never locked in to one or the other. What the designers of the scroll language in the browser had to get exactly right is the angles at which the recognizer designates the scroll as vertical, horizontal, or neither. Neither of the authors was there, but no doubt this was done through extensive user testing to tweak these values. Evidence of this tweaking is evident in a subtle difference between horizontal and vertical scrolling: Scroll a little bit vertically, and the recognizer locks in immediately (the "recognition" phase ends and moves on to the "continuation" phase of specifying how much to scroll, to use the parlance of Chapter 18). Try scrolling a little vertically and then switch to horizontally, and it's no dice: you're locked in. This isn't true in the case of horizontal scrolling, however: start sliding your finger horizontally, and then switch direction to a vertical scroll. Unlike vertical scrolling, if you scroll a little bit horizontally, you can still switch to vertical scrolling. The recognition phase for horizontal is longer.

This asymmetry is obvious evidence of tweaking. It's likely that the designers and researchers at Apple discovered that users sometimes move a little horizontally before they start to scroll diagonally or vertically, most likely when scrolling down with the thumb, and so lengthened the recognition phase to prevent a false-positive detection of horizontal scrolling.

User Guessing and Learning

As we have described, rookie designers tend to overemphasize making gestures "guessable," hoping to reduce false negatives by making it likely that a user will guess right every time. As we described in detail in Chapters 17 and 19, the goal of a NUI designer is to create a set of gestural primitives that is learnable and, through scaffolding (Chapter 10) feedback and affordances (Chapters 14 and 20), guide the user to perform them correctly.

Thus, your goal in addressing user guessing and learning is *not* to try to make your gesture language guessable without help. Instead, your goal is to create an internally consistent set that can be applied again and again when prompted by appropriate affordances and guided with appropriate feedback.

Pruning your Gesture Language

Another likely cause of false recognition (positive or negative) is a gesture language with too crowded a gesture space. An example of this can also be found in the iPhone's *delete* gesture (hold on, now, iPhone zealots: you knew that eventually we'd point out some flaws). In our experience, only a subset of iPhone users knows about the *delete* gesture. In some lists, such as the list of e-mail messages in the mail client, the user can slide her finger horizontally across the message in the list and a little "delete" button will pop up. The user can then tap the button to delete the message.

It is clear that the delete gesture suffers from both false-positive and false-negative user errors. The case of false-negative errors is easy to see: many iPhone users complain that, despite a great deal of practice, they can never quite "get" the delete gesture. This is because the angle at which delete is recognized (vs. a scroll) is very narrow—slide your finger up even a little and the system recognizes the action as a scroll, and the delete never triggers. This is evidence of a dense gesture space in this case: vertical scrolling has been assigned so much of the range of angles in the gesture space that there is very little room left for the delete gesture. It may also be an example where tweaking was done to reduce false-positive recognition of delete.

The case of false positives is equally obvious to the trained designer of gesture systems: The fact that there is a delete button at all reflects a belief that this gesture is likely to be performed accidentally, and so a confirmation step was added. Another aspect to consider is called "proportional effect." When something large or decisive occurs, the gesture for it should be proportionately large or decisive. A two-phase gesture fits the bill nicely.

That there is so much evidence for false-positive and false-negative recognition of the delete gesture makes it somewhat remarkable that it was included at all. The case in its favor, however, is an obvious one: with sufficient practice, users are eventually able to perform this gesture with few errors (as has been the experience of one of the two authors). This means that the expert user will feel like a natural, one goal of a NUI. Where the delete gesture fails as a design element, however, is in the novice users who are not able to perform the gesture correctly. Chapter 20 provides details about how novices and experts can both be supported in a gestural system.

Inconsistent Gesture Languages

An obvious source of false recognition is when gestures are inconsistently available. Picking again on the iPhone's delete gesture, consider its inconsistent use. There are many lists that a user encounters when using the iPhone. Considering just a few of the built-in applications, the user will see lists of e-mail messages, cities for which they are configured to see the weather, songs, artists, albums, videos, bookmarks, and the home screen itself (a 2-D list). While each of these is a list, only a subset of them use the delete gesture. Want to delete an e-mail or video? You can happily swipe to the right and press the button. Want to remove a city from your weather app or delete a song from your music library? Your one-finger swipe to the right will get no response at all. Want to delete an application from the home screen? Your one-finger swipe will instead change the page.

An engineer might argue that the recognizer running in the weather, music browsing, and home screen applications simply was designed to not recognize the gesture; therefore, no such error has occurred. To an informed designer of a NUI system, however, this inconsistency is an example of false-negative recognition. The user believes that she has performed the gesture correctly, but the system has not recognized it. Worse still, the system doesn't give any feedback saying, "Yes, I see this gesture, but you can't do that here." It just sits there, inert. This leads us to our next topic: superstitious behavior.

Superstitious Behavior

Another reason that a user might not "get" the iPhone's delete gesture is one that seems to come from the users themselves. In our observations, users seem to consistently develop the superstitious belief that the gesture is somehow speed-based—that it's not enough to slide their finger horizontally; they also have to do it *quickly*. You might even believe this yourself. It's not true! Slow down! You will be more accurate and have fewer false-negative recognition errors.

We guess that this behavior comes from previous false-negative errors caused by other sources: users try it once, and a false-negative error occurs because they slid a little too much vertically. The next time they try it, they speed up, and it works—not because they went faster, but because they actually had the angle right this time. Because they know that they sped up, but didn't notice the change of angle, they attribute the accurate recognition to the change in speed.

As we described in detail in Chapter 14, superstitious behavior is the enemy of a designer of touch and gesture systems, and learning is her friend. In this case, the reason is obvious: moving too quickly makes it more likely that the user will input at the wrong angle and experience a false-negative recognition. The next time around, designers of the iPhone might ask themselves, "How can we get users to slow down when they are entering the delete gesture?" Understanding the difference between false negative and false positive errors, and the different causes of each we have described, will help you in designing your gesture language. Any time you observe an error in performing a gesture, classify the error in this way, and then apply the guidelines in this chapter to tweak or redesign your user experience.

DESIGN GUIDELINES

Must

- The question "Will the user guess this?" is a fine place to start, but it's definitely not where to stop. Ask this question, but make sure to do it rarely, usually for tweaking your feedback and affordances. This is not normally the question to be asking when defining the gesture primitives themselves.

- Consider both the false-positive rate and false-negative rate of your gestures. False positives occur because the actions of a user too readily resemble some unintended gesture in your language. False negatives occur because the precision with which you have constrained the allowed gesture is too narrow.

- Develop a good understanding of the recognizer for which you are building your natural user interface.

- Build affordances and feedback that teach users what gestures to perform (as explained in Chapter 20); then give them good feedback on their performance to continually improve (as explained in Chapter 14).

- Avoid the use of gestures that overlap with one another in a dense space—this is likely to generate a lot of cross talk where one gesture is falsely negatively recognized and another is falsely positively recognized.

Should

- Even better than *understanding* the recognizer is having the developers who are building it working together with the designers who are building the UI (or having them be the same person!).

- Aim for consistency in the cause (affordances) and effect (recognition and subsequent action) of your gestures. Avoid the iPhone delete mistake by avoiding modality. Ensure that all similar items (like lists) can have the same actions applied (like delete).

- If a gesture does not actually make sense in the context (e.g., you don't want users to delete music using the iPhone, but rather to delete it on the PC in iTunes), make sure you still recognize the gesture and give feedback. That feedback should say to the user, "Yes, I see that you performed that gesture, but that won't work here. And here's why."

Could

- Consider using only *manipulation*-based gestures, imitating naive physics, without gestures that get "recognized" at all. As we saw with the iPhone example, however, even manipulation-based gestures need a little recognition at times to tweak and compensate for physical effects, like the arc of a thumb's movement.

SUMMARY

False recognition of gestures, positive or negative, is the bane of a user's interaction with a gestural system. It makes the user more hesitant and less trusting and, worst of all, encourages the development of superstitious beliefs about the function of the system. Understanding and reducing false recognition are a key to the success of a touch and gestural system. While this may seem easy, the world is replete with examples of systems where this was not done well (yes, we claim that even the iPhone has moments where it does not achieve this as well as it could). Perhaps most important is that you avoid the mistake of a rookie designer—focusing too much on false negatives at the expense of making false-positive errors more likely. The goal is to balance and reduce both.

 ## FURTHER READING

Wickens, T. D. (2002) *Elementary Signal Detection Theory*. New York: Oxford University Press. The notion of false-negative and false-positive detection has been presented in any number of domains. In signal detection theory, a construct in psychology, a false negative is a "miss" and a false positive is a "false alarm." Wickens' text provides an in-depth introduction to the space.

RITE with a Purpose

29

> *We all have a few failures under our belt. It's what makes us ready for the successes.*
>
> —**Randy K. Milholland, Midnight Macabre, 10-18-05**

DESCRIPTION

The RITE (Rapid Iterative Testing and Evaluation) method is uniquely suited to the design and development of touch and gestural interfaces. Touch and gestural interfaces lack the conventions of more traditional interfaces like the GUI. They also must meet a higher bar; that is, they must feel natural and fun and encourage the learning of a new interaction paradigm. Making an interface "natural" requires more research effort and design thinking than making an unnatural interface (e.g., a logical but arcane command system) or mimicking a conventional interface like the GUI. Given these challenges and the perpetual commercial requirement to make progress quickly, the RITE method is a natural choice.

APPLICATION TO NUI

The RITE method has been applied to two core challenges in creating the a NUI interface using touch and gesture. The first challenge was what feedback and feed-forward should we provide to communicate the metaphor effectively. The second challenge was what metaphor should be chosen for the interface.

LESSONS FROM THE PAST

Historically, the challenge of creating or choosing a metaphor for the NUI has been relatively clear. One element of the GUI that contributed to its success was the **219** desktop metaphor. In the GUI, the computer screen became like a desktop. A presentation of documents on the screen was analogous to the way they might appear on a desk. For example, one could "open" folders on a desk and see the documents inside. On a physical desktop one could open a document (e.g., turn over the cover page) and then interact with it—making notes of changes, highlighting sections, adding comments, and the like. In the "metaphorical desktop" one opened a document and then could interact with it—making changes, highlighting parts, and adding comments. When confronting a NUI, the first question is "What metaphor should we employ that will appear natural and enhance learning?"

The challenge of creating a successful metaphor for a NUI can be divided into two parts. First, do the design elements of the system communicate the metaphor to the users? Second, does that metaphor make sense to users, helping them learn the system while retaining their enthusiasm for it? Historically, the RITE method has been applied to the problem of refining a design so that users will be able to complete tasks more easily and enjoy the system more. It does this by quickly uncovering problems that users have and generating fixes for subsequent testing. It has a similar function when applied to a metaphor for a system. That is, it allows the team to refine the elements of the design so that they more effectively communicate the metaphor. As the system evolves and the metaphor is effectively communicated, the second challenge becomes paramount, that is, does the metaphor help users learn and like the system? This second challenge requires some additional RITEs, that is, that users' understanding of and preference for a metaphor be assessed. Assessing understanding and preference is best done by comparing metaphors.

In a set of RITE tests for Microsoft Surface, the goals of refining the designs and assessing users' understanding and preferences were undertaken. Using a set of guiding principles that had been developed for the Surface product, the design team explored a large number of possible metaphors, which were narrowed down to three. These metaphors were "magnet," "sphere," and "unfold." The magnet metaphor was based on the idea of a magnet board in which placing physical objects on the surface created virtual objects and activated functions. In the sphere metaphor, the interface was depicted as open space with a series of spherical objects in which the primary interaction was dragging elements out of their sphere (orbit). In the unfold metaphor, the interface was depicted like a magazine foldout in which the users could unfold content.

Refining the interface took a traditional RITE approach. That is, changes were made as problems were uncovered. However, the changes were directed not only toward the goal of increasing performance on the task but also at making the metaphor clearer to users by removing confusing elements and increasing the salience of elements that supported the interface. Throughout the testing, we collected user descriptions and ratings of the individual metaphors.

The magnet board and sphere were both better understood and preferred as compared to unfold. We also found that each of those two metaphors had different strengths. The sphere metaphor was better for navigation, and the magnet board metaphor was better for interaction within a document. As a result, the team synthesized the two metaphors

DESIGN GUIDELINES

The success of a modified RITE approach to the design of the NUI for Microsoft Surface suggests that it would be an effective approach for any team developing a NUI.

Must

- First and foremost, any team considering a RITE test needs be aware of the factors that make RITE effective:

  - It must be technically possible to make changes quickly.

  - Team members must be present for tests.

  - Team members must be empowered to make decisions and committed to improving the interface.

- Second, when applying the RITE method to refining and choosing a metaphor for a NUI system:

  - As a lead up to the RITE tests, the design team must create a large number of possible metaphors and designs.

  - More than one metaphor must be tested.

  - Understanding and preference data need to be collected throughout the test.

  - The goal must be clear. Unlike a "traditional" RITE test, where the goal is to make the interface better, in this case the goal of the RITE is to choose the best metaphor.

Should

- In choosing metaphors to test, teams should choose the most distinctive metaphors. This will enable test participants to give better feedback and increase the opportunity of the team to learn.

- Each interface should be "rigorous" in its representation of the metaphor. This means that the interface should not be a compromise. The team should go so far as to retain elements that they think may be suboptimal in order to faithfully depict the metaphor.

- Initial tests should be directed at refining the metaphors. The goals of this refinement are to remove obstacles to interaction and to more clearly depict the metaphor.

- Metrics for comparison should be chosen before the tests and assessed throughout.

- Opinion questions should be used to understand the users' thinking.

Could

- Teams can segment the RITE test. That is, they can iterate in the early stages and then lock the interface halfway though the tests.

- The quantitative and qualitative data regarding the interfaces can be collected throughout, but the team may choose to focus on the data collected after the interface was "locked down."

SUMMARY

The choice of a metaphor for a NUI system is both important and challenging. RITE testing provides a way to refine the design of the interface so that it better conveys the underlying metaphor. In order to choose a metaphor, RITE testing needs to be complemented by a quantitative evaluation of user preference for the interface and by a set of qualitative open-ended questions that allows the team to assess user understanding of the metaphor.

FURTHER READING

The RITE method describes an approach to rapid iteration of designs. It is widely practiced and consistently shows measurable improvement in usability of products. The original description of the RITE method is contained in Medlock, M. C, Wixon, D., Romero, R., and Fulton, B. *Using the RITE Method to Improve Products: A Definition and Case Study.* Presented at the Usability Professional Association, 2002, Orlando, FL. Several examples are presented in Medlock, M., Wixon, D., McGee, M., and Welsh, D. (2005) The Rapid Iterative Test and Evaluation Method: Better products in less time. In Bias, G., and Mayhew, D. (eds.) *Cost Justifying Usability,* pp. 489–517. San Francisco: Morgan Kaufmann.

Hofmeester, K., and Wixon, D. *Using Metaphors to Create a Natural User Interface for Microsoft Surface.* Conference on Human Factors in Computing Systems. Proceedings of the 28th International Conference on Human Factors in Computing Systems, Atlanta, GA, pp. 4629–4644, 2010.

A Word About Engineering

30

The future ain't what it used to be.

—Yogi Berra

DESCRIPTION

Bringing a new human-computer interaction paradigm to life is no easy task. The history of innovation is littered with products that were "ahead of their time." Often these "failed" innovations contained a number of innovative attributes that found their way into subsequent successful products. Alternatively, these innovations were successful in niche markets but did not reshape an entire industry. Some simply failed and were forgotten.

In a sense, NUIs stand at a crossroads, and three possible options loom ahead. The first option is that NUIs will become the next paradigm for how people interact with computers. The second option is that NUIs succeed in niche markets. These niches may be large or small. The last option is that NUI elements get incorporated into existing products with varying degrees of success. To refer to these alternatives succinctly, let's call them dominant, niche, and assimilation. Our hope is that NUIs will be dominant and replace the GUI. But NUIs may only thrive in niche markets. Finally, assimilation would indicate the "death" of the NUI as a type of HCI and its rebirth as a facilitator of other dominant forms. In this scenario, the NUI could be a facilitator of the GUI.

Of these three outcomes (dominant, niche, assimilation), which one is most likely? One way to anticipate the future is to look at the past. Although this may seem like looking into a rear view mirror to see where you are going, it can be instructive. Examining the past becomes instructive when we extract some principles that we can apply to the future. These principles can be enriched if we also examine some concrete examples. Finally, which past should we consider? Probably the best place to look is the near-term history of HCI. If we look at the near-term history of computer-human interaction, three interface paradigms are instructive. The first is the GUI. The second is the World Wide Web. The web presented its own browsers, search engines, and hypertext links. The final paradigm is computerized gaming. The latter may seem an odd choice, but the computer gaming industry is huge and diverse. Gaming consoles represent state-of-the-art hardware. In many respects, gaming interfaces employ cutting-edge interactive approaches and represent an instructive if heterogeneous set of interaction techniques.

When we look at the recent history of HCI we need to take a holistic view. Technologists tend to focus narrowly. They would focus exclusively on Moore's law. While the ever-increasing power of computing is an important determinant of what made the GUI, the web, and computerized gaming possible, there are large social, economic, and cultural factors and trends that determined their relative dominance. In addition to these factors and trends, we need to consider some specific elements of the GUI products, web interfaces, and games. These specific elements enabled exemplary products not only to become widely used but also to become the dominant mindset in HCI. In fact, it is the combination of increasing computer power (with reduced cost), large social, cultural, and economic trends, and unique element design that has made computing a dominant force and shaped the ways we interact with this technology.

LESSONS FROM THE PAST

What are the dominant trends and design elements that have shaped HCI over the past 60 years and that will determine the success of the NUI?

First, computing power will increase and become cheaper. This will drive the computer industry to seek more diverse markets. The quest for new markets opens the space for new HCI paradigms and was one of the key drivers of the broad adoption of the GUI paradigm. Computer companies knew that costs were coming down and that they needed to broaden their market to a mass market. Ease of learning and use were significant barriers to widespread adoption of the GUI, the World Wide Web, and computer games.

However, lowered costs also facilitated the evolution and adoption of a number of niche technologies and interfaces. For example, laser scanners were adopted in retail and deskilled retail work to the point that customers are now asked to perform the retail work for their own transactions. For example, ATMs employed a menu interface of limited choices and thereby enabled 24-hour banking at lower costs; provided you wanted to be your own teller. But menu interfaces did not become the new paradigm of HCI. Similarly, laser scanning did not emerge as the technological base of new millennium human-computer interaction. They were highly successful in their niches, but they stayed confined to these niches.

Second, the form factors of computing changed. The original mainframe with its limited interface gave way to time sharing, which provided more flexibility. Time sharing was supplanted by PCs. The form factor of the PC was very well suited to office work. In many ways its keyboard and screen mimicked the typewriter of the time and thus fit naturally into the office environment. However, a well-adapted form factor would not have been sufficient to induce a paradigm shift. Instead, a family of applications emerged that were well suited to office work. Most office work consisted of dealing with documents in one form or another and keeping track of money. Hence, word processing and spreadsheet applications adopted the GUI paradigm and made office work accessible to "the rest of us." This combination of form factor and applications that could do economically useful work drove broad adoption of the GUI, and it became a dominant mode of interacting with computers.

Third, the world was shrinking and becoming more interdependent. Commerce was becoming international. Communication became global. Time and distance between people shrank. In that fertile environment the World Wide Web flourished. Prior to that, the basic technology of the Internet was a comparatively obscure DARPA (Defense Advanced Research Projects Agency) project that was intended to create a computing and communication network that could survive a nuclear holocaust. Connecting computers and giving them a simple way to exchange information provided the technological underpinnings of the World Wide Web. Supplement that with a simple way of accessing information (click a link) and the fact that such information could take any form (text, images, videos) and you have the formula for increasing the diversity of people producing information and those consuming it. Mix in the first factor of more power and lower cost (for every base technology— information, richness of information, low cost storage, and easy transfer), and you have a recipe for widespread use and adoption.

Fourth, the GUIs actually assimilated interface elements from other systems and incorporated useful features that propelled them to dominance. Menus were not new. They solved the problem of remembering and reproducing a large number of commands and memorizing an elaborate syntax of commands and their qualifiers and elements. Combined with dialog boxes, they made functionality accessible. But the dominant GUI systems also eliminated the gap between input and output and reduced the gap between screens and printing.

APPLICATION TO NUI

What do these four trends—more computer power at lower cost, an emergence and proliferation of form factors, the shrinking of time and distance, and the tendency of new paradigms to borrow from other models—mean for the NUI paradigm?

First, the trend of ever-shrinking costs and ever-increasing power of the computers will not simply make NUIs possible; it will drive their broad adoption. The computer industry will seek to entice more people to use more computers to do a wider range of activities. Many of these people do not work in offices, sit at desks, and produce documents and spreadsheets. The industry will create offerings that fit with the environments they work in and the things they need to do. These environments and activities will transcend the domain of the typical GUI, that is, office work. These new offerings will have to provide a quick and seamless transition from novice to expert. People will expect them to be intuitive, efficient, and enjoyable.

Second, emerging form factors will need to be streamlined and simple. They will be without mediating devices like mice and keyboards. They will fit into their contexts naturally. We are already seeing this trend with book readers like the Kindle and touch platforms like the iPad. Similarly, form factors for entertainment devices will diversify, and with that diversification will come a broader range of apps appealing to a broader range of users. A few years ago the idea that folks in retirement homes would be playing computer games seemed far-fetched. But a platform that provided a more natural way of interacting—the Wii with its gestural interface, combined with some appealing games such as bowling—was very appealing to people who retained their passion for bowling despite some minor but critical infirmities, for example, the loss of grip strength. These and other NUI platforms and accompanying applications will gain wide and unanticipated popularity because they will make use of a wider range of human capabilities and modalities than traditional interfaces and will compensate for infirmities of the same that preclude unassisted play and use. In these contexts the NUI plays an interesting role: It must retrain the "fun" of the interaction while removing the constraints. The success of the Wii is proof that this is possible.

Third, the World Wide Web with its proliferation of information and entertainment and its widespread distribution drives adoption of NUIs. Information exchange comes in many diverse forms, from farmers in third-world countries checking commodities on their cell phones to commuters watching videos as they ride high-speed trains. One hardly needs a mouse and keyboard to consume information or to be entertained. Simple, natural, and direct interfaces not only will fill the need, but also are easier to learn, more flexible to use, and more fun than traditional interfaces.

Finally, successful NUIs will borrow from existing interfaces. Such borrowing will have certain characteristics. First, it will morph beyond easy recognition. The GUI adopted menus as a way of making choices, but these menus bore little resemblance to the previous menus. There were many more of them. They used a new input device—the mouse. They were always present and did not represent a "mode." In short, they looked and acted nothing like the menus of the previous systems such as the WANG word processor or the IBM display writer. Indeed, only a student of HCI would see the logical similarity between menus at an ATM and the menus of Microsoft Office. Similarly, choosing functions in a NUI may be logically equivalent to menus in a GUI (or any other system, for that matter). In other words, they allow a choice of functions without relying on recall memory, but their form, their activation, and their behavior could and should be different. Making them like a GUI menu simply recreates a GUI with a different (and less efficient) input device. Just as it would have been nonsense for the GUI to copy the menu of an IBM display writer it would be insanity for a NUI to reproduce the GUI. Similarly, activating items by touching would seem to make sense for a NUI, but to make that the default action would render NUIs merely the web interfaces with a different (and less efficient) pointer. Instead, a responsive system that shows affordances and leads the user to the next logical step is a true NUI. That next logical step may be one of several, but to the user the choice and its implications will be clear. A true NUI will not produce frustrating cul-de-sacs so common on the web. It will also avoid the long searches for the location of the intended action common to the GUI. A true NUI will not leave its users wondering what the advantage of the NUI is over and above a GUI.

SUMMARY

Our bias (or aspiration) is clear. We hope and expect that NUIs will become the dominant form of human-computer interaction over the next few years. The realization of that hope will depend on the pioneers who create innovative NUIs and the settlers who build on those ideas and designs in a practical and compelling way. Our intent in writing this book was to facilitate that process. We don't underestimate its difficulty. That is why we did not write a "NUI for dummies" or imply that one could create a NUI by following a simple 10-step process. Instead, we've provided a variety of essays on the NUI and grounded these essays in specific recommendations. We do provide an overarching broad process that is outlined in Figure 1.1 in Chapter 1. Here our aim was to segment and structure the challenge of creating a NUI. We also provided a general flow for approaching the creation of a NUI. Both the structure and the process flow emerged out of our struggles in creating NUIs. While we don't dwell on the mistakes we made, our concrete recommendations and abstract reflections emerge from them.

In the end, we implore you to do two things. Learn from us. Apply our learnings to your challenges and build on or transcend what we have said. Second, share what you have learned. Ultimately the fate of your efforts, be it a commercial product, a research effort, or a platform, and the fate of the NUI in general will depend on you.

Index

229